Christian Leaders [...]
by Jerry [...]

"I believe [*The Pursuit of Holiness*] is a modern classic. Few books have had the influence on me that this one has."
— CHARLES COLSON, Founder, Prison Fellowship Ministries

"For the believer seriously considering the lordship of Christ in his life, *Respectable Sins* is must reading!"
— JONI EARECKSON TADA, Founder and CEO,
Joni and Friends International Disability Center

"The price Jerry Bridges has had to pay in the pursuit of holiness has not been small. His pain has been our gain."
— JOHN PIPER, Pastor for Preaching,
Bethlehem Baptist Church, Minneapolis, Minnesota

"[*The Pursuit of Holiness*] is surely one of the most important books produced in the past fifty years."
— JOHN MacARTHUR, Pastor-Teacher,
Grace Community Church, Sun Valley, California

"[*Growing Your Faith* is] solid. Practical. Needed. Shows readers why and how to come under the influence of God's Word. I'm so thankful we have another book by this man of God."
— KAY ARTHUR, Cofounder, Precept Ministries International

"Biblical, informed, accessible, and rooted in Jerry's own deep experience as a disciple of Jesus and as a teacher. If you are seeking the way forward in Christlikeness, or wish to show that way to others, *Growing Your Faith* is a book you can count on for substantial help."
— DALLAS WILLARD, Professor, School of Philosophy,
University of Southern California

"Jerry Bridges continues to be a leading communicator of the truths of God's Word to believers — young and mature. In his clear, concise writing style, he makes spiritual truth easily accessible to everyone."
— STEVE DOUGLASS, President, Campus Crusade for Christ

Transformational Thoughts
for Your Spiritual Journey

HOLINESS
DAY BY DAY

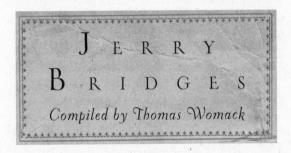

JERRY
BRIDGES

Compiled by Thomas Womack

NAVPRESS
Discipleship Inside Out®

NavPress is the publishing ministry of The Navigators, an international Christian organization and leader in personal spiritual development. NavPress is committed to helping people grow spiritually and enjoy lives of meaning and hope through personal and group resources that are biblically rooted, culturally relevant, and highly practical.

For a free catalog go to www.NavPress.com
or call 1.800.366.7788 in the United States or 1.800.839.4769 in Canada.

© 2008 by Jerry Bridges

ISBN-13: 978-1-61747-087-5

Cover design by Arvid Wallen
Cover image by Shutterstock

Some of the anecdotal illustrations in this book are true to life and are included with the permission of the persons involved. All other illustrations are composites of real situations, and any resemblance to people living or dead is coincidental.

Italics in Scripture quotations are the author's emphasis. Unless otherwise indicated, Scripture quotations are from: The Holy Bible, *English Standard Version* (ESV) © 2001 by Crossway Bibles, a division of Good News Publishers. Used by permission. All rights reserved. Other Scripture quotations are from: *The Holy Bible,* New International Version (NIV) © 1973, 1984 by International Bible Society, used by permission of Zondervan Publishing House; *New American Standard Bible* (NASB) © 1960, 1977 by the Lockman Foundation; *The Holy Bible,* King James Version (KJV); the *Amplified Bible* (AMP) © The Lockman Foundation 1954, 1958, 1962, 1964, 1965, 1987;. *The New Testament: A Translation in the Language of the People,* Charles B. Williams (WMS) copyright 1937 by Bruce Humphries, Inc., copyright renewed 1965 by Edith S. Williams, Moody Bible Institute; and the New King James Version (NKJV). Copyright © 1982 by Thomas Nelson, Inc. Used by permission. All rights reserved.

Printed in the United States of America

2 3 4 5 6 7 8 9 10 / 18 17 16 15 14 13 12

We can begin each day with the deeply encouraging realization, *I'm accepted by God, not on the basis of my personal performance, but on the basis of the infinitely perfect righteousness of Jesus Christ.*

INCREDIBLE INHERITANCE

> *To me . . . this grace was given, to preach to*
> *the Gentiles the unsearchable riches of Christ.*
> (EPHESIANS 3:8)

Years ago our pastor told about a southern plantation owner who left a $50,000 inheritance (perhaps equivalent to half a million dollars today) to a former slave who'd served him faithfully all his life. The estate's lawyer duly notified the old man and told him the money was deposited at a local bank.

Weeks went by, and the former slave never called for any of his inheritance. Finally, the banker called him in and told him again he had $50,000 available to draw on at any time. "Sir," the old man replied, "do you think I can have fifty cents to buy a sack of cornmeal?"

That story illustrates the plight of many Christians today. Paul wrote of preaching "the unsearchable riches of Christ" (Ephesians 3:8) — referring not to financial wealth but to the glorious truths of the gospel. It's as if each of us has $50,000 available in the gospel, yet most of us are hoping we can squeeze out fifty cents' worth. We don't understand the riches of the gospel any more than the former slave understood his inheritance.

Suppose also that the slave was not only poverty-stricken but also deep in debt for back rent. With his inheritance, he could not only pay off the debt but also buy his house. His inheritance far surpasses his debt. This is the truth of the gospel. We owe an enormous spiritual debt to God; there's no way we can repay it. The gospel tells us Jesus Christ paid our debt, but it also tells us far more: We're no longer enemies and objects of God's wrath. We're now His sons and daughters, heirs with Christ to all His unsearchable riches. This is the good news of the gospel.

The Gospel for Real Life

HOLINESS AND GRACE

Strive for . . . the holiness without which no one will see the Lord.

(HEBREWS 12:14)

The Holy Spirit's work in transforming us more and more into the likeness of Christ is called sanctification. Our involvement and cooperation with Him in His work is what I call the pursuit of holiness. That expression is taken from Hebrews 12:14: "Strive for [literally: *pursue*] . . . the holiness without which no one will see the Lord."

This pursuit requires sustained, vigorous effort. It allows for no indolence, no lethargy, no halfhearted commitment, and no laissez-faire attitude toward even the smallest sins. In short, it demands the highest priority in a Christian's life because to be holy is to be like Christ — God's goal for every Christian.

The word *pursue* in this context means to strive to gain or accomplish. In Philippians 3:12-14, this word is translated "press on." In the New Testament it is most commonly translated "persecute," carrying the word's common meaning — to track down in order to harm or destroy.

At the same time, however, the pursuit of holiness must be anchored in the grace of God; otherwise it is doomed to failure. That statement probably strikes many people as strange. A lot of Christians seem to think the grace of God and the vigorous pursuit of holiness are antithetical — in direct and unequivocal opposition.

To some, the pursuit of holiness sounds like legalism and man-made rules. To others, an emphasis on grace seems to open the door to irresponsible behavior based on the notion that God's unconditional love means we're free to sin as we please.

Grace and the personal discipline required to pursue holiness, however, go hand in hand. An understanding of how grace and personal, vigorous effort work together is essential for a lifelong pursuit of holiness.

The Discipline of Grace

BANKRUPT

No one does good, not even one.
(ROMANS 3:12)

Bankrupt! The word has a dreadful ring to it. Even in our lax and permissive society, being bankrupt still conveys some degree of disgrace and shame.

In the moral realm, the word *bankrupt* has an even more disparaging connotation. To say a person is morally bankrupt is to say he or she is completely devoid of any decent moral qualities. It's like comparing that person to Adolf Hitler.

You may never have thought of it this way, but *you* are bankrupt. You and I and every person in the world are *spiritually* bankrupt. Except for Jesus Christ, every person who has ever lived has been spiritually bankrupt. In Romans 3:10-12, Paul declared our spiritual bankruptcy in its most absolute state. We were spiritually destitute, owing God a debt we couldn't pay. Then we learned salvation is a gift from God, entirely by grace through faith (Romans 6:23; Ephesians 2:8-9). We renounced confidence in any supposed righteousness of our own and turned in faith to Jesus Christ alone for our salvation. In that act, we essentially declared spiritual bankruptcy.

But what kind of bankruptcy did we declare? In the business world, financially troubled companies can declare bankruptcy according to "chapter 7" — if it has no future as a viable business — or "chapter 11," for companies that, given time, can work through their financial problems.

So what kind of bankruptcy did we declare — permanent or temporary? I think most of us actually declared temporary bankruptcy. Having trusted in Christ alone for our salvation, we have subtly and unconsciously reverted to a works relationship with God in our Christian lives. We recognize that even our best efforts cannot get us to heaven, but we do think they earn God's blessings in our daily lives.

Transforming Grace

Dust to Glory

You were dead in the trespasses and sins in which you once walked. . . .
But God . . . made us alive together with Christ.

(Ephesians 2:1,4-5)

The word *gospel* essentially means "good news," specifically about our relationship with God. We all like good news, especially if it addresses bad news we've just received. If you've just been told you have cancer, it's good news when the doctor tells you it's a type that readily responds to treatment.

The gospel is like that. It's good news that directly addresses our ultimate bad news. The Bible tells us we were in deep trouble with God; we were unrighteous and ungodly, and God's wrath is revealed "against all the godlessness and wickedness of men"; in fact, we were "by nature objects of [God's] wrath" (Romans 1:18, NIV; Ephesians 2:3, NIV). Coming into the world as a baby, before you'd ever done anything bad, you were an object of God's wrath. That's the bad news.

Then the Bible tells us that God has provided a solution far surpassing our problem. The Good News always outweighs the bad — as in Ephesians 2:1-9. After telling us we were objects of God's wrath, Paul added: "But . . . God, who is rich in mercy . . . raised us up with Christ, and seated us with him in the heavenly realms in Christ Jesus" (NIV). That is surely a dust-to-glory story. What greater contrast could there be than an object of God's wrath seated with His Son in glory?

This good news doesn't begin when we die. It's for now. We don't have to feel guilt-ridden and insecure before God. We don't have to wonder if He likes us. We can begin each day with the deeply encouraging realization, *I'm accepted by God, not on the basis of my personal performance, but on the basis of the infinitely perfect righteousness of Jesus Christ.*

The Gospel for Real Life

WARMTH AND DESIRE

As a deer pants for flowing streams, so pants my soul for you, O God.
(PSALM 42:1)

In the life of the godly person, this desire for God produces an aura of warmth. Godliness is never austere and cold. Such an idea comes from a false sense of legalistic morality erroneously called godliness. The person who spends time with God radiates His glory in a manner that is always warm and inviting, never cold and forbidding.

This longing for God also produces a desire to glorify God and to please Him. In the same breath, Paul expressed the desire to know Christ as well as to be like Him (Philippians 3:10). This is God's ultimate objective for us and is the object of the Spirit's work in us. In Isaiah 26:9, the prophet proclaimed his desire for the Lord: "My soul yearns for you in the night; my spirit within me earnestly seeks you." Immediately before this expression of desire for the Lord, he expresses a desire for His glory: "Your name and renown are the desire of our hearts" (verse 8, NIV). *Renown* has to do with one's reputation, fame, and eminence — or in God's case, with His glory. The prophet could not separate in his heart his desire for God's glory and his desire for God Himself. These two yearnings go hand in hand.

This is devotion to God — the fear of God, which is an attitude of reverence and awe, veneration, and honor toward Him, coupled with an apprehension deep within our souls of the love of God for us, demonstrated preeminently in Christ's atoning death. These two attitudes complement and reinforce each other, producing within our souls an intense desire for this One who is so awesome in His glory and majesty, yet so condescending in His love and mercy.

The Practice of Godliness

ON A BAD DAY

> *How much more will the blood of Christ . . .*
> *purify our conscience from dead works to serve the living God.*
> (HEBREWS 9:14)

What should we do when we've had a "bad" day spiritually, when it seems we've done everything wrong and are feeling very guilty? We must go back to the cross and see Jesus there bearing our sins in His own body (1 Peter 2:24). We must by faith appropriate for ourselves the blood of Christ that will cleanse our guilty consciences (Hebrews 9:14).

In a bad-day scenario, we might pray something like this: "Father, I've sinned against You. I've been negligent in the spiritual disciplines that I know are necessary and helpful for my spiritual growth. I've been irritable and impatient toward those around me. I've allowed resentful and unkind thoughts to lodge in my mind. I repent of these sins and claim Your forgiveness.

"You have said You justify the wicked (Romans 4:5). Father, in view of my sins today, I acknowledge that in myself I am wicked. In fact, my problem is not merely the sins I've committed, some of which I may not even be aware of, but the fact that my heart is sinful. These sins I'm now so painfully conscious of are merely expressions of my sinful heart.

"But despite my sinfulness, You have said, 'There is therefore now no condemnation for those who are in Christ Jesus' (Romans 8:1). Given my acute awareness of my sin, that's an incredible statement. How can I be without condemnation when I've so flagrantly and willfully sinned against You today?

"O Father, I know it's because Jesus bore those sins in His body on the cross. He suffered the punishment I deserve, so I might experience the blessings He deserved. So I come to You, dear Father, in Jesus' name."

The Discipline of Grace

ON A GOOD DAY

Be perfect, as your heavenly Father is perfect.
(MATTHEW 5:48)

Consider what you would probably call a "good" day spiritually — when
your spiritual disciplines are all in place and you're reasonably satisfied
with your Christian performance. Have you thereby earned God's blessing that day? Will God be pleased to bless you because you've been good?
You're probably thinking, *Well, when you put it like that, the answer's no.
But doesn't God only work through clean vessels?* Yet how good do you have
to be to be "clean"? How good is good enough?

When a Pharisee asked Jesus which of the Law's commandments was
the greatest, He replied, "'Love the Lord your God with all your heart and
with all your soul and with all your mind.' This is the first and greatest
commandment. And the second is like it: 'Love your neighbor as yourself'" (Matthew 22:37-39, NIV).

Using that as a standard, how good has your good day been? Have
you perfectly kept those two commandments? If not, does God grade on
a curve? Is 90 percent a passing grade with God? We know the answers to
those questions, don't we? We know that Jesus said, "You therefore must
be perfect, as your heavenly Father is perfect" (Matthew 5:48). And we
remember that James wrote, "For whoever keeps the whole law and yet
stumbles at just one point is guilty of breaking all of it" (James 2:10, NIV).

Regardless of our performance, we're always dependent on God's
grace, His undeserved favor to those who deserve His wrath. Some days
we may be more acutely conscious of our sinfulness and our need of His
grace, but there's never a day when we can stand before Him on our own
two feet of performance and be worthy enough to deserve His blessing.

The Discipline of Grace

BEST KEPT SECRET

Having begun by the Spirit, are you now being perfected by the flesh?

(GALATIANS 3:3)

One of the best kept secrets among Christians today is this: Jesus paid it all. I mean *all*. He not only purchased your forgiveness of sins and your ticket to heaven, *He purchased every blessing and every answer to prayer you will ever receive*. Every one of them — no exceptions.

Why is this such a well-kept secret? The core issue is that we don't believe we're still spiritually "bankrupt." Having come into God's kingdom by grace alone solely on the merit of Another, we're now trying to pay our own way by our performance. We declared only *temporary* bankruptcy; we're now trying to live by good works rather than by grace.

After we become Christians, we begin to put away our more obvious sins. We also start attending church, put money in the offering plate, and maybe join a small group Bible study. We see some positive change in our lifestyle, and we begin to feel pretty good about ourselves. We're now ready to emerge from bankruptcy and pay our own way in the Christian life.

Then the day comes when we fall on our face spiritually. We lapse back into an old sin or fail to do what we should have done. And we assume we've forfeited all blessings from God for some undetermined period of time. Our expectation of God's blessing depends on how well we feel we're living the Christian life. We think we can and must "pay our own way" with God.

Try this test: Think of a time recently when you really fell on your face spiritually. Then imagine that immediately afterward you encountered a terrific opportunity to share Christ with a non-Christian friend. Could you have done it with complete confidence in God's help?

Transforming Grace

IMPOSSIBLE DEBT

And since he could not pay, his master ordered him to be sold,
with his wife and children and all that he had, and payment to be made.

(MATTHEW 18:25)

We can't begin to appreciate the good news of the gospel until we see our deep need. Most people, even believers, have never given much thought to how desperate our condition is outside of Christ. Few ever think about the dreadful implications of being under the wrath of God. And none of us even begins to realize how truly sinful we are.

Jesus once told a story (Matthew 18:21-35) about a king's servant who owed his master ten thousand talents. (Just *one* talent was equal to about twenty years' wages for a working man.) Why would Jesus use such an unrealistically large amount when He knew that in real life it would have been impossible for any servant to accumulate such a debt?

Jesus was fond of using hyperbole to make His point. That immense sum represents a spiritual debt every one of us owes to God. It's the debt of our sins. For each of us, it's a staggering amount.

This is what the gospel is all about. Jesus paid our debt to the full. And He did far more. He also purchased for us an eternal inheritance of infinite worth. That's why Paul wrote of the "unsearchable riches of Christ" (Ephesians 3:8). And God wants us to enjoy those unsearchable riches in the here and now, even in the midst of difficult and discouraging circumstances.

Without some heartfelt conviction of our sin, we can have no serious feeling of personal interest in the gospel. What's more, this conviction should actually grow throughout our Christian lives. In fact, one sign of spiritual growth is an increased awareness of our sinfulness.

The Gospel for Real Life

GOD-CENTERED HOLINESS

You shall be holy, for I am holy.
(1 PETER 1:16)

If holiness is so basic to the Christian life, why do we not experience it more in daily living? Why do so many Christians feel constantly defeated in their struggle with sin? Why does the church of Jesus Christ so often seem to be more conformed to the world around it than to God?

Our first problem is that our attitude toward sin is more self-centered than God-centered. We're more concerned about our own "victory" over sin than we are about the fact that our sins grieve God's heart. We cannot tolerate failure in our struggle with sin chiefly because we are success-oriented, not because we know it's offensive to God.

W. S. Plumer said, "We never see sin aright until we see it as against God. . . . All sin is against God in this sense: that it is His law that is broken, His authority that is despised, His government that is set at naught. . . . Pharaoh and Balaam, Saul and Judas each said, 'I have sinned'; but the returning prodigal said, 'I have sinned against heaven and before thee'; and David said, 'Against Thee, Thee only have I sinned.'"[1] God wants us to walk in obedience — not victory. Obedience is oriented toward God; victory is oriented toward self. This may seem to be merely splitting hairs over semantics, but there's a subtle, self-centered attitude at the root of many of our difficulties with sin. Until we deal with this attitude, we won't consistently walk in holiness.

Victory is a by-product of obedience. As we concentrate on living an obedient, holy life, we'll certainly experience the joy of victory over sin. Will you begin to look at sin as an offense against a holy God, instead of as a personal defeat only?

The Pursuit of Holiness

Falling into the Trap

Whatever you ask in my name, this I will do.
(John 14:13)

I struggle with legalistic tendencies even though I know better. Several years ago I was scheduled to speak at a large church on the West Coast. Arriving about fifteen minutes before the Sunday morning service, I learned that one of the pastoral staff had died suddenly the day before. The staff and congregation were in a state of shock and grief.

Sizing up the situation, I realized the "challenge to discipleship" message I'd prepared was inappropriate. The congregation that day needed comfort and encouragement, not challenge. Knowing I needed a new message, I silently began to pray, asking God to bring to my mind something suitable for the occasion. Then I began to add up my merits and demerits for the day: Had I had a quiet time that morning? Had I entertained any lustful thoughts or told any half-truths? I'd fallen into the performance trap.

I quickly recognized what I was doing. "Lord," I said, "I don't know the answer to those questions, but it doesn't matter. I come to You today in the name of Jesus and, by His merit alone, ask for Your help." A verse of Scripture came to my mind and with it a brief outline for an appropriate message. I went to the pulpit and literally prepared the message as I spoke. God did answer prayer.

Why did God answer? Was it because I had a quiet time that morning or fulfilled other spiritual disciplines or hadn't entertained any sinful thoughts that day? No, God answered my prayer for only one reason: Jesus Christ had already purchased that answer to prayer two thousand years ago on a Roman cross. God answered on the basis of His grace alone, not because of my merits or demerits.

Transforming Grace

WHY THE CROSS?

Jesus . . . endured the cross, despising the shame.
(HEBREWS 12:2)

At the time of Christ's death, the cross was an instrument of incredible horror and shame. It was a most wretched and degrading punishment, inflicted only on slaves and the lowliest of people. If free men were at any time subjected to crucifixion for great crimes such as treason or insurrection, the sentence could not be executed until they were put in the category of slaves by degradation and their freedom taken away by flogging.[2]

How could it be that the eternal Son of God — by whom all things were created and for whom all things were created (Colossians 1:15-16) — would end up in His human nature dying one of the most cruel and humiliating deaths ever devised by man?

We know that Jesus' death on the cross did not take Him by surprise. He continually predicted it to His disciples. (See Luke 18:31-33 for one example.) And with His impending crucifixion before Him, Jesus Himself said, "What shall I say? 'Father, save me from this hour'? No, it was for this very reason I came to this hour" (John 12:27, NIV). Jesus said He came to die.

But why? Why did Jesus come to die? The apostles Paul and Peter gave us the answer in clear, concise terms. Paul wrote, "Christ died for our sins in accordance with the Scriptures," and Peter wrote, "For Christ died for sins once for all, the righteous for the unrighteous, to bring you to God" (1 Corinthians 15:3; 1 Peter 3:18, NIV).

Christ died for our sins. Jesus Christ, the eternal Son of God, took upon Himself a human nature and died a horrible death on our behalf. That is the reason for the cross. He suffered what we should have suffered. He died in our place to pay the penalty for our sins.

The Gospel for Real Life

DOES HE CARE?

Try to discern what is pleasing to the Lord.
(EPHESIANS 5:10)

The good news of the gospel is that God's grace is available on our worst days. That's true because Christ fully satisfied the claims of God's justice and fully paid the penalty of a broken law when He died on the cross in our place. Because of that, Paul could write, "He forgave us all our sins" (Colossians 2:13, NIV).

Does this mean God no longer cares whether we obey or disobey? Not at all. The Scripture speaks of our grieving the Holy Spirit through our sins (Ephesians 4:30). And Paul prayed that we "may please [God] in every way" (Colossians 1:10, NIV). Clearly, He cares about our conduct and will discipline us when we refuse to repent of conscious sin. But God is no longer our Judge. Through Christ He is now our heavenly Father who disciplines us only out of love and only for our good.

If God's blessings were dependent on our performance, they would be meager indeed. Even our best works are shot through with sin — with varying degrees of impure motives and lots of imperfect performance. We're always, to some degree, looking out for ourselves, guarding our flanks, protecting our egos. It's because we don't realize the utter depravity of the principle of sin remaining in us and staining everything we do that we entertain any notion of earning God's blessings through our obedience. And because we don't fully grasp that Jesus paid the penalty for all our sins, we despair of God's blessing when we've failed to live up to even our own desires to please God.

Your worst days are never so bad that you're beyond the reach of God's grace. And your best days are never so good that you're beyond the need of God's grace.

The Discipline of Grace

WHAT IS GRACE?

Where sin increased, grace abounded all the more.

(ROMANS 5:20)

What, then, is the grace by which we're saved and under which we live? Grace is God's free and unmerited favor shown to guilty sinners who deserve only judgment. It's the love of God shown to the unlovely. It is God reaching downward to people who are in rebellion against Him.

Grace stands in direct opposition to any supposed worthiness on our part. To say it another way: Grace and works are mutually exclusive. As Paul said in Romans 11:6, "If it is by grace, it is no longer on the basis of works; otherwise grace would no longer be grace." Our relationship with God is based on either works or grace. There's never a works-plus-grace relationship with Him.

Furthermore, grace doesn't first rescue us from the penalty of our sins, furnish us with some new spiritual abilities, then leave us on our own to grow in spiritual maturity. Rather, as Paul said, "He who began a good work in you [by His grace] will [also by His grace] carry it on to completion until the day of Christ Jesus" (Philippians 1:6, NIV).

Paul asks us today, as he asked the Galatian believers, "After beginning with the Spirit, are you now trying to obtain your goal by human effort?" (Galatians 3:3, NIV). Although the issue of circumcision was the specific problem Paul was addressing, notice that he didn't say, "Are you trying to attain your goal by circumcision?" He generalized his question and dealt not with the specific issue of circumcision, but with the broader problem of trying to please God by human effort, any effort — even good Christian activities and disciplines performed in a spirit of legalism.

Transforming Grace

THE BOOKENDS

Grow in the grace and knowledge of our Lord and Savior Jesus Christ.
(2 PETER 3:18)

As we consider various means by which Christians grow, think of each one of them as a book you're putting on the shelf of your life. In order to keep those books in place, you need two bookends.

The first bookend we need is *the righteousness of Christ*. The most important question any person can ask is: How can I, a sinful person, be accepted by an infinitely holy and righteous God? Paul told us that it's by trusting in the righteousness of Christ. Paul counted all his impressive religious credentials as rubbish in order that he might "gain Christ and be found in him, not having a righteousness of my own that comes from the law, but that which is through faith in Christ—the righteousness that comes from God and is by faith" (Philippians 3:8-9, NIV). Paul found his acceptance with God not in his own imperfect obedience, as impressive as it was, but by trusting in the perfect righteousness of Jesus Christ, which God credits to all who trust in Him as Savior. This is what faith is—trusting in Jesus Christ alone as one's Savior.

The second bookend we must set in place is *the power of Christ*. Just as our acceptance with God must come through the righteousness of Christ, so our power to live the Christian life must come from Christ as well. As Jesus indicated in John 15:5, we have no ability within ourselves to grow. All of the ability must come from Him.

The common element in these two bookends is the word *dependence*. We're dependent upon the righteousness of Christ for our acceptance with God, and upon the power of Christ for our ability to pursue spiritual growth.

Growing Your Faith

ADAM'S SIN IS OURS

In Adam all die.
(1 CORINTHIANS 15:22)

The consequences of Adam and Eve's sin went far beyond their own banishment from the Garden of Eden and the presence of God. God had appointed Adam as the federal head or legal representative of the entire human race. Consequently his fall brought guilt and depravity on all his descendants. That is, all people (except Jesus) after Adam and Eve are born with a sinful nature. David spoke of this fact when he said in Psalm 51:5, "Behold, I was brought forth in iniquity, and in sin did my mother conceive me." David's sinfulness while still in his mother's womb was not in acts of sin committed. He was referring to his sinful nature acquired at conception.

The apostle Paul explained it like this: "Therefore, just as sin came into the world through one man, and death through sin, and so death spread to all men because all sinned" (Romans 5:12). Note that Paul's sentence appears to be broken off before he finished his thought. What did Paul mean in saying that "all sinned"? We could easily assume that he was speaking of the individual sins of each of us, but that is not what he had in mind. Rather he was speaking of the fact that Adam was the legal representative of all his descendants. In that sense, what he did, we did. Therefore the consequences of his sin, in terms of both guilt and original sin, fell on all of us.

In Romans 5:18-19, Paul wrote that "the result of one trespass was condemnation for all men" and that "through the disobedience of the one man the many were made sinners" (NIV). It's clear in Paul's theology that Adam was appointed by God to act on behalf of all his posterity. That's why you and I, like David, were born with original sin, and why we were by nature objects of God's wrath.

The Gospel for Real Life

A LIFETIME MESSAGE

The word of the cross . . . is the power of God.

(1 CORINTHIANS 1:18)

If it's true our relationship with God is based on His grace instead of our performance, why are we so prone to fall into good-day–bad-day thinking? It's because we've relegated the gospel to the unbeliever.

Regardless of when you trusted Christ, the cross divides your life into two periods: "unbeliever" and "believer." What one word describes the Bible message you most needed to hear as an *unbeliever*? It's the *gospel,* the power of God for salvation (Romans 1:16). And what one word describes the message we most need to hear as *believers*? I get many different answers to that question, but most can be summed up with the word *discipleship*—demands and duties such as the spiritual disciplines, holiness, and service.

I don't question our emphasis on discipleship. Jesus did say, "Go therefore and make disciples" (Matthew 28:19). If anything, we need more challenge and instruction on this. But there's something more basic than discipleship, something that provides the necessary atmosphere in which discipleship can be practiced—the *gospel.*

We need to continue to hear the gospel every day of our Christian lives. Only a continuous reminder of God's grace through Christ will keep us from falling into good-day–bad-day thinking, where we view our daily relationship with God as based on how good we've been.

Only the joy of hearing the gospel, being reminded that our sins are forgiven in Christ, will keep the demands of discipleship from becoming drudgery. Only the gratitude and love to God that come from knowing He no longer counts our sins against us (Romans 4:8) will provide the proper motive for responding to the claims of discipleship.

The Discipline of Grace

GRACE AND MERIT

Grace and truth came through Jesus Christ.

(JOHN 1:17)

Paul sometimes used the grace of God and the merit of Christ almost interchangeably. For example: "If you let yourselves be circumcised, Christ will be of no value to you at all. . . . You who are trying to be justified by law have been alienated from Christ; you have fallen away from grace" (Galatians 5:2,4, NIV). Notice the parallel statements Paul used: *Christ will be of no value to you. You have been alienated from Christ. You have fallen away from grace.*

In Ephesians 2:4-7, Paul wrote, "But because of his great love for us, God, who is rich in mercy, made us alive with Christ even when we were dead in transgressions — it is by grace you have been saved. And God raised us up with Christ and seated us with him in the heavenly realms in Christ Jesus, in order that in the coming ages he might show the incomparable riches of his grace, expressed in his kindness to us in Christ Jesus" (NIV).

Again note the close connection between Christ and grace. *We're made alive with Christ. It's by grace we've been saved.* And God wants to express to us the incomparable riches of His grace in Christ.

Though the grace of God and the merit of Christ are not the same, they always go together in our relationship with God. We cannot experience one without the other. In terms of order, God's grace comes first. Because of His grace, the Father sent His only Son to die in our place. To say it another way, Christ's death was the result of God's grace; grace is not the result of Christ's death.

Transforming Grace

NEVER DIRECTLY

We have confidence to enter the holy places by the blood of Jesus.
(HEBREWS 10:19)

Pharisee-type believers unconsciously think they've earned God's bless-ing through their behavior. Guilt-laden believers are sure they've forfeited God's blessing through disobedience or lack of discipline. Both have forgotten the meaning of grace — God's unmerited favor to those who deserve only His wrath.

Most of us probably entertain either of these attitudes on different days. On a good day (as we perceive it), we tend toward self-righteous Pharisaism. On a not-so-good day, we allow ourselves to wallow in a sense of failure and guilt. Either way we've moved away from the gospel of God's grace, trying to relate to God directly on the basis of our perfor-mance rather than through Christ.

God never intended that we relate to Him directly. Our own perfor-mance is never good enough to be acceptable. The only way we can relate to Him is through the blood and righteousness of Jesus Christ. Only the blood of Jesus will cleanse us from a guilty conscience and give us confi-dence to enter into God's presence (Hebrews 10:19-21).

The gospel, applied every day to our hearts, frees us to be brutally honest with ourselves and with God. The assurance of His total forgive-ness through Christ's blood means we don't have to play defensive games anymore. We don't have to rationalize and excuse our sins. We can say we told a lie instead of saying we exaggerated a bit. We can admit an unforgiving spirit instead of continuing to blame others for our emotional distress. We can call sin exactly what it is, however ugly and shameful it may be, because we know Jesus bore that sin in His body on the cross. We have no reason to hide from our sins anymore.

The Discipline of Grace

CONDUCT AND CHARACTER

The mature . . . have their powers of discernment trained by
constant practice to distinguish good from evil.

(HEBREWS 5:14)

The relationship between conduct and character is an intimate one. In the form of repeated actions over time, conduct produces character. That's the teaching of 2 Peter 2:14 and Romans 6:19. But it's also true that character determines actions. What we do, we become; what we are, we do.

Conduct is always feeding character, but character is also always feeding conduct. Paul's experience while shipwrecked on the island of Malta furnishes a good example of this relationship. The islanders built the refugees a fire because of the rain and cold. Luke related in Acts 28 that Paul gathered a pile of brushwood, and, as he put it on the fire, a snake came out of the brushwood and fastened itself on Paul's hand. Under the adverse circumstances of shipwreck, why would Paul have gone about gathering fuel for a fire built and tended by someone else? Why not just stand by the fire and warm himself? Because it was his character to serve (Acts 20:33-35; 1 Thessalonians 2:7-9). He'd learned well the lesson Jesus taught when He washed His disciples' feet. Because it was Paul's character to serve, he gathered the brushwood instinctively.

Because conduct determines character, and character determines conduct, it's vitally important — extremely necessary — that we practice godliness every day. That's why Peter said, "Make every effort to supplement your faith with . . . godliness" (2 Peter 1:5-6). There can be no letup in our pursuit of godly character. Every day that we're not practicing godliness we're being conformed to the world of ungodliness around us. Granted, our practice of godliness is imperfect and falls far short of the biblical standard. Nevertheless, let us press on to know Christ and to be like Him.

The Fruitful Life

TWO STANDARDS

On these two commandments depend all the Law and the Prophets.

(MATTHEW 22:40)

Have you thought about what it means to "love the Lord your God with all your heart and with all your soul and with all your mind" (Matthew 22:37, NIV)?

Here are a few obvious aspects: You seek fellowship with Him and long to gaze upon His beauty (Psalm 27:4). You rejoice in meditating on His Word and rise early to pray (Psalm 119:97; Mark 1:35). You always delight to do His will (Psalm 40:8). A regard for His glory governs and motivates everything you do (1 Corinthians 10:31) — eating and drinking, working and playing, buying and selling, reading and speaking, even driving. You're never discouraged or frustrated by adverse circumstances because you're confident God is working all things together for your good (Romans 8:28). You're always content because you know He'll never leave you or forsake you (Hebrews 13:5).

Or look at what Jesus called the "second" commandment: "Love your neighbor as yourself" (Matthew 22:39, NIV). Among other things, this would mean that you never show selfishness, irritability, peevishness, or indifference in your dealings with others. You take a genuine interest in their welfare and seek to promote their interests, honor, and well-being. You never regard them with prideful superiority or talk about their failings. You never resent any wrongs they do to you, but instead are always ready to forgive. You always treat them as you would have them treat you.[3]

Do you begin to grasp some of the implications of what it means to obey these two commandments? Most of us don't even think about them in the course of a day, let alone aspire to obey them. Instead we content ourselves with avoiding major outward sins and performing accepted Christian duties.

The Gospel for Real Life

AT THE KING'S TABLE

You shall eat at my table always.

(2 SAMUEL 9:7)

There's a beautiful story in the life of King David illustrating God's grace to us through Christ. Mephibosheth was the son of David's bosom friend, Jonathan, son of Saul. He'd been crippled in both feet at age five. After David was established as king over all Israel, he desired to show kindness to anyone remaining of Saul's family, "for Jonathan's sake." So Mephibosheth — crippled and destitute, unable to care for himself and living in someone else's house — was brought into David's house and "ate at David's table like one of the king's sons" (2 Samuel 9:11, NIV).

Why was Mephibosheth treated this way? It was for Jonathan's sake. We might say Jonathan's loyal friendship with David "earned" Mephibosheth's seat at David's table. Mephibosheth, in his crippled and destitute condition, unable to improve his lot and wholly dependent on the benevolence of others, is an illustration of you and me, crippled by sin and unable to help ourselves. David, in his graciousness, illustrates God the Father, and Jonathan illustrates Christ.

Just as Mephibosheth was elevated to a place at the king's table for Jonathan's sake, so you and I are elevated to the status of God's children for Christ's sake. And just as being seated at the king's table involved not only daily food but other privileges as well, so God's salvation for Christ's sake carries with it all the provisions we need, not only for eternity but for this life as well.

This account both begins and ends with the statement that Mephibosheth was crippled in both feet (verses 3,13). Mephibosheth never got over his crippled condition. He never got to the place where he could leave the king's table and make it on his own. And neither do we.

Transforming Grace

OUR HIGHEST MOMENT

Far be it from me to boast except in the cross of our Lord Jesus Christ.
(GALATIANS 6:14)

Mutua Mahiaini, leader of The Navigators ministry in Kenya, addressed eloquently the issue of performance versus God's grace:

"In talking with many believers, I get the impression that most of us consider the on-going repentance of the saved as a not-so-glorious experience. A sort of sad necessity.

"Sin grieves God. We must not down-play the seriousness of it in the life of a believer. But we must come to terms with the fact that God's Grace is greater than all our sins. Repentance is one of the Christian's highest privileges. A repentant Christian focuses on God's mercy and God's grace. Any moment in our lives when we bask in God's mercy and grace is our highest moment. Higher than when we feel smug in our decent performance and cannot think of anything we need to confess.

"Whenever we fail — and fail we will — the Spirit of God will work on us and bring us to the foot of the cross where Jesus carried our failures. That is potentially a glorious moment. For we could at that moment accept God's abundant Mercy and Grace and go forth with nothing to boast of except Christ Himself, or else we struggle with our shame, focusing on that as well as our track record. . . . One who draws on God's Mercy and Grace is quick to repent, but also slow to sin."[4]

Are you and I willing to live like Mutua and the apostle Paul? Are we willing to rely on God's grace and mercy alone instead of our performance, to boast in nothing except the cross? If so, we can bask every day in the grace of God. And in the joy and confidence of that grace we can vigorously pursue holiness.

The Discipline of Grace

NO PLACE TO HIDE

I was brought forth in iniquity.

(PSALM 51:5)

Our fallen sinful nature affects and pollutes everything we do. Our very best deeds are stained with sin. Even our acts of obedience fall so far short of perfection, defiled as they are by remaining sin, that they are but as "filthy rags" (Isaiah 64:6, NIV) when compared with the righteousness God's Law requires.

If we limit our attention to single sins to the neglect of our sinful nature, we'll never discover how deeply infected with sin we really are. When David prayed his memorable prayer of Psalm 51, after he'd committed adultery with Bathsheba and had her husband murdered, he traced his heinous actions back to their original cause — his sinful nature acquired in his mother's womb.

You might be thinking, *Why devote so much attention to sin? It just makes me feel guilty.* My reason is to cause us all to realize we have no place to hide. Only against the dark backdrop of our sinfulness can we see the glory of the cross shining forth in all its brilliance and splendor.

We often resort to euphemisms to mitigate the severity of our sins. I sat with some friends across the table from a Christian leader who said, "I've had an affair." Of course we all knew what he meant, but I later wished I'd had the presence of mind to respond, "Bob, look me in the eye and say, 'I've committed adultery.'" We need to call sin what the Bible calls it and not soften it with expressions borrowed from our culture.

Furthermore, even a deep, penetrating sense of our sinfulness does not do justice to the reality of our predicament. Our situation was so desperate that only the death of God's own Son on a cruel and shameful cross was sufficient to resolve the problem.

The Gospel for Real Life

KEEP YOUR EYE ON THE GOAL

*I press on toward the goal for the prize of
the upward call of God in Christ Jesus.*

(PHILIPPIANS 3:14)

All of us face the pressure of more to do than we have time for. So we have
to set priorities. We have to determine what's most important in our lives.
We have to ask, "Do I really want to grow spiritually?"

Get your goal clearly in mind and keep focused on that. Paul used the
analogy of the competitive races of his day to challenge the Corinthians to
pay the price of growth: "Do you not know that in a race all the runners
run, but only one receives the prize? So run that you may obtain it. Every
athlete exercises self-control in all things. They do it to receive a perishable wreath, but we an imperishable. So I do not run aimlessly; I do not
box as one beating the air" (1 Corinthians 9:24-26).

In our case, we have an advantage over those Grecian runners. In
a given race, only one received the prize, and it was only a wreath that
would soon fade. But we're not in competition with anyone. We can all get
the prize, and it will last forever.

What is your spiritual goal? Do you really want to get the prize? Do
you want to grow to be the man or woman God wants you to be? Do you
want to pay the price of the spiritual disciplines you need to practice in
order to grow? Or will you be content to sort of muddle through your
Christian life and, at the end, have to sum it all up as no more meaningful
than a trip to the corner store for a loaf of bread?

The choice is yours. What will it be?

Growing Your Faith

A BIBLICAL VIEW OF GRACE

We appeal to you not to receive the grace of God in vain.

(2 CORINTHIANS 6:1)

I once heard a definition of grace as God's making up the difference between the requirements of His righteous Law and what we lack in meeting those requirements. No one is good enough to earn salvation by himself, this definition said, so God's grace simply makes up what we lack. Some receive more grace than others, but all receive whatever they need to obtain salvation. No one ever need be lost because whatever grace he needs is his for the taking.

This definition of grace sounds very generous of God, doesn't it, making up whatever we lack? The problem with this definition, though, is that it isn't true. It represents a grave misunderstanding of the grace of God and a very inadequate view of our plight as sinners before a holy God. We need to be sure we have a biblical view of grace, for grace is at the very heart of the gospel. It is certainly not necessary for someone to understand all the theology of grace to be saved, but if a person has a false notion of grace, it probably means he or she does not really understand the gospel.

For *living* by grace, we need to be sure we first understand *saving* grace. It would be a fatal injustice if I allowed you to believe that all the wonderful provisions of God's grace are yours apart from salvation through Jesus Christ.

Grace is always the same, whether God exercises it in saving us or in dealing with us as believers. In whatever way the Bible defines saving grace, that same definition applies in the arena of living the Christian life day by day.

Transforming Grace

SAINT OR SINNER?

To all the saints in Christ Jesus . . .
(PHILIPPIANS 1:1)

As Christians, should we view ourselves as saints or sinners? My answer is both. Paul often referred to believers as saints (Ephesians 1:1; Philippians 1:1), and we really are — not only in our standing before God but in our essential persons as well. We really are new creations in Christ. A fundamental change has occurred in the depths of our being. The Holy Spirit has come to dwell within us, and we've been freed from sin's dominion. But despite this we still sin every day, many times a day. And in that sense we're sinners.

We should always view ourselves both in terms of what we are in Christ (saints) and what we are in ourselves (sinners). To help us understand this twofold view of ourselves, consider Jesus as an analogy. In His own person He was sinless, but as our representative He assumed our guilt. However, He never had any of the personal feelings associated with guilt. He was fully conscious of His own sinlessness even when bearing our sins and the curse of our sins in our place.

Just as Christ could maintain a separate sense of His personal sinlessness and His official bearing of our sin, so we must distinguish between the righteousness we have in Him and the sinfulness we see in ourselves. We should always rejoice in the righteousness we have in Christ and never cease to feel deeply our own sinfulness and consequent unworthiness.

If we refuse to identify ourselves as sinners as well as saints, we risk the danger of deceiving ourselves about our sin and becoming self-righteous. Our hearts are deceitful (Jeremiah 17:9), and we all have moral "blind spots." We have a difficult enough time seeing our sin without someone insisting that we no longer consider ourselves as "sinners."

The Discipline of Grace

GOING OUR OWN WAY

You were straying like sheep.

(1 PETER 2:25)

One of the most damning indictments of mankind is found in Isaiah 53:6: "We all, like sheep, have gone astray, each of us has turned to his own way" (NIV). Going our own way is the very essence, the very core, of sin. Your way may be to give money to charity; another person's way may be to rob a bank. But neither is done with reference to God; both of you have gone your own way. And in a world governed by a sovereign Creator, that is rebellion.

When a particular territory rebels against a nation's central government, the citizens of that territory may be generally decent individuals. But all their goodness is irrelevant to the central government, to whom there's only one issue: the state of rebellion. Sometimes governments are so corrupt, we may applaud a rebellious territory. But God's government is perfect and just. His moral law is "holy, righteous and good" (Romans 7:12, NIV). No one has a valid reason to rebel against His government. We rebel for only one reason: We were born rebellious, with a perverse inclination to go our own way, to set up our own internal government rather than submit to God.

It's not that some become sinful because of an unfortunate childhood environment while others are blessed with a highly moral upbringing. Rather we're all born sinners with a corrupt nature, a natural inclination to go our own way. As David wrote, "I was brought forth in iniquity, and in sin did my mother conceive me" (Psalm 51:5). David acknowledges he was sinful while still in his mother's womb, even during the period of pregnancy when as yet he had performed no actions, either good or bad.

Transforming Grace

THE CROSS AND GOD'S HOLINESS

His wrath is poured out like fire.

(NAHUM 1:6)

Many people think that God can just forgive our sins because He's loving. Nothing could be further from the truth. The cross speaks to us not only about our sin but about God's holiness.

We usually think of God's holiness as His infinite moral purity, but there's more to it than that. The basic meaning of the word *holy* is "separate," and when used of God it means, among other things, that He's eternally separate from any degree of sin. He does not sin Himself, and He cannot abide or condone sin in His moral creatures.

He's not like the proverbial indulgent grandfather who winks at or ignores a grandchild's mischievous disobedience. Instead, God's holiness responds to sin with immutable and eternal hatred. To put it plainly, God hates sin. The psalmist said, "The boastful shall not stand before your eyes; you hate all evildoers," and "God is a righteous judge, a God who expresses his wrath every day" (Psalm 5:5; 7:11, NIV). God always hates sin and inevitably expresses His wrath against it.

The cross expresses God's holiness in His determination to punish sin, even at the cost of His Son. And it expresses His love in sending His Son to bear the punishment we so justly deserved.

We cannot begin to understand the true significance of the cross unless we understand something of the holiness of God and the depth of our sin. And a continuing sense of the imperfection of our obedience, arising from the constant presence and remaining power of indwelling sin, drives us more and more as believers to an absolute dependence on the grace of God given to us through His Son, our Lord Jesus Christ.

The Gospel for Real Life

PERSONAL RESPONSIBILITY

Consecrate yourselves, therefore, and be holy, for I am the LORD your God.
(LEVITICUS 20:7)

Another reason that we do not experience more holiness in daily living is that we have misunderstood "living by faith" (Galatians 2:20) to mean no effort at holiness is required on our part. In fact, sometimes we've even suggested that any effort on our part is "of the flesh."

The words of J. C. Ryle, bishop of Liverpool from 1880 to 1900, are instructive to us on this point: "Is it wise to proclaim in so bald, naked, and unqualified a way as many do, that the holiness of converted people is by faith only, and not at all by personal exertion? Is it according to the proportion of God's Word? I doubt it. That faith in Christ is the root of all holiness . . . no well-instructed Christian will ever think of denying. But surely the Scriptures teach us that in following holiness the true Christian needs personal exertion and work as well as faith."[5]

We must face the fact that we have a personal responsibility for our walk of holiness. One Sunday our pastor in his sermon said words to this effect: "You can put away that habit that has mastered you if you truly desire to do so." Because he was referring to a particular habit which was no problem to me, I quickly agreed with him in my mind. But then the Holy Spirit said to me, "And you can put away the sinful habits that plague you if you will accept your personal responsibility for them." Acknowledging that I did have this responsibility turned out to be a milestone for me in my own pursuit of holiness.

Will you begin to take personal responsibility for your sin, realizing that as you do, you must depend on the grace of God?

The Pursuit of Holiness

INIQUITY OF HOLY THINGS

> *God, I thank you that I am not like other men . . .*
> *or even like this tax collector.*
>
> (LUKE 18:11)

With whom do we identify, the Pharisee or the tax collector? The prodigal son or the older brother? Obviously no one wants to identify with the Pharisee or the older brother. But are we willing to identify with the tax collector and the prodigal son, as sinners deeply in need of the grace and mercy of God? Are we willing to say, "God, be merciful to me the sinner" or "I am no longer worthy to be called Your son"? Are we willing to acknowledge that even our righteous acts are no more than filthy rags in the sight of God (Isaiah 64:6)?

John Owen, known as the prince of Puritan theologians, wrote these words way back in 1657: "Believers obey Christ as the one by whom our obedience is accepted by God. Believers know all their duties are weak, imperfect and unable to abide in God's presence. Therefore they look to Christ as the one who bears the iniquity of their holy things, who adds incense to their prayers, gathers out all the weeds from their duties and makes them acceptable to God."[6]

Owen speaks of Christ bearing the iniquity of our holy things — the sinfulness of even our good works. As another Puritan preacher was reputed to have said, "Even our tears of repentance need to be washed in the blood of the Lamb." Our best works can never earn us one bit of favor with God. Let us then turn our attention from our own performance — whether it seems good or bad — and look to the gospel of Jesus Christ, which is God's provision for our sin, not only on the day we trusted Christ for salvation but every day of our Christian lives.

The Discipline of Grace

MAKING UP OUR DEFICIENCIES?

God, be merciful to me, a sinner!

(LUKE 18:13)

Sin is more than actions; it's an attitude that ignores God's Law. It's more than a rebellious attitude; sin is a state of corruption in our inmost being, of vileness, even of filthiness in God's sight. For this reason the Bible never speaks of God's grace as simply making up our deficiencies — as if salvation consists in so much good works plus so much of God's grace. Rather the Bible speaks of a God "who justifies the ungodly" (Romans 4:5), who is found by those who do not seek Him, who reveals Himself to those who do not ask for Him (Romans 10:20).

In Jesus' parable in Luke 18:9-14 the tax collector did not ask God to simply make up his deficiencies. Rather, he beat his breast — a sign of his deep anguish — and said, "God, be merciful to me, a sinner!" (verse 13). He declared total spiritual bankruptcy, and on that basis, he experienced the grace of God. Jesus said the man went home justified — declared righteous by God.

Like the tax collector, we don't just need God's grace to make up for our deficiencies; we need His grace to provide a remedy for our guilt, a cleansing for our pollution. We need His grace to provide a satisfaction of His justice, to cancel a debt we cannot pay.

It may seem that I'm belaboring the point of our guilt and vileness before God. But we can never rightly understand God's grace until we understand our plight as those who need His grace.

As Dr. C. Samuel Storms said, "The first and possibly most fundamental characteristic of divine grace is that it presupposes sin and guilt. Grace has meaning only when men are seen as fallen, unworthy of salvation, and liable to eternal wrath."[7]

Transforming Grace

QUALITY OBEDIENCE

He committed no sin.
(1 PETER 2:22)

There are times when our inward desires do not match our outward conduct. We act very proper on the outside, but sin in our hearts. This was never the case with Jesus. Through one of the messianic psalms He could say, "I delight to do your will, O my God; your law is within my heart" (Psalm 40:8). He not only perfectly obeyed the Law of God; He always desired to do so and, in fact, delighted in doing it. Once He even said, "My food . . . is to do the will of him who sent me" (John 4:34, NIV).

If we think about it, we realize that obedience that isn't delighted in is not perfect obedience. Yet that was the quality of obedience Jesus rendered throughout His life.

In one of His many confrontations with His chief antagonists, the Jewish religious leaders, Jesus could unself-consciously and without any pretentiousness say, "I always do what pleases [the Father]" (John 8:29, NIV). Such a claim must include not only Jesus' outward actions and speech, but also His inward thoughts (Psalm 139:1-4). Even more important, it must include His motives, for God not only knows our thoughts but understands our motives as well (1 Chronicles 28:9; 1 Corinthians 4:5).

A little later in the same confrontation Jesus asked, "Which one of you convicts me of sin?" (John 8:46). Jesus dared His critics to name a single sin He had committed, knowing full well how eager they would have been to do so if it were possible.

It's no wonder that at the beginning of His ministry and again toward the end of it, a voice came from heaven saying, "This is my beloved Son, with whom I am well pleased" (Matthew 3:17; 17:5).

The Gospel for Real Life

PREACH THE GOSPEL TO YOURSELF

I would remind you, brothers, of the gospel.

(1 CORINTHIANS 15:1)

To preach the gospel to yourself means that you continually face up to your own sinfulness and then flee to Jesus through faith in His shed blood and righteous life. It means that you appropriate, again by faith, the fact that Jesus fully satisfied the Law of God. In both its precepts and penalty, He fulfilled the Law of God in its most exacting requirements. And He did this in our place as our representative and our substitute. He is your propitiation, so that God's holy wrath is no longer directed toward you.

To preach the gospel to yourself means that you take at face value the precious words of Romans 4:7-8: "Blessed are those whose lawless deeds are forgiven, and whose sins are covered; blessed is the man against whom the Lord will not count his sin." You believe on the testimony of God: "There is therefore now no condemnation for those who are in Christ Jesus" (Romans 8:1). You believe that "Christ redeemed us from the curse of the law by becoming a curse for us" (Galatians 3:13). You believe He forgave you all your sins (Colossians 2:13), that He reconciled you "to present you holy and blameless and above reproach before him" (Colossians 1:22).

To preach the gospel to yourself means you appropriate by faith the words of Isaiah 53:6: "The LORD has laid on him the iniquity of us all." It means you dwell upon the promise that God has removed your transgressions from you as far as the east is from the west (Psalm 103:12), that He has blotted out your transgressions and remembers your sin no more (Isaiah 43:25).

The Discipline of Grace

THE HEARTBEAT OF THE GODLY

My soul thirsts for God, for the living God.
(PSALM 42:2)

In Psalm 27:4, David expressed an intense desire for God: "One thing have I asked of the LORD, that will I seek after: that I may dwell in the house of the LORD all the days of my life, to gaze upon the beauty of the LORD and to inquire in his temple." David yearned intensely for God Himself that he might enjoy His presence and His beauty. Because God is a spirit, His beauty obviously refers not to a physical appearance but to His attributes. David enjoyed dwelling upon the majesty and greatness, the holiness and goodness of God. But David did more than contemplate the beauty of God's attributes; he sought God Himself, for elsewhere he says, "Earnestly I seek you; my soul thirsts for you, my body longs for you" (Psalm 63:1, NIV).

The apostle Paul also experienced this longing for God: "I want to know Christ" (Philippians 3:10, NIV). The *Amplified Bible* forcefully catches the intensity of Paul's desire in this passage: "[For my determined purpose is] that I may know Him [that I may progressively become more deeply and intimately acquainted with Him, perceiving and recognizing and under-standing the wonders of His Person more strongly and more clearly]."

This is the heartbeat of the godly person. As he contemplates God in the awesomeness of His infinite majesty, power, and holiness, and then as he dwells upon the riches of His mercy and grace poured out at Calvary, his heart is captivated by this One who could love him so. He is satisfied with God alone, but he is never satisfied with his present experience of God. He always yearns for more.

The Fruitful Life

No Cross, No Gospel

*Through him we have also obtained access by faith
into this grace in which we stand.*

(Romans 5:2)

When you set yourself to seriously pursue holiness, you'll begin realizing
what an awful sinner you are. If you aren't firmly rooted in the gospel
and haven't learned to preach it to yourself every day, you'll soon become
discouraged and will slack off. In the pursuit of holiness, nothing's more
important than learning to preach the gospel to yourself every day.

In doing so, we must be careful not to preach a gospel without a cross.
All the wonderful promises of forgiveness in Scripture are based upon
Christ's atoning death. Through it He satisfied God's justice and averted
from us God's wrath. We must be careful not to rely on the so-called
unconditional love of God without realizing His love can flow to us only
as a result of Christ's atoning death.

This is the gospel by which we were saved, and the gospel by which we
must live every day of our Christian lives.

In Romans 3:24, Paul said we are justified by grace, referring to
what we might call our point-in-time salvation, the day we trusted in
Christ. In Romans 5:2, however, Paul spoke of this grace in which we
now stand. Here he refers to our day-to-day standing before God as
being on the same basis as our justification — the basis of grace. But
this grace — unmerited favor to those who deserve wrath — comes to us
through the Lord Jesus Christ.

God is the "God of all grace" (1 Peter 5:10) and is disposed to deal
with us by grace, but not at the expense of His justice. But with justice
satisfied, God can now deal with us in grace, both in our salvation and in
our day-to-day relationship with Him.

The Discipline of Grace

WHO NEEDS GRACE MOST?

You are all partakers with me of grace.
(PHILIPPIANS 1:7)

All of us need grace, the saint as well as the sinner. The most conscientious, dutiful, hardworking Christian needs God's grace as much as the most dissolute, hard-living sinner. All of us need the same grace. The sinner doesn't need more grace than the saint, nor does the immature and undisciplined believer need more than the godly, zealous missionary. We all need the same amount because the "currency" of our good works is debased and worthless before God.

Grace considers all people as totally undeserving and unable to do anything to earn the blessing of God. C. Samuel Storms has aptly written, "Grace ceases to be grace if God is compelled to bestow it in the presence of human merit. . . . Grace ceases to be grace if God is compelled to withdraw it in the presence of human demerit. . . . [Grace] is treating a person . . . solely according to the infinite goodness and sovereign purpose of God."[8]

This description of God's grace cuts both ways: It can neither be earned by your merit nor forfeited by your demerit. If you feel you deserve an answer to prayer or a particular blessing from God because of your hard work or sacrifice, you're living by works, not by grace. But it's just as true that if you despair of experiencing God's blessing because of your demerits, you're also casting aside the grace of God.

I seldom think of merit on my part, but I'm often painfully aware of my demerits. Therefore, I need to be reminded frequently that my demerits do not compel God to withdraw His grace from me, but rather He treats me with no regard whatsoever to what I deserve. I'd much rather stake my hope of His blessing on His infinite goodness than on my good works.

Transforming Grace

EVERYTHING FOR US

He laid down his life for us.
(1 JOHN 3:16)

The Law of God set forth in Scripture is a transcript of God's own moral nature. It's the law that was fully imprinted on Adam's heart as part of his being created in God's image. It's the same law that the apostle Paul said is still written on people's hearts regardless of how obscured it may now be (Romans 2:12-16). It's a universal law applicable to all people of all times.

The apostle Paul was referring to this universal moral will of God when he wrote that Christ was "born under the law" (Galatians 4:4). Jesus was born under the Law because He came to perfectly obey it in our place. He came to do what we, because of our sinful nature, could not do.

There is, however, another significant dimension to Jesus' obedience. As our representative, He not only was obligated to obey the precepts of the Law, but also to suffer its penalty for our violation of it. This obligation He freely assumed in obedience to the Father's will.

So Jesus not only obeyed the Father's universal moral will, which we call the Law of God; He also obeyed the Father's specific will for Him, namely to suffer the penalty for our sin. The writer of Hebrews referred to this specific will of God for Jesus when he wrote, "And by that will, we have been made holy through the sacrifice of the body of Jesus Christ once for all" (Hebrews 10:10, NIV).

In recent years Christians have tended to focus on the death of Christ almost to the neglect of His sinless life. Jesus' life of perfect obedience has been seen mostly as a necessary precondition to His death. However, Jesus not only died for us; He also lived for us. All that Christ did in both His life and death, He did in our place as our substitute.

The Gospel for Real Life

SAY NO

The grace of God has appeared . . . training us
to renounce ungodliness and worldly passions.
(TITUS 2:11-12)

Grace teaches us to say no to ungodliness. Ungodliness in its broadest form basically comprises disregarding God, ignoring Him, or not taking Him into account in one's life. It's a lack of fear and reverence for Him. The wickedness portrayed by Paul in Romans 1:18-32 all starts with the idea that "although they knew God, they neither glorified him as God nor gave thanks to him" (verse 21, NIV). A person may be highly moral and even benevolent and still be ungodly.

When we trust in Christ as our Savior, we bring a habit of ungodliness into our Christian lives. We were accustomed to living without regard for God. As unbelievers, we cared neither for His glory nor His will. Basically, we ignored Him. But now that we have been delivered from the dominion of sin and brought under the reign of grace, grace teaches us to renounce this attitude (as well as actions) of ungodliness. Obviously this training does not occur all at once. In fact, God will be rooting out ungodliness from our lives as long as we live on this earth.

Grace also teaches us to say no to worldly passions, the inordinate desire for and preoccupation with the things of this life, such as possessions, prestige, pleasure, or power. "For this world in its present form is passing away" (1 Corinthians 7:31, NIV).

Saying no to ungodliness and worldly passions basically means a decisive break with those attitudes and practices. In one sense, this decisive break is a divine act that occurred when we died to the dominion of sin in our lives. In another sense, we're to work out this breach with sin by putting to death the misdeeds of the body (Romans 8:13).

The Discipline of Grace

PUT OFF, PUT ON

Put off your old self . . . and . . . put on the new self.

(EPHESIANS 4:22,24)

Sometimes we get the impression that the Christian life consists mainly of negative prohibitions. These are definitely an important part of our spiritual discipline, as attested by the fact that eight of the Ten Commandments are prohibitions (Exodus 20:1-19). We need the prohibitions set forth not just in the Ten Commandments but in all the life-application sections of the New Testament. Indwelling sin needs the constant restraint of being denied its gratification.

The Christian life, however, should also be directed toward positive expressions of Christian character. All of Paul's ethical teaching is characterized by this twofold approach of putting off the old self and putting on the new self (as in Ephesians 4:21-24).

I like to think of this twofold approach as represented by the two blades of a pair of scissors. A single scissors blade is useless as far as doing the job for which it was designed. The two blades must work in conjunction with each other to be effective. And we must work both at putting off the characteristics of our old selves and putting on the characteristics of the new selves. One without the other is not effective.

Some believers seem to focus on putting off sinful practices but give little attention to what they are to put on. Too often their lives become hard and brittle and probably self-righteous, because they tend to equate godliness with a defined list of "don'ts." Other believers tend to focus on putting on certain positive traits such as love, compassion, and kindness, but they can become careless in morality and ethics. We need the dual focus of "putting off" and "putting on" — each should receive equal attention from us.

The Discipline of Grace

SAY YES

The grace of God has appeared . . . training us . . .
to live self-controlled, upright, and godly lives.
(TITUS 2:11-12)

In Titus 2:11-12 , Paul expressed both the negative and positive aspects of what grace accomplishes in the Christian life: "For the grace of God has appeared, bringing salvation for all people, training us to [*negatively*] renounce ungodliness and worldly passions, and to [*positively*] live self-controlled, upright, and godly lives in the present age."

Those three words — *self-controlled, upright,* and *godly* — are considered by most Bible commentators to refer to actions with regard to one's self, one's neighbor, and God.

Self-control expresses the self-restraint we need to practice toward the good and legitimate things of life, as well as the outright denial of things clearly sinful.

Upright or righteous conduct refers to just and right actions toward other people, doing to them what we would have them do to us (Matthew 7:12).

Godliness is having a regard for God's glory and God's will in every aspect of our lives, doing everything out of reverence and love for Him. Matthew Henry has a helpful description of godliness in his commentary on Titus 2:12: "Personal and relative duties must be done in obedience to his commands, with due aim at pleasing and honouring him, from principles of holy love and fear of him. But there is an express and direct duty also that we owe to God, namely, belief and acknowledgment of his being and perfections, paying him internal and external worship and homage, — loving, fearing, and trusting in him, — depending on him, and devoting ourselves to him, — observing all those religious duties and ordinances that he has appointed, — praying to him, praising him, and meditating on his word and works."[9]

The Discipline of Grace

AMAZING FOR ALL

The grace of the Lord Jesus be with all. Amen.
(REVELATION 22:21)

John Newton, the debauched and dissolute slave trader, after his conversion, wrote the wonderful old hymn "Amazing Grace." He never tired of contemplating with awed amazement the wonder of a grace that would reach even to him. But the person who grew up in a godly Christian family, who trusted Christ at an early age, and who never indulged in any so-called "gross" sins should be just as amazed at the grace of God as was John Newton.

Here's a spiritual principle regarding the grace of God: To the extent that you're clinging to any vestiges of self-righteousness or putting any confidence in your own spiritual attainments, to that degree you are not living by the grace of God in your life. This principle applies both in salvation and in living the Christian life. Grace and good works (that is, works done to earn favor with God) are mutually exclusive. We cannot stand, as it were, with one foot on grace and the other on our own works of merit. If you're trusting to any degree in your own morality or religious attainments, or if you believe God will somehow recognize any of your good works as merit toward your salvation, you need to seriously consider if you're truly a Christian. We must be absolutely clear about the truth of the gospel of salvation.

More than two hundred years ago, Abraham Booth (1734–1806), a Baptist pastor in England, wrote, "Let the reader . . . carefully remember, that grace is either absolutely free, or it is not at all: and, that he who professes to look for salvation by grace, either believes in his heart to be saved entirely by it, or he acts inconsistently in affairs of the greatest importance."[10]

Transforming Grace

A SUFFERING LIFE

He learned obedience through what he suffered.

(HEBREWS 5:8)

The suffering of Christ was not limited to the hours He hung on the cross. It actually began at His incarnation when He laid aside His divine glory. and assumed a human nature subject to the same physical weaknesses and infirmities we are exposed to.

He was born into a poor family in a nation under the heel of a foreign empire. His first crib was an animal's feed trough. During His three years of public ministry, His brothers did not believe in Him and on at least one occasion mocked Him (John 7:1-5). He was misunderstood, criticized, and harassed by the Jewish religious leaders. In the words of Isaiah, "He was despised and rejected by men, a man of sorrows, and familiar with suffering" (Isaiah 53:3, NIV).

In Galatians 6:7, Paul stated a universal moral principle: A man reaps what he sows. Sin has consequences, both spiritual and temporal. Jesus, in a sense, reaped what we have sown.[11] His entire life was one of suffering obedience and obedient suffering. Of course, His suffering reached its climax on the cross, but even there we see His perfect obedience when he prayed the night before: "My Father, if it is possible, may this cup be taken from me. Yet not as I will, but as you will" (Matthew 26:39, NIV).

Jesus actively obeyed even in His death, when He "offered himself without blemish to God" (Hebrews 9:14), functioning as both high priest and sacrifice. Further, even before His death He said, "I lay down my life for the sheep. . . . No one takes it from me, but I lay it down of my own accord" (John 10:15,18). In that sense Jesus obeyed as actively on the cross as He had throughout His life.

The Gospel for Real Life

PRACTICAL CHRISTIAN LIVING

Let your light shine before others.
(MATTHEW 5:16)

In a series of moral exhortations in Titus 2:1–3:2 we find three instances where Paul emphasized the importance of our Christian testimony before unbelievers. In verse 5, he said, "that the word of God may not be reviled." In verse 8: "so that an opponent may be put to shame, having nothing evil to say about us." And in verse 10: "so that in everything they may adorn the doctrine of God our Savior."

Paul was obviously concerned about the witness by life of the believers. In Romans he said to the Jews, "God's name is blasphemed among the Gentiles because of you" (2:24, NIV), and he must have had a similar concern about the Cretan Christians to whom Titus ministered.

What would Paul say about us today? As the unbelieving world becomes increasingly hostile to true Christianity, it will be even more eager to find inconsistencies in our lives so it can ridicule God and His Word.

More than four hundred years ago, the great reformer John Calvin voiced a similar concern: "Everything bad [the ungodly] can seize hold of in our life is twisted maliciously against Christ and His teaching. The result is that by our fault God's sacred name is exposed to insult. The more closely we see ourselves being watched by our enemies, the more intent we should be to avoid their slanders, so that their ill-will strengthens us in the desire to do well."[12]

As believers we should seek to be exemplary in every aspect of our lives, doing our best for the sake of Christ and His gospel. Our work, play, driving, and shopping should all be done with a view that unbelievers will be attracted to the gospel that they see at work in our lives.

The Discipline of Grace

HUMILITY BEFORE GOD

He humbled himself.

(PHILIPPIANS 2:8)

Humility toward God is akin to the fear of God: It begins with a high view of God's person. As we see God in His majesty, awesomeness, and holiness, we are humbled before Him. In every occasion in the Scriptures in which man was privileged to view God in His glory, he was brought low or humbled in His presence. Moses bowed to the ground and worshipped; Isaiah cried, "Woe is me!"; Ezekiel fell face down; John fell at His feet as though dead. Even the four living creatures and the twenty-four elders in heaven of Revelation fell down before the throne of the glorified Lamb.

Humility in every area of life, in every relationship with other people, begins with a right concept of God as the One who is infinite and eternal in His majesty and holiness. We are to humble ourselves under God's mighty hand, approaching every relationship and every circumstance in reference to Him. When relationships with people are good and circumstances are favorable, we are to humbly receive these blessings from His gracious hand. When people are mistreating us and circumstances are difficult, we are to humbly accept them as from an infinitely wise and loving heavenly Father.

This humility before God is basic to all our relationships in life. We cannot begin to experience humility in any other relationship until we experience a deep and profound humility in our attitude toward God. When we are conscious of our (sinful) creature relationship to an infinitely majestic and holy God, we will not wish to selfishly compare ourselves with others. And to the extent that our awareness of our lowly place before God is an abiding one, we will avoid the temptations of pride and competition.

The Fruitful Life

GRACE TO OTHERS

> *Should not you have had mercy on your*
> *fellow servant, as I had mercy on you?*
> (MATTHEW 18:33)

We're brought into God's kingdom by grace; we're sanctified by grace; we receive both temporal and spiritual blessings by grace; we're motivated to obedience by grace; we're called to serve and enabled to serve by grace; we receive strength to endure trials by grace; and we're glorified by grace. The entire Christian life is lived under the reign of God's grace.

This grace is not only to be received by us; it is, in a sense, to be extended to others. I say "in a sense" because our relationship to other people is different from God's relationship to us. He is the infinitely superior Judge and moral Governor of the universe. We are all sinners and are on an equal plane with one another. So we cannot exercise grace as God does, but we can relate to one another as those who have received grace and who wish to operate on the principles of grace.

In fact, we won't experience the peace with God and the joy of God if we aren't willing to extend grace to others. This is the point of Jesus' parable of the unmerciful servant in Matthew 18:23-34.

The person who is living by grace sees the vast contrast between his own sins against God and the offenses of others against him. He forgives others because he himself has been so graciously forgiven. He realizes that by receiving God's forgiveness through Christ he has forfeited the right to be offended when others hurt him. He practices the admonition of Paul: "Be kind to one another, tenderhearted, forgiving one another, as God in Christ forgave you" (Ephesians 4:32).

Transforming Grace

OUR PERFECT LIFE

By the one man's obedience the many will be made righteous.

(ROMANS 5:19)

How can Jesus take our place both in obeying God's Law and in suffering the consequences of our disobeying it? How can the innocent suffer for the guilty?

Because God appointed Adam as the federal head or legal representative of the entire human race (except for Jesus, of course), we all suffered the consequences of Adam's disobedience. In the same manner, Jesus was appointed as the legal representative of all who would ever trust in Him.

This legal representation is the basis on which Christ's life and death become effective for us. There would be absolutely no benefit to us if Jesus lived and died merely as a private person. His work brings us benefit only because He lived and died as our representative.

Paul used again and again the expressions *in Christ, in Him,* and *in the Lord,* referring to our union with Christ. In a spiritual but nevertheless real way we're united to Him, both legally and vitally. This "legal union" is the basis on which we can say Christ lived and died as our representative and substitute.

Paul has this in view when he wrote that we were crucified with Christ, died with Him, were buried with Him, were made spiritually alive with Him, and will ultimately be united with Him in His resurrection (see Galatians 2:20; Romans 6:4-5,10; Ephesians 2:5). All that Christ did in His life and death is effective for us because we're legally united to Him.

Therefore we can accurately say that when Jesus lived a perfect life, *we* lived a perfect life. When He died on the cross to suffer the penalty of sin, *we* died on the cross. All that Jesus did, we did, because of our legal union with Him.

The Gospel for Real Life

GRACE TEACHES US

For the grace of God has appeared . . . training us.

(TITUS 2:11-12)

When I first became a Christian, I regarded the Bible largely as a rule book. The Bible would tell me what to do or not do, and I would simply obey. It was as easy as that — so I thought.

The practical precepts of the Bible were to me no more than statements of the Law of God. They commanded but gave no ability to obey. Furthermore, they condemned me for my failure to obey them as I knew I ought. It seemed the more I tried, the more I failed. I knew nothing of God's grace in enabling me to live the Christian life. I thought it was all by sheer grit and willpower. And just as importantly, I understood little of His forgiving grace through the blood of Christ. I felt both guilty and helpless — guilty because of recurring sin patterns in my life and helpless to do anything about them.

My experience was not unusual. I would say it is fairly typical, even among many who have been Christians for years. That's why we need to understand that it is grace — not law — that disciplines us. Of course, it is actually *God* in His grace, or by His grace, who disciplines us. Or to put it more plainly, God's parental training of His children is based on the principles of grace and administered in the realm of grace.

What are the principles of grace? Basically there are two. The first is the forgiveness of all our sins and the unconditional acceptance of our persons through the atoning work of Jesus Christ. The second is the deliverance from the dominion of sin and the enabling power of the Holy Spirit in us through our union with Christ.

The Discipline of Grace

GENEROSITY BEYOND COMPARE

How will he not also with him graciously give us all things?
(ROMANS 8:32)

The fact that God deals with His children on the basis of grace without regard to merit or demerit is a staggering concept. It's opposed to almost everything we've been taught about life. We've been generally conditioned to think that if we work hard and "pay our dues," we'll be rewarded in proportion to our work: "You do so much, you deserve so much."

But God's grace doesn't operate on a reward-for-works basis. It's much better than that. God is generous beyond all measure or comparison. The Scripture says, "God so loved the world, that he gave his only Son"; and Paul spoke of this as God's "inexpressible gift" (John 3:16; 2 Corinthians 9:15). God's inexpressible generosity, however, does not stop at saving us; it provides for all our needs and blessings throughout our entire lives. As Paul said in Romans 8:32, "He who did not spare his own Son but gave him up for us all, how will he not also with him graciously give us all things?" Paul used the argument of the greater to the lesser to teach us God's generosity. No blessing we'll ever receive can possibly compare with the gift of God's Son dying for us. God demonstrated His gracious generosity to the ultimate at the cross. And Paul based the assurance that we can expect God to meet all our other needs throughout life on the fact that God has already met our greatest need.

Note that Paul said God will "graciously" or freely give us all things. Just as salvation is given freely to all who trust in Christ, so all blessings are given freely to us, also through faith in Christ.

Transforming Grace

TAKING SIN SERIOUSLY

> *The wages of sin is death.*
>
> (ROMANS 6:23)

Yet another reason we don't experience more holiness in our daily lives is that we don't take some sin seriously. We've mentally categorized sins into that which is unacceptable and that which may be tolerated a bit.

In commenting on some of the more minute Old Testament dietary laws God gave to the children of Israel, Andrew Bonar said, "It is not the importance of the thing, but the majesty of the Lawgiver, that is to be the standard of obedience. . . . Some, indeed, might reckon such minute and arbitrary rules as these as trifling. But the principle involved in obedience or disobedience was none other than the same principle which was tried in Eden at the foot of the forbidden tree. It is really this: Is the Lord to be obeyed in all things whatsoever He commands? Is He a holy Lawgiver? Are His creatures bound to give implicit assent to His will?"[13]

But the Scripture says it is "the little foxes that ruin the vineyards" (Song of Solomon 2:15, NIV). It is compromise on the little issues that leads to greater downfalls. And who is to say that a little ignoring of civil law is not a serious sin in the sight of God?

Are we willing to call sin "sin" not because it is big or little, but because God's law forbids it? We cannot categorize sin if we are to live a life of holiness. God will not let us get away with that kind of attitude.

Take time to settle this issue in your heart right now. Will you decide to obey God in all areas of life, however insignificant the issue may be?

EMBRACED

We have come to share in Christ.

(HEBREWS 3:14)

Christ's work is not effective for everyone because not everyone is in union with Him. We're united to Christ by faith — that is, by trusting in Him as our Savior. And the moment we trust in Christ, we become partakers of and beneficiaries of all that He did in both His life and death.

We're united to Christ both *legally* and *vitally*. We can distinguish these two aspects in this way: Our legal union with Christ entitles us to all that Christ did *for* us as He acted in our place, as our substitute. Our vital union with Christ is the means by which He works *in* us by His Holy Spirit. The legal union refers to His *objective* work outside of us that is credited to us through faith. The vital union refers to His *subjective* work in us, which is also realized through faith as we rely on His Spirit to work in and through us.

Though our union with Christ has both these aspects, it is one union. We cannot have legal union without also having vital union. If through faith we lay hold of what Christ did for us, we'll also begin to experience His working in us.

Have you ever thought about the wonderful truth that Christ lived His perfect life in your place and on your behalf? Has it yet gripped you that when God looks at you today He sees you clothed in the perfect, sinless obedience of His Son? And that when He says, "This is my beloved Son, with whom I am well pleased" (Matthew 3:17; 17:5), He includes you in that warm embrace? The extent to which we truly understand this is the extent to which we will begin to enjoy those unsearchable riches that are found in Christ.

The Gospel for Real Life

GIVING YOU WINGS

You yourselves have been taught by God.

(1 THESSALONIANS 4:9)

God administers His discipline in the realm of grace. What does that mean? It means that all His teaching, training, and discipline are administered in love and for our spiritual welfare. It means God is never angry with us, though He's often grieved at our sins. It means He doesn't condemn us or count our sins against us. All that He does in us and to us is done on the basis of unmerited favor. To use the words of William Hendricksen, "God's grace is his active favor bestowing the greatest gift upon those who have deserved the greatest punishment."[14]

Where the Law condemns, grace forgives through the Lord Jesus Christ. Where the Law commands but gives no power, grace commands but does give power through the Holy Spirit who lives and works within us.

Here's a helpful little verse from centuries ago that summarizes this truth: "'Run, John, run,' the law commands, but gives neither feet nor hands. Better news the gospel brings; it bids me fly and gives me wings."[15] It's easy to memorize, and if you do so, it will help you capture the essence of what it means to be disciplined by grace.

How do you perceive God's parental training? Is it by law or by grace? How are you seeking to respond? Do you accept the forgiveness of His grace, or labor under the burden of guilt? Are you relying on your union with Christ and the indwelling Spirit for the power to respond to God's training, or is the Bible only a rule book that you struggle to obey by your own willpower?

The grace that brought you salvation is the same grace that teaches you. But you must respond on the basis of grace, not law.

The Discipline of Grace

THE GENEROUS LANDOWNER

Am I not allowed to do what I choose with what belongs to me?
(MATTHEW 20:15)

God's reward is out of all proportion to our service and sacrifice. In the kingdom of heaven, God's reward system is based not on merit but on grace, and grace always gives far more than we have "earned." As R. C. H. Lenski wrote, "The generosity and the magnanimity of God are so great that he accepts nothing from us without rewarding it beyond all computation. . . . The vast disproportion existing between our work and God's reward of it already displays his boundless grace, to say nothing of the gift of salvation which is made before we have even begun to do any work."[16]

In the parable Jesus told in Matthew 20:1-16, a landowner was progressively more generous with each group of workers he hired throughout the day. Each worker, regardless of how long he'd worked, received a day's wages. He received not what he'd earned on an hourly basis, but what he needed to sustain his family for a day. The landowner chose to pay them according to their need, not according to their work. He paid according to grace, not debt.

The parable focuses particularly on those workers hired at the eleventh hour. They were treated extremely generously, each one receiving twelve times what he'd earned on a strict hourly basis. They'd been standing all day waiting for someone to hire them so they could earn money to support their families. They needed employment more than the landowner needed their services. He hired them, not because of *his* need, but *their* need. He represents God in His gracious awareness of our needs and His continuous work to meet them.

God calls us to serve Him, not because He needs us, but because we need Him.

Transforming Grace

JUSTICE HONORED

It is appointed for man to die once, and after that comes judgment.

(HEBREWS 9:27)

All of us will eventually face judgment before a holy and just God. As we think of that inevitable day, do we want to see justice done, or mercy? Except for the most arrogantly self-righteous among us, we would all hope for mercy. Here, however, is our dilemma: God's justice is certain, and it is inflexible.

Paul says in 2 Thessalonians 1:6-8, "God is just: He *will* pay back. . . . He *will* punish those who do not know God" (NIV). And in Romans 12:19: "'It is mine to avenge; I *will* repay,' says the Lord" (NIV). Though often delayed, God's justice is nonetheless certain.

Justice may be defined as rendering to everyone according to one's due. Justice means getting exactly what we deserve — nothing more, nothing less. In our human experience a tension often exists between justice and mercy. Sometimes one prevails at the expense of the other. But with God, justice always prevails. His justice must be satisfied; otherwise His moral government would be undermined.

God does not exalt His mercy at the expense of His justice. And in order to maintain His justice, all sin without exception must be punished. Contrary to popular opinion, with God there's no such thing as mere forgiveness. There is only justice.

The death of Jesus was a complete and full satisfaction of divine justice for all who trust in Him. At the cross there's no tension between justice and mercy; instead, they meet in full harmony. While mercy has full expression, justice has been honored and magnified. It has exacted its penalty and been completely satisfied. Therefore, as believers we can rejoice in the abundant mercy of God through Christ, while also fully honoring the inviolate nature of His holy justice.

The Gospel for Real Life

More Love

It is my prayer that your love may abound more and more.
(Philippians 1:9)

How can we fulfill our responsibility to love "more and more" (1 Thessalonians 4:9-10)? Recognizing that love is an inner disposition of the soul produced only by the Holy Spirit, what can we do to fulfill our responsibility? First, the Spirit of God uses His Word to transform us. If we want to grow in love, we must saturate our minds with Scriptures that describe love and show its importance. First Corinthians 13:1-3, for example, tells us of the emptiness of all knowledge, abilities, and zeal apart from love. First Corinthians 13:4-7 describes love in terms of specific attitudes and actions. Romans 13:8-10 describes love in terms of fulfilling the Law of God in our lives.

The second thing we must do is pray for the Holy Spirit to apply His Word to our hearts and to our daily lives. Paul did not just exhort the Thessalonians to grow in love; he looked to the Lord to work in their hearts: "May the Lord make your love increase and overflow for each other and for everyone else, just as ours does for you" (1 Thessalonians 3:12, NIV). As we see instances in our lives of failing to love, we should confess them to God, asking Him to help us grow in those specific areas.

Finally, we must obey. We must do those things that love dictates. We must do no harm to our neighbor (Romans 13:10); we must meet our neighbor's needs and forgive our neighbor's wrongs against us; we must put his interests before our own; and we must reach out and embrace our brother in Christ. But we must do all this in dependence upon the Holy Spirit, who works in us to will and act according to His good purpose.

The Fruitful Life

CRUISE CONTROL OR RACE CAR?

For this is the love of God, that we keep his commandments.

(1 JOHN 5:3)

If we're to love God with all our heart and soul and mind, and if obedience is a major part of such love, it follows that we're to obey Him with all our heart, soul, and mind. We're to put everything we have into obedience to Him.

Most of us believers practice what I call a "cruise-control" approach to obedience. We press the pedal of obedience until we've brought our behavior up to a certain level or speed, which is most often determined by the behavior standard of other Christians around us. We don't want to lag behind them, nor are we eager to forge ahead. We want to just comfortably blend in. Once we have arrived at this comfortable level of obedience, we push the cruise-control button in our hearts, ease back, and relax. We don't have to watch the speed limit signs in God's Word, and we certainly don't have to experience the fatigue that comes with striving to obey Him with all our heart, soul, and mind.

By contrast consider race-car drivers. They wouldn't think of using cruise control. They're not interested in blending in with those around them. They want to win the race. So they're totally focused on their driving. They try to push their car to the outer limits of its mechanical ability and endurance, and press themselves to the limits of their skill. They're driving with all their heart, soul, and mind.

This is what it means to love and obey God with all our heart, soul, and mind. It means *striving* for holiness, in the words of Hebrews 12:14. It means *making every effort* to add to our faith the various facets of Christian character, in the words of 2 Peter 1:5-7.

The Discipline of Grace

GOD DELIGHTS TO DO GOOD

I will rejoice in doing them good.

(JEREMIAH 32:41)

When I married my first wife — who is now with the Lord — we asked that the following Scripture be read at our wedding. Note the many expressions of God's goodness: "They will be my people, and I will be their God. I will give them singleness of heart and action, so that they will always fear me *for their own good* and the *good* of their children after them. I will make an everlasting covenant with them: I will *never stop doing good* to them, and I will inspire them to fear me, so that they will never turn away from me. I will *rejoice in doing them good* and will assuredly plant them in this land with all my heart and soul" (Jeremiah 32:38-41, NIV). This sounds appropriate, doesn't it, for two young people committed to serving God full time?

But this assurance was originally given to a group of people described by God as those who "have done nothing but evil in my sight from their youth" (verse 30, NIV). They were in captivity in Babylon because of their sins over many generations.

Just a few chapters earlier, God had said to them: "This is what the LORD says: 'When seventy years are completed for Babylon, I will come to you and fulfill my gracious promise to bring you back to this place. For I know the plans I have for you,' declares the LORD, 'plans to prosper you and not to harm you, plans to give you hope and a future'" (Jeremiah 29:10-11, NIV). If anyone qualified for demerits, surely the Israelites in captivity did. Yet God promised to prosper them, to rejoice in doing them good.

Transforming Grace

JUSTICE SATISFIED

When justice is done, it is a joy to the righteous.

(PROVERBS 21:15)

What are we to expect when we stand before God's bar of judgment? Most people think God will somehow relax His inflexible justice and pardon all of us by mere sovereign prerogative. But God, by the perfection of His nature, cannot do that. He cannot exalt one of His glorious attributes (such as mercy) at the expense of another. Justice must be satisfied.

Through His death on the cross Jesus fully satisfied the justice of God on our behalf. Therefore everyone who has trusted in Christ as Savior can say, "God's justice toward me is satisfied." As believers we must steadily keep this in mind. Never again should we fear the retributive justice of God.

Yet many believers live under a sense of fear of God's justice. We know we sin continually, and sometimes that painful awareness almost overwhelms us. At such times we're still prone to view God as our judge meting out absolute justice. We fail to grasp by faith the fact that Christ Jesus has fully satisfied God's justice for us.

One morning in my private devotions I was reflecting on my sin, which seemed particularly painful to me that day. In my discouragement I blurted out, "God, You would be perfectly just in sending me to hell." Immediately on the heel of those words, though, came this thought: *No, You wouldn't because Jesus satisfied Your justice for me.*

This is the stand we must take as believers. We must not allow the accusations of Satan or the condemning indictments of our consciences to bring us under a sense of God's unrequited justice. Instead, we should by faith lay hold of the wonderful truth that God's justice has been satisfied for us by our Lord Jesus Christ.

The Gospel for Real Life

THE ACCEPTABLE MOTIVE

We love God and obey his commandments.

(1 JOHN 5:2)

Although obedience is the primary way we express love to God, it's not the same as love. Love is essentially a motive. "Love is a verb, not a feeling," the saying goes. Indeed, Jesus said we're to love our enemies (Matthew 5:44).

In another sense, however, love is not a verb but the motive that prompts and guides other verbs — certain actions. I love my enemies first by *forgiving* them for their harmful actions toward me, then by *seeking* their welfare in appropriate ways. Love needs other verbs to give it hands and feet. This can be seen in 1 Corinthians 13 where Paul used *love* as a noun, the subject of a whole list of action statements: Love is patient, love is kind, it does not envy, it does not boast, and so on.

The converse truth is that love gives validity to my actions and makes them acceptable to God. I can seek my enemies' welfare so they won't harm me again. That's manipulation, not love. It's looking out for my welfare under the guise of looking out for theirs.

Love for God is the only acceptable motive for obeying Him. This love may express itself in reverence for Him and a desire to please Him, but those expressions must spring from love. Without love, my apparent obedience may be essentially self-serving. I may fear God's punishment or His withholding of blessing, or I may conform to a certain standard of conduct because I want to fit in with the Christian culture around me. I might even obey simply because I have a compliant temperament.

All these motives may result in outward obedience, but not obedience from the heart. Only conduct arising from love is worthy of the name *obedience*.

The Discipline of Grace

When God Is Irrelevant

Whatever you do, do all to the glory of God.

(1 Corinthians 10:31)

When I talk about specific areas of our subtle, "acceptable" sins, one comment I often hear is that pride is their root cause. While I agree pride plays a major role, I believe there's another sin even more basic, more widespread, and more apt to be the root cause of other sins. It's the sin of ungodliness, of which we're all guilty to some degree.

We don't think of ourselves as ungodly. After all, we're Christians, not atheists or wicked people. How can I say that we believers are all, to some extent, ungodly?

Ungodliness may be defined as living one's everyday life with little or no thought of God, God's will, God's glory, or our dependence on God. You can readily see that someone can lead a respectable life and still be ungodly in the sense that God is essentially irrelevant in his or her life.

The sad fact is that many of us believers tend to live our daily lives with little or no thought of God. We may read our Bibles and pray at the beginning of each day, but then go out into the day's activities and basically live as though God doesn't exist. We seldom think of our dependence on God or our responsibility to Him. We might go for hours with no thought of God at all. I believe that all our other acceptable sins can ultimately be traced to this root sin of ungodliness. Ungodliness ultimately gives life to our more visible sins.

Pray that God will make you more conscious of the fact that you live every moment of every day under His all-seeing eye, knowing that He sees your every deed, hears your every word, and knows your every thought.

LOST YEARS RESTORED

How great is his goodness!
(ZECHARIAH 9:17)

Joel prophesied God's judgment upon Judah through a plague of locusts that would devour all the trees and plants, resulting in widespread famine. Then, in the midst of a prophecy of restoration, God made the following promise: "I will restore to you the years that the swarming locust has eaten, the hopper, the destroyer, and the cutter, my great army, which I sent among you" (Joel 2:25).

Consider the amazing generosity of God. He did not limit His promise merely to restoring the land to its former productivity. He said He'll *repay* them for the years the locusts have eaten, years they themselves forfeited to the judgment of God. God could well have said, "I'll restore your land to its former productivity, but too bad about those years you lost! They are gone forever. That's the price you pay for your sin." He would have been generous just to have restored them — but He went beyond that. He would cause their harvests to be so abundant they would recoup the losses from the years of famine. He said He'll repay them, though He obviously owed them nothing.

From time to time I have opportunity to minister individually to people who in some way have really "blown it" in life. Usually these people lament their "lost" years, the years when they served sin instead of God, or years that were wasted as Christians. I try to encourage them about the grace of God. I cannot promise them God will restore those lost years as He did the Israelites, but I can assure them that it is God's nature to be gracious. I encourage them to pray to this end and to realize, as they pray, that they are coming to a God who does not withhold His grace because of demerits.

Transforming Grace

THE CUP JESUS EMPTIED

My Father, if this cannot pass unless I drink it, your will be done.

(MATTHEW 26:42)

In the Garden of Gethsemane Jesus prayed, "My Father, if it is possible, may this cup be taken from me. Yet not as I will, but as you will." A little later, at His arrest, He said to Peter, "Put your sword away! Shall I not drink the cup the Father has given me?" (Matthew 26:39, NIV; John 18:11, NIV). The cup was very much on Jesus' mind that night.

What was in the cup? We generally associate it with His crucifixion. We assume that when He prayed that the cup might be taken away, He was asking to be spared from that horrible and demeaning death on the cross. There's truth in that assumption, and certainly the cup was connected with the crucifixion. But still — what was in it?

In both Old and New Testaments the cup of God is a reference to His judgment. For example, in Psalm 75:8 we read, "In the hand of the LORD is a cup full of foaming wine mixed with spices; he pours it out, and all the wicked of the earth drink it down to its very dregs" (NIV).

Jeremiah 25:15 is even more specific: "Take from my hand this cup of the wine of my wrath, and make all the nations to whom I send you drink it." And Revelation 14:10, looking out into the future, speaks of the ungodly who "will drink the wine of God's wrath, poured full strength into the cup of his anger."

So we see that the cup is a metaphorical expression referring to the judgment of God as expressed in the pouring out of His wrath on sinful nations and people.

What was in the cup Jesus drank at His crucifixion? It was the wrath of God.

The Gospel for Real Life

GROWING IN LOVE

The LORD is on my side.
(PSALM 118:6)

How can we develop our love for God so that our obedience is prompted by love instead of some lesser motive? The Scripture gives us our first clue, or beginning point, when it says, "We love because he first loved us" (1 John 4:19). Our love to God can only be a response to His love for us. If I don't believe God loves me, I cannot love Him. To love God, I must believe that He is for me, not against me (Romans 8:31) and that He accepts me as a son or a daughter, not a slave (Galatians 4:7).

What would keep us from believing God loves us? The answer is a sense of guilt and condemnation because of our sin. The same tender conscience that enables us to become aware of sins that lie deep beneath the level of external actions can also load us down with guilt. When we're under that burden and sense of condemnation, it is difficult to love God or believe that He loves us.

We cannot love God if we think we're under His judgment and condemnation. James Fraser said, "But whilst the conscience retains the charge of guilt, condemnation, and wrath, there cannot be purity, or sincerity of heart toward God, or sincerity of the love of God. Human nature is so formed, that it cannot love any object that is adverse and terrible to it."[17]

This means we must continually take those sins that our consciences accuse us of to the cross and plead the cleansing blood of Jesus. Only the blood of Christ cleanses our consciences so that we may no longer feel guilty (Hebrews 9:14; 10:2).

The Discipline of Grace

ONE BLESSING AFTER ANOTHER

May grace and peace be multiplied to you.

(1 PETER 1:2)

John wrote that Jesus was "full of grace and truth" and that "from his fullness we have all received, grace upon grace" (John 1:14,16). The idea portrayed is analogous to the ocean waves crashing upon the beach. One wave has hardly disappeared before another arrives. They just keep coming from an inexhaustible supply. So it is with the grace of God through Christ. He's full of grace and truth, and from His inexhaustible fullness we receive one blessing after another.

William Hendriksen commented on this passage as follows: "The meaning of verse 16 is that believers are constantly receiving grace in the place of grace. One manifestation of the unmerited favor of God in Christ is hardly gone when another arrives; hence grace upon grace. . . . The concept grace upon grace, an incessant supply of grace, harmonizes better with the idea from his fulness than does the simple term grace. The limitless supply or reservoir indicated by the words his fulness would seem to suggest a limitless outflow: grace upon grace."[18]

The God who was gracious to Adam and Eve both before and after the Fall, who rejoiced in doing good to the Jewish nation in captivity, who was the "God of all grace" to Peter (1 Peter 5:10) is the same gracious and generous God today. Grace is part of the very nature of God, and He cannot change. He is indeed the generous landowner of the parable in Matthew 20:1-16, continually going to the marketplace of life to find those in need of a day's wages so He can bring them into His vineyard and then reward them out of all proportion to their labors.

Transforming Grace

JOY'S STEPPING STONES

You received the word . . . with the joy of the Holy Spirit.

(1 THESSALONIANS 1:6)

Joy is a fruit of the Spirit, the effect of His ministry in our hearts. Paul wrote, "May the God of hope fill you with all joy and peace as you trust in him, so that you may overflow with hope by the power of the Holy Spirit" (Romans 15:13, NIV). It's by the power of the Holy Spirit that we experience the joy of salvation and are enabled to rejoice even in the midst of trials.

The Spirit uses His Word to create joy in our hearts. Romans 15:4 speaks of the endurance and encouragement that come from the Scriptures; the next verse says that God gives endurance and encouragement. God is the Source; the Scriptures are the means. The same truth applies to joy. Verse 13 speaks of God filling us with joy and peace as we trust Him. How would we expect God to do this? The reasonable answer is by means of the Scriptures.

When I've experienced the Lord's discipline, Hebrews 12:6 has been a means of restoring joy: "The Lord disciplines the one he loves." When I was once experiencing a severe trial, Psalm 50:15 became a source of comfort: "Call upon me in the day of trouble; I will deliver you, and you will honor me" (NIV). On another occasion when I thought my future looked bleak, I was enabled to rejoice in the Lord through the assurance of Jeremiah 29:11, "'I know the plans I have for you,' declares the LORD, 'plans to prosper you and not to harm you, plans to give you hope and a future'" (NIV).

The Spirit will use these words to promote our joy if they're in our hearts through regular exposure to and meditation upon them.

The Fruitful Life

GOD'S NECESSARY WRATH

> *The wrath of God is coming.*
>
> (COLOSSIANS 3:6)

The wrath of God is a subject ignored by most believers. Perhaps we shy away from it because of the violent emotions and behavior we frequently associate with the word *wrath* when used of sinful human beings. We're reluctant, rightly so, to attribute that same attitude and activity to God.

I suspect, however, that the more basic reason we avoid or ignore the subject is that we simply don't think of our sinfulness as warranting that degree of judgment. Frankly, most people don't think they're that bad. A divine reprimand or an occasional slap on the wrist may be needed — but an outpouring of divine wrath? That's much too severe. Perhaps another reason we avoid the subject is that we don't want to think of our nice, decent, but unbelieving neighbors and relatives as subject to God's wrath.

The Bible, however, doesn't give us that option. Again and again it asserts that the wrath of God is expressed in both temporal and eternal judgment. Noted biblical scholar Leon Morris pointed out that in the Old Testament alone, more than twenty words are used for the wrath of God, while the number of references to His wrath exceeds 580.[19]

Although God's wrath does not contain the sinful emotions associated with human wrath, it does contain a fierce intensity arising from His settled opposition to sin and His determination to punish it to the utmost. God, by the very perfection of His moral nature, cannot but be angry at sin — not only because of its destructiveness to humans, but, more important, because of its assault on His divine majesty. This is not the mere petulance of an offended deity because His commands are not obeyed. It's rather the necessary response of God to uphold His moral authority in His universe.

The Gospel for Real Life

FORGIVEN MUCH, LOVING MUCH

Though your sins are like scarlet, they shall be as white as snow.
(ISAIAH 1:18)

Jesus said, "He who is forgiven little, loves little" (Luke 7:47). In the context of that statement He essentially said the converse is also true: Those who are forgiven much, love much. The extent to which we realize and acknowledge our own sinfulness, and the extent to which we realize the total forgiveness and cleansing from those sins, will determine the measure of our love to God.

Charles Hodge said, "The great difficulty with many Christians is that they cannot persuade themselves that Christ (or God) loves them; and the reason they cannot feel confident of the love of God, is, that they know they do not deserve his love, on the contrary, that they are in the highest degree unlovely. How can the infinitely pure God love those who are defiled with sin, who are proud, selfish, discontented, ungrateful, disobedient? This, indeed, is hard to believe."[20]

But when our sense of guilt is taken away because our consciences are cleansed by the blood of Christ, we're freed up to love Him with all our hearts and souls and minds. We're motivated in a positive sense to love Him in this wholehearted way. Our love will be spontaneous in an outpouring of gratitude to Him and fervent desire to obey Him.

So if we want to grow in our love for God and in the acceptable obedience that flows out of that love, we must keep coming back to the cross and the cleansing blood of Jesus Christ. That is why it is so important that we keep the gospel before us every day. Because we sin every day, and our consciences condemn us every day, we need the gospel every day.

The Discipline of Grace

EXPERIENCING GOD'S GRACE

I came that they may have life and have it abundantly.

(JOHN 10:10)

Why do we not experience more of the endless supply of God's grace? Why do we so often seem to live in spiritual poverty instead of experiencing life to the full as Jesus promised (John 10:10)? There are several reasons that may or may not apply to a particular believer. One that might apply to most of us is our frequent misperception of God as the divine equivalent of Ebenezer Scrooge, demanding the last ounce of work out of His people and then paying them poorly. That may sound like an overstatement of our perception of God, but I believe it's a fairly accurate representation of how many Christians think.

Consider the following words from one of John Newton's hymns: "Thou art coming to a King, large petitions with thee bring; for His grace and pow'r are such none can ever ask too much."[21] How many Christians really believe those words? How many really believe His grace and power are such that we can never ask too much? Rather, we tend in the direction of believing God is reluctant to answer prayer and His grace and power aren't sufficient to fulfill our needs, let alone our requests.

We should not forget that Satan's very first temptation of mankind was based on questioning the goodness and generosity of God (Genesis 3:1-5). And his vicious attack on the patriarch Job was designed to cause Job to question God's goodness so that he would then curse God (Job 1:6-11). Satan has not changed his strategy today. This perception of God as the reluctant giver comes right from Satan and must be resisted by us if we are to experience the fullness of God's grace.

Transforming Grace

WRATH REVEALED

The wrath of God is being revealed from heaven
against all the godlessness and wickedness of men.

(ROMANS 1:18, NIV)

Some people like to think that although the wrath of God is a reality in the Old Testament era, it disappears in the teaching of Jesus, where God's love and mercy become the only expressions of His attitude toward His creatures. Jesus clearly refuted that notion: "Whoever rejects the Son will not see life, for God's wrath remains on him" (John 3:36, NIV).[22] And He frequently referred to hell as the ultimate, eternal expression of God's wrath. (See, for example, Matthew 5:22; 18:9; Mark 9:47; Luke 12:5.)

In the inspired letters of Paul, we read of God's wrath being "stored up" for the day of judgment (Romans 2:5) and that God's wrath is coming because of sin (Colossians 3:6). And the whole tenor of Revelation warns us of the wrath to come.

Having then established the grim reality of God's wrath, how are we to understand it? God's wrath arises from His intense, settled hatred of all sin and is the tangible expression of His inflexible determination to punish it. We might say God's wrath is His justice in action, rendering to everyone his just due, which, because of our sin, is always judgment.

Why is God so angry because of our sin? Because our sin, regardless of how small or insignificant it may seem to us, is essentially an assault on His infinite majesty and sovereign authority. As nineteenth-century theologian George Smeaton wrote, God is angry at sin "because it is a violation of His authority, and a wrong to His inviolable majesty."[23]

Here we begin to realize the seriousness of sin. All sin is rebellion against God's authority, a despising of His Law, and a defiance of His commands.

The Gospel for Real Life

Week 12 / THURSDAY

OUR HOLY GOD

> *Who is like you, majestic in holiness?*
>
> (EXODUS 15:11)

God has called every Christian to a holy life. There are no exceptions to this call. This call to a holy life is based on the fact that God Himself is holy. Holiness is nothing less than conformity to the character of God.[24]

Holiness in Scripture describes both the majesty of God and the purity and moral perfection of His nature. Holiness is one of His attributes[25] — an essential part of the nature of God. His holiness is as necessary as His existence — as necessary, for example, as His wisdom or omniscience. Just as He cannot but *know* what is right, so He cannot but *do* what is right.

The absolute holiness of God should be of great comfort and assurance to us. If God is perfectly holy, we can be confident that His actions toward us are always perfect and just. We're often tempted to question God's actions and complain that He is unfair in His treatment of us. This is the Devil's lie, the same thing he essentially told Eve: "God is being unfair to you" (Genesis 3:4-5). But it is impossible in the very nature of God that He should ever be unfair. Because He is holy, all His actions are holy.

We must accept by faith the fact that God is holy, even when trying circumstances make it appear otherwise. To complain against God is in effect to deny His holiness and to say He is not fair. As Stephen Charnock said, "It is less injury to Him to deny His being, than to deny the purity of it; the one makes Him no God, the other a deformed, unlovely, and a detestable God . . . he that saith God is not holy speaks much worse than he that saith there is no God at all."[26]

The Pursuit of Holiness

FAITH AND LOVE

> *In Christ Jesus neither circumcision nor uncircumcision counts for*
> *anything, but only faith working through love.*
>
> (GALATIANS 5:6)

There's an inextricable link between faith and love. It's impossible to please God without faith (Hebrews 11:6) and also impossible to please Him without love. This love arises in our hearts only as we, by faith, lay hold of the great truths of the gospel. To do this, our faith must be constantly nourished by feeding on the gospel. It's not the only message we need; we must also hear the requirements of discipleship. But the gospel is most important because it alone provides both the proper motive and the only enduring motivation to respond to our Lord's call to discipleship.

John Owen, the prince of Puritan theologians, wrote three masterful treatises on sin. He also wrote a book titled *Communion with God* in which he made this statement: "The greatest sorrow and burden you can lay on the Father, the greatest unkindness you can do to him, is not to believe that he loves you."[27] Owen wasn't soft on sin. In fact, his work on indwelling sin is almost scary as he exposes the nature, power, and deceitfulness of the sin that still resides in us. But Owen was more concerned that we keep before us the gospel: the love of God revealed in His Son Jesus Christ.

To the degree that we live with an abiding sense of His love for us in Christ, to that degree will we love God with all our heart and soul and mind. So let us not put the gospel "on the shelf" of our lives. Let us review it daily, and in the joy that it brings, pursue these disciplines.

The Discipline of Grace

ACKNOWLEDGING UNWORTHINESS

I am not worthy to have you come under my roof.

(LUKE 7:6)

I was talking one day with a man whose mother, a faithful servant of God for more than forty years, was dying of painful cancer. He said, "After all she's done for God, this is the thanks she gets." Such a statement sounds irreverent, but the man didn't intend it to be that way. He simply thought God owed his mother a better life. He only verbalized what many people feel.

There are other occasions when we remind God of the sacrifices we've made to serve Him and expect an answer to prayer in return. With such an attitude we may grumble about blessings not received instead of being grateful for those we have received.

We need to adopt the attitude of the Roman centurion described in Luke 7. This man sent some Jewish elders to Jesus asking Him to come and heal his sick servant. The elders pleaded with Jesus: "He is worthy to have you do this for him, for he loves our nation, and he is the one who built us our synagogue" (verses 4-5).

The centurion surely was a remarkable man. But his attitude about himself is even more remarkable than his deeds. Instead of thinking of what he should receive because of what he deserved, he freely confessed he didn't deserve anything. He sent word to Jesus: "Lord, do not trouble yourself, for I am not worthy to have you come under my roof. Therefore I did not presume to come to you" (verses 6-7). Because of this attitude, the centurion not only experienced the joy of having his request granted but also the added joy of knowing he had received what he didn't deserve.

Transforming Grace

WRATH AND LOVE

He himself bore our sins in his body on the tree.
(1 PETER 2:24)

While Jesus hung on the cross, darkness came over the land from noon until three o'clock. During those awful three hours, Jesus drank the cup of God's wrath in our place — the cup that we should have drunk. He drained it to its dregs.

We do not know all that transpired during those terrible hours. Scripture draws a veil over them for the most part. We do know that the physical suffering Jesus endured was only a feeble picture of the suffering of His soul. And part of that suffering was the very real forsakenness by His Father. Toward the end of that time He cried out, "My God, my God, why have you forsaken me?" (Matthew 27:46). The night before, He had been strengthened by divine assistance (Luke 22:43), but now He was left alone. God turned His back on His own dearly loved Son.

We can perhaps better understand what transpired that day by considering Paul's words in 2 Corinthians 5:21: "God made him who had no sin to be sin for us, so that in him we might become the righteousness of God" (NIV). Christ was "made sin" for us by a judicial act of God; He charged the guilt of our sin to Jesus.

However, we must always keep in mind the distinction between Christ's sinlessness in His personal being and His sin-bearing in His official liability to God's wrath. He was the sinless sin-bearer. Though officially guilty as our representative, He was personally the object of the Father's everlasting love and delight.

Should this not make us bow in adoration at such matchless love, that the Father would subject the object of His supreme delight to His unmitigated wrath for our sake?

The Gospel for Real Life

DEPENDENT DISCIPLINE

Train yourself for godliness.

(1 TIMOTHY 4:7)

Just as it's impossible for an airplane to fly with only one wing, so is it impossible for us to successfully pursue holiness with only dependence on God *or* discipline. We absolutely must have both.

Discipline, as I am now using it, refers to activities designed to train a person in a particular skill. In urging Timothy to train or discipline himself to be godly (1 Timothy 4:7), Paul borrowed a term originally referring to the training of young athletes. It later came to include both mental and moral training. Paul used it to refer to spiritual training. And Paul told Timothy, "Train yourself."

But we must not try to carry out our responsibilities in our own strength and willpower. We must depend on the Holy Spirit to enable us. At the same time we must not assume we have no responsibility simply because we're dependent. God enables us to work, but He doesn't do the work for us.

"Unless the LORD builds the house," we read in Psalm 127:1, "those who build it labor in vain. Unless the LORD watches over the city, the watchman stays awake in vain." Here the psalmist recognizes God's intimate involvement in the building and watching; he doesn't say, "Unless the LORD helps the builders and the watchman," but, "Unless the LORD builds . . . Unless the LORD watches . . . "

Yet it's just as obvious that the psalmist envisions the builders laboring and the watchman standing guard. The builders cannot put away their tools and go fishing and expect God to build the house. Neither can the watchman retire to his bed and expect God to sound the alarm if an enemy approaches. The builders must work, the watchman must stand guard; but they all must carry out their responsibilities in total dependence on God.

The Discipline of Grace

WHY WE WORRY

Do not be anxious about your life.
(MATTHEW 6:25)

Why do we worry? Because we don't believe. We're not really convinced the same Jesus who can keep a sparrow in the air knows where our lost luggage is, or how we'll pay that car repair bill. Or if we believe He *can* deliver us through our difficulties, we doubt if He *will*. We let Satan sow seeds of doubt in our minds about God's love and care for us.

The great antidote to anxiety is to come to God in prayer about everything. "Do not be anxious about anything, but in everything by prayer and supplication with thanksgiving let your requests be made known to God. And the peace of God, which surpasses all understanding, will guard your hearts and your minds in Christ Jesus" (Philippians 4:6-7). Nothing's too big for Him to handle or too small to escape His attention. Paul said we're to come to God "with thanksgiving." We should thank Him for His past faithfulness in delivering us from troubles. We should thank Him for the fact that He's in control of every circumstance of our lives and that nothing can touch us that He doesn't allow. We should thank Him that in His infinite wisdom He's able to work in this circumstance for our good. We can thank Him that He won't allow us to be tempted beyond what we can bear (1 Corinthians 10:13).

The promised result is not deliverance, but the peace of God. One of the reasons we don't find this peace is that all too often we won't settle for anything other than deliverance from the trouble. But God, through Paul, promises us peace, a peace that is unexplainable. It will guard our hearts and minds against the anxiety to which you and I are so prone.

The Fruitful Life

IN NO ONE'S DEBT

> *Who has first given to me, that I should repay him?*
> *Whatever is under the whole heaven is mine.*
>
> (JOB 41:11)

We can never obligate God by our obedience or sacrificial service. Even if we're perfectly obedient in all our Christian duties, we would still be forced to say, "We are unworthy servants; we have only done what was our duty" (Luke 17:10).

Suppose you perfectly obey all the traffic laws of your state. You always stay within the speed limit, always come to a complete stop at stop signs, always drive in the proper lane, always use your turn signals. Do you receive any reward? Not at all; that's the way you're supposed to drive. By perfect obedience of the traffic laws, you don't obligate the state to reward you in any manner. All you can say is "I have done my duty."

As the Sovereign Ruler of the universe, God has the right to require perfect obedience and faithful service from all of us without in the least obligating Himself. We owe Him that obedience and service. If we were to perfectly obey every command God has given and faithfully perform every duty — which, of course, we never do — we still could only say, "I have merely done my duty."

Through the inspired pen of the apostle Paul, the Holy Spirit again asserts God's freedom from obligation to anyone: "Who has given a gift to him that he might be repaid?" (Romans 11:35). This assertion wasn't made in a vacuum. Paul had been dealing with the difficult question of the Jews' future in the face of God's apparent spurning of them in favor of the Gentiles. Regardless of how we understand that future, the principle stated by the Holy Spirit through Paul is crystal clear: God doesn't owe anyone anything.

Transforming Grace

PROPITIATION? WHAT'S THAT?

He is the propitiation for our sins.

(1 JOHN 2:2)

The Bible uses a strange word to describe what Christ did for us when He drank the cup of God's wrath in our place: *propitiation.*

What does *propitiation* mean? I believe that the word *exhausted* forcefully captures the essence of Jesus' work of propitiation. Jesus exhausted the wrath of God. He bore the full, unmitigated brunt of it. God's wrath against sin was unleashed in all its fury on His beloved Son. He held nothing back.

Isaiah foretold this: "We esteemed him *stricken, smitten* by God, and *afflicted.* But he was *wounded* for our transgressions; he was *crushed* for our iniquities" (Isaiah 53:4-5). The italicized words describe the pouring out of God's wrath on His Son. During those awful hours when Jesus hung on the cross, the cup of God's wrath was turned upside down. Christ exhausted God's wrath. For all who trust in Him, there is nothing more in the cup. It is empty.

At the end of those terrible hours Jesus cried out, "It is finished" (John 19:30; see also Mark 15:37).[28] This was not a cry of relief, but one of triumph. He had accomplished what He came to do, to save His people from the wrath of God. And He did this by consuming it in His own person.

That's why Paul could write of our being "saved from God's wrath through him" and say that "God did not appoint us to suffer wrath but to receive salvation through our Lord Jesus Christ" (Romans 5:9, NIV; 1 Thessalonians 5:9, NIV). All who trust in Jesus need never fear the possibility of experiencing the wrath of God.[29] It was exhausted on His Son as He stood in our place, bearing the guilt of our sin.

The Gospel for Real Life

PRAY OR WORK?

For we are God's fellow workers.

(1 CORINTHIANS 3:9)

Nehemiah understood well the principle that we're both dependent and responsible. In rebuilding the wall around Jerusalem, he faced great opposition from certain enemies of the Jews. When the Jews had rebuilt the wall to half its height, these enemies "all plotted together to come and fight against Jerusalem and to cause confusion in it. And we prayed to our God and set a guard as a protection against them day and night" (Nehemiah 4:8-9).

Note Nehemiah's response to the threatened attack. His people prayed and posted a guard. He recognized his dependence on God, but he also accepted his responsibility to work — to stand guard.

Today, we would tend to divide into two camps. The more "spiritual" people would call an all-night prayer meeting. To them, posting a guard would be depending on human effort instead of God. The "practical" ones among us would do a fine job organizing the guard and assigning everyone to various watches, but they would be too busy to pray.

Nehemiah and his people did both. They recognized their dependence on God, but they also understood they were depending on Him to enable and help them, not to do their work for them.

There are instances in the Old Testament where God miraculously intervened and actually fought the battle for Israel (such as 2 Chronicles 20). But these are the exception, not the rule. However — and this is an important statement — there is not a single instance in New Testament teaching on holiness where we are taught to depend on the Holy Spirit without a corresponding exercise of discipline on our part.

The Discipline of Grace

GIVING TO GOD

What do you have that you did not receive?

(1 CORINTHIANS 4:7)

We actually cannot give God anything that He has not first given to us. David recognized this fact when the leaders of Israel gave so generously for the building of the temple. In his prayer of praise to God he said, "Who am I, and what is my people, that we should be able thus to offer willingly? For all things come from you, and of your own have we given you. O LORD our God, all this abundance that we have provided for building you a house for your holy name comes from your hand and is all your own" (1 Chronicles 29:14,16).

David knew he and his people had not given anything to God that wasn't His already. Even our service to God comes from His hand. As the prophet Isaiah said, "LORD, . . . all that we have accomplished you have done for us" (Isaiah 26:12, NIV). Paul summed it up rather conclusively when he said of God, "Nor is he served by human hands, as though he needed anything, since he himself gives to all mankind life and breath and everything" (Acts 17:25). When our every breath is a gift from God, there's really nothing left to give that hasn't been first given to us.

Where does that leave us? It leaves us in the blessed position of being eleventh-hour workers in God's kingdom (Matthew 20:1-16). It leaves us going home at the end of the day from God's vineyard profoundly grateful, knowing that the gracious landowner has been generous beyond all measure. In a word, it leaves us content, and "there is great gain in godliness with contentment" (1 Timothy 6:6).

Transforming Grace

THE SIN OF ANXIETY

He cares for you.

(1 PETER 5:7)

When we tell someone, "Don't be anxious," we're simply trying to encourage or admonish that person in a helpful way. But when God in His Word tells us, "Don't be anxious," it has the force of a moral command. It's His moral will that we not be anxious. Or to say it more explicitly, *anxiety is sin.*

Anxiety is sin for two reasons. First, it's a distrust of God. In Matthew 6:25-34, Jesus said that if our heavenly Father takes care of the birds of the air and the lilies of the field, will He not much more take care of our temporal needs? When I give way to anxiety, I'm in effect believing that God won't take care of me.

Anxiety is also a lack of acceptance of God's providence — His orchestrating all circumstances and events in His universe for His glory and the good of His people. Some believers have difficulty accepting the fact that God does in fact do this, and even those who believe this glorious truth often lose sight of it. Instead we focus on immediate causes of our anxiety rather than remembering that those causes are under God's control.

Anxiety is one of my most persistent temptations. If you're frequently tempted to anxiety as I am, can you recognize the types of circumstances that tend to make you anxious? Do you identify with me in chafing under God's providential will for you when it differs from your own agenda? If so, I encourage you to ask God to give you faith to believe that His providential will for you in these circumstances flows from His infinite wisdom and goodness and is ultimately intended for your good. Ask Him to give you a heart that is submissive to His providential will.

Respectable Sins

THIS IS LOVE

For God so loved the world, that he gave his only Son.
(JOHN 3:16)

Jesus' propitiatory work was initiated by the Father because of His great love for us. "In this the love of God was made manifest among us," the apostle John wrote, "that God sent his only Son into the world, so that we might live through him. In this is love, not that we have loved God but that he loved us and sent his Son to be the propitiation for our sins" (1 John 4:9-10).

Sometimes the work of Christ is erroneously depicted as a kind and gentle Jesus placating the wrath of a vengeful God, as if Jesus needed to persuade the Father not to pour out His wrath on us. Nothing could be further from the truth. God the Father sent His Son on this great errand of mercy and grace. Though Jesus came voluntarily and gladly, He was sent by the Father.

Scripture consistently affirms the Father's love as the compelling cause of Jesus' great work of atonement. "God demonstrates his own love for us in this: While we were still sinners, Christ died for us" (Romans 5:8, NIV). Though we all "were by nature children of wrath, like the rest of mankind," God saved us "because of the great love with which he loved us" (Ephesians 2:3-4).

Herein lies the glory of the cross. Justice and mercy are reconciled; wrath and love are both given full expression — and all so that we might experience the unsearchable riches of Christ.

What great humility and gratitude this should produce in us: humility that we were the cause of our Savior's unimaginable suffering, and gratitude that He so willingly and lovingly experienced God's wrath that we might not suffer it ourselves.

The Gospel for Real Life

WORK OR TRUST?

Trust in him at all times.

(PSALM 62:8)

We often speak of "letting the Lord live His life through me." I'm personally uncomfortable with this expression because it suggests a passivity on our part. He doesn't live His life through me. Rather, as I depend on Him, He enables *me* to live a life pleasing to Him.

Some years ago when I was following this more passive approach, which seemed more spiritual to me at the time, I was struggling to love a Christian brother. One evening God really dealt with me about my lack of love, and I sensed God saying to me, "If I love him, can you?" I responded, "Lord, I can't, but I'm willing for You to love him through me."

What happened? Over time my attitude toward this brother did change. In fact, we became good friends. Did Jesus then love him through me? No, He enabled *me* to love the man. We are not passive in the pursuit of holiness. We are the ones who love. We are the ones who clothe ourselves with compassion, kindness, humility, gentleness, and patience (Colossians 3:12). But we do this in utter dependence on Him who gives us strength.

Some would say that God's part is to work, man's part is to trust, and that the believer can do nothing but trust. But this idea that we can do *nothing* but trust is particularly troubling to me. I believe the psalmist and Nehemiah and Paul would say, "Man's part is to trust *and* work. God's part is to enable the man or woman to do the work." Or perhaps it's more helpful to say, "Our part is to work, but to do so in reliance upon God to enable us to work."

The Discipline of Grace

SOME THINGS DON'T CHANGE

I have learned in whatever situation I am to be content.

(PHILIPPIANS 4:11)

Contentment with what we have is worth far more than all the things we don't have. The person living on the basis of merit is never content. One day he thinks he isn't being rewarded fairly by God; the next day he's afraid he has forfeited all hope for any reward. Far better to adopt the biblical attitude that grace doesn't depend on merit at all, but on the infinite goodness and sovereign purpose of God. I would much rather entrust my expectations of blessings and answers to prayer to the infinite goodness of God and His sovereign purpose for my life than rely on all the merit points I could ever accumulate.

With this emphasis on contentment, I'm not suggesting we should always be satisfied with the status quo in every area of our lives and not pray for or seek improvement. Remember, God by His nature is graciously disposed to give us all good things (Romans 8:32). But for all of us, there are certain things that simply aren't going to change. In those areas, we must learn to be content, always accepting the fact that God doesn't owe us something different.

Frankly, I've had to struggle to learn this myself. God has given me a physical body that, in a number of ways, is less than average. He has given me spiritual gifts that lie largely outside the mainstream ministry of the organization I'm called to serve with. Neither of these circumstances is going to change, so I've had to learn to be content with what God has given me. I've learned this by focusing on two facts: He doesn't owe me anything, and what He has given me was given by His grace alone.

Transforming Grace

THE SCAPEGOAT

> *The goat shall bear all their iniquities on itself to a remote area.*
>
> (LEVITICUS 16:22)

The greatest scapegoat in all of history is the Lord Jesus Christ.

The word is never used of Him in the Bible, but it is used of a male goat in the Old Testament sacrificial system which pictured the one great sacrifice of Jesus in His death. Each year this elaborate system of sacrifices reached its climax on the great Day of Atonement, when two male goats were selected.

One was to be killed and its blood sprinkled on and before the mercy seat in the Most Holy Place where God symbolically dwelt (Leviticus 16:15-19). This goat's death as a sacrifice to God symbolized our Lord's propitiatory sacrifice for us on the cross.

The priest would lay his hands on the head of the second goat "and confess over it all the iniquities of the people of Israel, and all their transgressions, all their sins." Then the goat would be led "away into the wilderness," never to be seen again. This goat was called the scapegoat because all the guilt of the people was symbolically transferred to it, and their sins carried away into the desert (verses 20-22).

The death of the first goat symbolized the means of propitiating the wrath of God through the death of an innocent victim substituted in the sinner's place. The sending away of the second goat set forth the effect of this propitiation, the complete removal of the sins from the presence of the Holy God and from His people.

Since both goats represented Christ, we may say Christ became our scapegoat, bearing the guilt of our sins in His propitiatory sacrifice and by that act bearing them away from the presence of His holy Father.

The Gospel for Real Life

PATIENCE WITH OTHERS' SHORTCOMINGS

Bear one another's burdens, and so fulfill the law of Christ.

(GALATIANS 6:2)

In the Scriptures, forbearance, or tolerance, is associated with love, the unity of the believers, and the forgiveness of Christ. In Ephesians 4:2-3, Paul said that we're to live "with all humility and gentleness, with patience, *bearing with one another in love,* eager to maintain the unity of the Spirit in the bond of peace." Peter told us that "love covers a multitude of sins" (1 Peter 4:8); love for the other person causes us to overlook or tolerate his shortcomings.

I recall an instance when a friend of mine forgot an appointment we had together. Rather than being peeved, I simply shrugged it off. Later I tried to determine why I'd had such a tolerant reaction to his failure. I concluded it was because I deeply loved and appreciated this person, and the principle that "love covers a multitude of sins" was at work.

Paul said we're to bear with one another "to maintain the unity of the Spirit" — the unity applied by the Spirit to the body of Christ. We're to consider the unity of the body far more important than the petty irritants or disappointments of others. Here, Romans 12:5 is very helpful: "Each member belongs to all the others" (NIV). When I'm tempted to become irritated with my brother in Christ, remembering that he belongs to me and I to him helps quell that exasperation.

In Colossians 3:13, Paul equated forbearance with forgiveness: "Bear with each other and forgive whatever grievances you may have against one another" (NIV). Instead of letting others' actions irritate us, we're to use them as an opportunity to forgive as the Lord forgave us.

The Fruitful Life

GRACE OR DUTY?

Trust in him, and he will act.

(PSALM 37:5)

There's no question that we're responsible to pursue holiness with all the intensity the word *pursue* implies. Every moral imperative in the Bible addresses itself to our responsibility to discipline ourselves unto godliness. We aren't just to "turn it all over to the Lord" and let Him live His life through us. Rather, we're to love one another, to put to death the misdeeds of the body, and to put off the old man and put on the new man.

If we're to make any progress in the pursuit of holiness, we must assume our responsibility to discipline or train ourselves. But we're to do all this in total dependence on the Holy Spirit to work in us and strengthen us with the strength that is in Christ.

Sometimes we don't sense that we're experiencing His strength. Instead we experience deep, agonizing failure. We may even weep over our sins and wonder why the Holy Spirit doesn't come to our aid and strengthen us against the onslaught of temptation. We identify with Paul when he said, "I do not understand what I do. For what I want to do I do not do, but what I hate I do" (Romans 7:15, NIV).

Why doesn't the Spirit always strengthen us? There are several possible reasons. He may be letting us see the sinfulness of our own hearts. He may be causing us to realize how weak we are in ourselves and how dependent on Him we really are. Perhaps He is curbing a tendency toward spiritual pride and causing us to grow in humility. Whatever the reason, which we may never know, our responsibility is to utterly depend on Him. Sovereignly and with infinite wisdom, He determines how best to respond to our dependence.

The Discipline of Grace

THE PERIL OF COMPARING

When they . . . compare themselves with one another,
they are without understanding.

(2 CORINTHIANS 10:12)

We constantly see believers around us who seem more blessed by God than we are. Some are more gifted in spiritual abilities; others always succeed with little effort; others seem to have few problems or concerns. Probably none of us is exempt from the temptation to envy someone else's blessings and secretly grumble at God, or even charge Him with rank injustice, for giving another person more in some way than He has given us.

Yet God in His sovereignty has the right to bless each of us as He chooses. Consider these words from the apostle Paul: "But who are you, O man, to answer back to God? Will what is molded say to its molder, 'Why have you made me like this?' Has the potter no right over the clay, to make out of the same lump one vessel for honorable use and another for dishonorable use?" (Romans 9:20-21).

Regardless of how we understand the particular application of Paul's teaching, we cannot escape its basic principle: God is sovereign. And He's sovereign in every area of life. Our Creator has the right to endow each of us at birth with different physical and mental abilities, different temperament characteristics, and different natural talents. He also has the right to give each of us different spiritual gifts. And it's obvious God exercises those rights. We're not created equal nor given equal opportunities throughout life. Each of us has his or her own unique set of circumstances, some appearing much more favorable than others. Since God is under no obligation to any of us, He's free to bless some more than others as He chooses. He has the right to do what He wants with His blessings.

Transforming Grace

BEHIND GOD'S BACK

I am he who blots out your transgressions for my own sake.

(ISAIAH 43:25)

God uses several metaphors and colorful expressions to assure us that our sins have been literally carried away by our Lord Jesus Christ. One of them is in Psalm 103:12: "As far as the east is from the west, so far has he removed our transgressions from us" (NIV). Here was an infinite distance, as great as human vocabulary could express.

Jesus not only bore our sins on the cross, He carried them away an infinite distance. He removed them from the presence of God and from us forever. They can no longer bar our access to God's holy presence. Now "we have confidence" — or "boldness" as the King James Version more strikingly puts it — to enter God's presence (Hebrews 10:19).

Reinforcing this message is Isaiah 38:17, where King Hezekiah said to God, "You have cast all my sins behind your back." When something's behind your back, you can't see it anymore. It's out of sight. This is how He has completely dealt with our sin and put it away.

There's an emphatic ring to Hezekiah's words. They suggest a deliberate, decisive action on God's part. God Himself has cast our sins behind His back, and He is not hesitant or reluctant in doing this. He has taken the initiative, and He did so joyfully and gladly. God takes pleasure in putting our sins behind His back because He takes pleasure in the work of His Son.

Do we believe this? Do we believe the testimony of Scripture, or do we believe our guilty feelings? Only to the extent we believe God has indeed put our sins behind His back will we be motivated and enabled to effectively deal with those sins in our daily lives.

The Gospel for Real Life

THE SELF-DISCIPLINE APPROACH

Neither he who plants nor he who waters is anything,
but only God who gives the growth.

(1 CORINTHIANS 3:7)

There's no doubt that disciplined people, both believers and unbelievers, can effect change in themselves. But in the self-discipline approach to holiness, a major temptation is to rely on a regimen of spiritual disciplines instead of on the Holy Spirit.

I believe in spiritual disciplines, and I seek to practice them. But those disciplines are not the source of our spiritual strength. The Lord Jesus Christ is, and the Spirit's ministry is to apply His strength in our lives. To paraphrase 1 Corinthians 3:7, we can plant and water, but we cannot make things grow. Only the Spirit can do that. We *must* plant and water if we're to make progress in holiness, but only the Spirit can change us more and more into the likeness of Jesus.

Jonathan Edwards compiled a series of seventy resolutions to govern his own spiritual disciplines and conduct. Talk about spiritual discipline! His resolutions would make most of our present-day disciplines look like spiritual kindergarten. But at the beginning of his list he wrote these words: "Being sensible that I am unable to do any thing without God's help, I do humbly entreat him, by his grace, to enable me to keep these Resolutions, so far as they are agreeable to his will, for Christ's sake."[30] Edwards was disciplined, but he was also dependent.

I'm sure those of us who tend toward the self-discipline school of holiness agree that we must depend on the enabling power of the Spirit. We give lip service to it, but do we practice it? Do we each day and throughout the day acknowledge our dependence on Him? Or do we in fact seek to pursue holiness in the strength of our own willpower?

The Discipline of Grace

NOT AN OPTION

Strive . . . for the holiness without which no one will see the Lord.

Scripture speaks of both a holiness which we have in Christ before God and a holiness which we are to strive after. These two aspects of holiness complement one another, for our salvation is a salvation to holiness: "For God did not call us to be impure, but to live a holy life" (1 Thessalonians 4:7, NIV). To the Corinthians Paul wrote: "To the church of God in Corinth, to those sanctified in Christ Jesus and called to be holy" (1 Corinthians 1:2, NIV). The word *sanctified* here means "made holy." We are, through Christ, made holy in our standing before God and called to be holy in our daily lives.

In Hebrews 12:14 we're told to take seriously the necessity of personal, practical holiness. When the Holy Spirit comes into our lives at our salvation, He comes to make us holy in practice. If there is not, then, at least a yearning in our hearts to live a holy life pleasing to God, we need to seriously question whether our faith in Christ is genuine.

This desire for holiness may be only a spark at the beginning. But that spark should grow till it becomes a flame — a desire to live a life wholly pleasing to God. When God saves us through Christ, He not only saves us from the penalty of sin but also from its dominion. Bishop Ryle said, "I doubt, indeed, whether we have any warrant for saying that a man can possibly be converted without being consecrated to God. More consecrated he doubtless can be, and will be as his grace increases; but if he was not consecrated to God in the very day that he was converted and born again, I do not know what conversion means."[31]

The Pursuit of Holiness

GRACE FOR THE UNWORTHY

> *We are unworthy servants.*
> (LUKE 17:10)

God often blesses those who, in our opinion, seem most unworthy. We see this demonstrated forcefully in Jesus' words in Luke 4:25-27: "But in truth, I tell you, there were many widows in Israel in the days of Elijah, when the heavens were shut up three years and six months, and a great famine came over all the land, and Elijah was sent to none of them but only to Zarephath, in the land of Sidon, to a woman who was a widow. And there were many lepers in Israel in the time of the prophet Elisha, and none of them was cleansed, but only Naaman the Syrian."

Luke then recorded, "When they heard these things, all in the synagogue were filled with wrath" (verse 28). Why were these Jews so enraged that they wanted to kill Jesus (verse 29)? The widow of Zarephath and Naaman the Syrian were despised Gentiles — and therefore unworthy, in the Jews' opinion. How could God bless those Gentile dogs instead of more deserving Jews?

God blessed those two Gentiles while passing right by His own chosen people. Were the widow and Naaman more "deserving" than anyone in Israel? Not at all. Naaman, by his anger and haughtiness, was very undeserving. God often blesses people who seem unworthy to us. But that's what grace is all about, because we're all unworthy.

We rejoice in God's generosity as long as it's directed toward us or our family or friends. But how do we feel when God blesses someone we view as undeserving? Are we envious? Do we feel, as did the workers in the parable of Matthew 20, that we "have borne the burden of the day and the scorching heat" (verse 12), yet someone else has been blessed more than we have?

Transforming Grace

NEVER AGAIN REMEMBERED

I will not remember your sins.

(ISAIAH 43:25)

Not only has God blotted out our sins, He has further promised never to remember our sins, never to bring them to His mind again.

What an overwhelming thought! What joy this should bring to our hearts. Think of one of your more recent sins, of which you're now ashamed. It may have been an unkind word, a resentful attitude, or a lustful thought. Whatever it might be, God says He has put it out of His mind; He remembers it no more.

To remember no more is God's way of expressing absolute forgiveness. In Hebrews 8:12 (which quotes Jeremiah 31:34), God said, "For I will forgive their wickedness and will remember their sins no more" (NIV). And again in Hebrews 10:17-18, He said, "'Their sins and lawless acts I will remember no more.' And where these have been forgiven, there is no longer any sacrifice for sin" (NIV). Note that in both passages "remembering no more" is equated with forgiveness.

Psalm 130:3-4 states that same truth in a somewhat different way: "If you, O LORD, should mark iniquities, O Lord, who could stand? But with you there is forgiveness, that you may be feared." Here the psalmist considered the prospect that God does remember our sins, that He does keep a record of them. If such were true, it would be a terrifying thought. The psalmist said, "Who could stand?" It's a rhetorical question. None of us could successfully stand before God's bar of judgment. But then the psalmist went on to exclaim, "But with you there is forgiveness."

God does not keep a record of our sins. Instead He forgives. This, of course, anticipates the sacrifice of Christ for our sins, for "without the shedding of blood there is no forgiveness" (Hebrews 9:22).

The Gospel for Real Life

THE DISCIPLINE OF PRAYER

Give me life according to your word!
(PSALM 119:25)

How can we grow in a conscious sense of dependence on Christ? Through the discipline of prayer. Prayer is the tangible expression of our dependence. We may think we're dependent on Christ, but if our prayer life is meager or perfunctory, we thereby deny it. We're in effect saying we can handle our spiritual life through self-discipline and our innate goodness. Or perhaps we're not even committed to the pursuit of holiness.

The writer of Psalm 119 teaches us about the discipline of prayer in pursuing holiness. We usually think of it as the psalm about the Word of God, but more accurately it's an expression of the psalmist's ardent desire and commitment in pursuing holiness. Twenty-two times the psalmist pleaded for God's help in obeying His law, as in these words of prayer: "Teach me, O LORD, the way of your statutes. . . . Give me understanding, that I may keep your law and observe it with my whole heart. Lead me in the path of your commandments. . . . Incline my heart to your testimonies, and not to selfish gain!" (Psalm 119:33-36).

But notice also the psalmist's exercise of spiritual discipline with regard to God's Word: "I have stored up your word in my heart. . . . With my lips I declare all the rules of your mouth. . . . I will meditate on your precepts and fix my eyes on your ways. I will delight in your statutes; I will not forget your word" (119:11,13,15-16).

Here was both a man of discipline and a man of prayer. His discipline did not cause him to neglect prayer for God to work nor did his prayer cause him to neglect his own work. He practiced discipline *and* dependence.

The Discipline of Grace

THE FIRST LAST, THE LAST FIRST

> *Friend, I am doing you no wrong.*
> (MATTHEW 20:13)

The parable of the generous landowner in Matthew 20 is sandwiched between two almost identical statements from Jesus: "But many who are first will be last, and the last first" (Matthew 19:30). "So the last will be first, and the first last" (Matthew 20:16). How should we understand these words?

I believe Jesus is asserting the sovereign prerogative of God to dispense His favors as He pleases. I don't think His words are meant to be taken in an absolute sense, as if this would always be the case; rather, there's often no apparent correlation between what one seemingly deserves and what he or she receives. The whole point of the parable was to respond to the attitude Peter expressed to Jesus in Matthew 19:27: "See, we have left everything and followed you. What then will we have?" R. C. H. Lenski summarized Peter's assumption with this statement: "The more we do, the more we earn, and the more God owes us."[32]

If we're to succeed in living by grace, we must come to terms with the fact that God is sovereign in dispensing His gracious favors, and He owes us no explanation when His actions don't correspond with our system of merits. Indeed, as Paul said, "How unsearchable His decisions, and how mysterious His methods! For who has ever understood the thoughts of the Lord, or has ever been His advisor?" (Romans 11:33-34, WMS).

We're left without any grounds for grumbling about the treatment we receive from God. At the same time, God reserves the right to treat each of us differently, bestowing blessings as He sovereignly chooses.

Transforming Grace

KIND AND GOOD

Jesus . . . went about doing good.
(ACTS 10:38)

Kindness is a sincere desire for the happiness of others; goodness is the activity calculated to advance that happiness. Kindness is the inner disposition, created by the Holy Spirit, that causes us to be sensitive to the needs of others, whether physical, emotional, or spiritual. Goodness is kindness in action — words and deeds.

I tend to think of kindness in terms of our awareness of those around us and the thoughtfulness we can express to them, almost incidentally. Kindness may be as simple as a smile, a thank-you, or a word of encouragement or recognition. None of these expressions is costly in time or money. But they do require a sincere interest in the happiness of those around us. Apart from God's grace, most of us naturally tend to be concerned about *our* responsibilities, *our* problems, *our* plans. But the person who has grown in the grace of kindness has expanded his thinking outside himself and developed a genuine interest in those around him.

Goodness, on the other hand, involves deliberate deeds that are helpful to others. Although the Bible uses the word *good* to refer to what is upright, honorable, and noble about our ethical or moral character, it also uses it to describe actions that are not only good in themselves but also beneficial to others.

George W. Bethune well observed, "The best practical definition of goodness is given in the life and character of Jesus Christ: 'Jesus of Nazareth, who went about doing good.' So far as we resemble Jesus, in his devotion to the welfare of men, do we possess the grace of goodness."[33]

Do we aspire to be Christlike? Then we must be continually sensitive to how we might meet the needs of those around us.

The Fruitful Life

OUR SINS HURLED AWAY

For sin will have no dominion over you.

(ROMANS 6:14)

In Micah 7:19 we find another powerful metaphor of how God deals with our sin through Jesus Christ: "You will cast all our sins into the depths of the sea."

The picture is of God vigorously disposing of our sins by hurling them overboard. He doesn't just drop them over the side; He hurls them as something to be rid of and forgotten.

God is eager to cast away our sins. Because the sacrifice of His Son is of such infinite value, He delights to apply it to sinful men and women. God is not a reluctant forgiver, but a joyous one. His justice having been satisfied and His wrath having been exhausted, He's now eager to extend His forgiveness to all who trust in His Son as their propitiatory sacrifice.

What a picture of the way God treats our sins — He hurls them overboard. "And then," as Corrie ten Boom, a dear saint of the last century, used to say, "God put up a sign saying, 'No fishing allowed.'" She knew that we tend to drag up our old sins, that we tend to live under a vague sense of guilt. She knew we aren't nearly as vigorous in appropriating God's forgiveness as He is in extending it. Consequently, instead of living in the sunshine of God's forgiveness through Christ, we tend to live under an overcast sky of guilt most of the time.

This is why God gave the Jews the picture of the scapegoat in Leviticus 16:20-22, symbolically bearing away their sins. In addition to being a picture of what Jesus would do at the cross, it was an assurance to the Israelites that God had indeed honored the sacrifice of the slain goat and had put away their sins.

The Gospel for Real Life

NEHEMIAH'S EXAMPLE

I continued fasting and praying before the God of heaven.
(NEHEMIAH 1:4)

Our prayers of dependence should be of two types: planned periods of prayer and unplanned, spontaneous prayer. We see both beautifully illustrated for us in the life of Nehemiah, who was one of the Jews in exile and was cupbearer to the Persian king Artaxerxes. The book begins with Nehemiah learning of the sad state of affairs of the Jews back in Judah and the fact that the wall of Jerusalem was in ruins. Hearing this, Nehemiah sat down and wept, then fasted and prayed for a period of several months.

We can assume Nehemiah set aside a certain time or times of the day during which he earnestly besought God for the welfare of Jerusalem. Most likely he would have had to schedule his times of prayer around his daily duties, just as we have to do. Because he prayed over a period of several months, we can describe this part of Nehemiah's prayer life as planned, protracted, persevering prayer.

Then one day, when Nehemiah brought the king his wine, the king noticed Nehemiah's sadness and inquired about the cause. After Nehemiah explained his concern for Jerusalem, King Artaxerxes asked, "What are you requesting?" (Nehemiah 2:4). At this crucial moment, before Nehemiah replied, he "prayed to the God of heaven." This quick, silent prayer was probably something like "Lord, help me to speak. Give me favor in the king's heart." It was unplanned, short, and spontaneous — in contrast to his planned, protracted, persevering prayer over the previous few months.

Both types of prayer were needed in Nehemiah's situation. Each gave validity to the other. And each reflected Nehemiah's consciousness of his total dependence on God. We can learn from his example how to pray for ourselves in the pursuit of holiness.

The Discipline of Grace

THE PROMISES OF GOD

Through him . . . we utter our Amen to God for his glory.

(2 CORINTHIANS 1:20)

The Bible is full of God's promises — to provide for us spiritually and materially, to never forsake us, to give us peace in times of difficult circumstances, to cause all circumstances to work together for our good, and to bring us safely home to glory. *Not one of those promises is dependent upon our performance.* They're all dependent on the grace of God given to us through Jesus Christ.

Paul wrote, "For all the promises of God find their Yes in him" (2 Corinthians 1:20). What did Paul mean by this?

First of all, Christ in His messianic mission is the personal fulfillment of all the promises in the Old Testament regarding a Savior and coming King. As Philip Hughes wrote, "In Christ is the yes, the grand consummating affirmative, to all God's promises. . . . In Him all things 'which are written in the law of Moses, and the prophets, and the psalms' achieve their fulfillment (Lk. 24:44)."[34]

Beyond the actual fulfillment of all the promises made about Him, Christ is also the meritorious basis upon which all of God's other promises depend. John Calvin wrote in his comments on 2 Corinthians 1:20, "All God's promises depend upon Christ alone. This is a notable assertion and one of the main articles of our faith. It depends in turn upon another principle — that it is only in Christ that God the Father is graciously inclined towards us. His promises are the testimonies of His fatherly goodwill towards us. Thus it follows that they are fulfilled only in Christ. . . . Secondly, we are incapable of possessing God's promises till we have received the remission of our sins and that comes to us through Christ."[35]

Transforming Grace

ATONEMENT DAY

I will confess my transgressions to the LORD.
(PSALM 32:5)

Put yourself in the shoes of a devout Jew on the Day of Atonement. He sees the high priest slay a goat as a propitiatory sacrifice. He watches as the priest disappears into the Tent of Meeting, to enter the Most Holy Place and to sprinkle the blood of the slain goat on and before the mercy seat. Only the high priest is allowed to enter that room (after ceremonial cleansing), and even then only once a year and only with the blood of the sacrificial animal.

The devout Jew waits with some degree of anxiety for the high priest to return, very conscious that atonement for his sins is conditioned on God's acceptance of the high priest's ministry.

Finally, the high priest comes out. He lays his hands on a live goat's head and confesses over it all the sins of the people, symbolically transferring those sins to the goat. He solemnly confesses, perhaps with weeping, the people's wickedness and rebellion. Then the goat is led away, bearing their sins into the desert.

Two things were necessary for this ritual to be meaningful to an individual Jew. First, he must identify with the sins the high priest was confessing. He must acknowledge them as his own personal sins. Then he must by faith believe that the goat did indeed carry those sins away. He probably didn't understand how a goat could do this, but he believed God had ordained this rite, and somehow his sins were removed from God's presence and no longer counted against him. His faith was not in the goat but in God, who had ordained this ritual.

The same attitudes of penitence and faith are necessary for all of us today—all who trust in Jesus as our scapegoat.

The Gospel for Real Life

PRAY, BECAUSE GOD IS SOVEREIGN

I cry out to God Most High, to God who fulfills his purpose for me.
(PSALM 57:2)

Prayer assumes the sovereignty of God. If God is not sovereign, we have no assurance that He's able to answer our prayers. Our prayers would become nothing more than wishes. But while God's sovereignty, along with His wisdom and love, is the foundation of our trust in Him, prayer is the expression of that trust.

The Puritan preacher Thomas Lye wrote, "As prayer without faith is but a beating of the air, so trust without prayer [is] but a presumptuous bravado. He that promises to give, and bids us trust his promises, commands us to pray, and expects obedience to his commands. He will give, but not without our asking."[36]

While imprisoned in Rome, Paul wrote to his friend Philemon, "Prepare a guest room for me, because I hope to be restored to you in answer to your prayers" (Philemon 22, NIV). Paul hoped to be restored but didn't presume to know God's secret will. He didn't say, "I will be restored." But he did know God in His sovereignty was well able to effect his release, so he asked Philemon to pray. Prayer was the expression of his confidence in the sovereignty of God.

John Flavel, another Puritan preacher, wrote a classic treatise titled *The Mystery of Providence*, first published in 1678.[37] He began this treatise on God's sovereign providence with a discourse on Psalm 57:2: "I cry out to God Most High, to God who fulfills his purpose for me." Flavel was saying that because God is sovereign, we should pray. God's sovereignty does not negate our responsibility to pray, but rather makes it possible to pray with confidence.

Is God Really in Control?

OUR HANDS ON CHRIST'S HEAD

He himself bore our sins in his body.

(1 PETER 2:24)

To subjectively benefit from the work of the high priest in the scape-goat ritual on the Day of Atonement (Leviticus 16:20-22), the individual Israelite had to exercise both penitence and faith. Penitence is a sincere and humble acknowledgment of one's sins. Faith, in this instance, is believing God's testimony that his sins were transferred to the goat and that the guilt of them no longer hung over his head.

Of course, the scapegoat could not itself carry away the sins of the people. It was only symbolic of the true scapegoat to come, Jesus Christ. Today we see the reality of the symbol. We see Jesus as the One who not only propitiated the wrath of God, symbolized by the sacrifice of the first goat, but who also removed our sins from God's presence, symbolized by the second goat led away into the desert, bearing the sins of the people.

Those same two attitudes, penitence and faith, are necessary for all of us today who rely on Christ for salvation. We must acknowledge ourselves as sinners before a holy God. We must, so to speak, lay our hands on Christ's head and confess over Him all our transgression and rebellion. We acknowledge ourselves as sinners before a holy God, and we face up to particular sins we're aware of.

This heartfelt penitence and faith should characterize our lives throughout every day. We not only come to God through faith in Christ as both our propitiation and our scapegoat, we must live in His presence every day on the same basis. We must believe that just as the Old Testament scapegoat symbolically carried away the sins of the Jews from the presence of God, so Jesus actually carried away our sins.

The Gospel for Real Life

PLANNED PRAYER

I give myself to prayer.

(PSALM 109:4)

We need to set aside time each day for planned, protracted, persevering prayer. We need to lay before the Lord any areas of persistent sin in our lives such as gossip, irritability, impatience, lack of love, and impure thoughts. These sins need to be the object of earnest prayer that God would work in us and *enable* us to deal with them. We are the ones who must deal with these sins, but the Holy Spirit must enable us to do it.

Note the dependent discipline Paul teaches in Romans 8:13: "If by the Spirit you put to death the deeds of the body, you will live." There's the discipline of putting to death the sins of the body, but we do this "by the Spirit." This means continual, fervent prayer for the Spirit to enable us to do our duty. As John Murray said, "The believer is not endowed with a reservoir of strength from which he draws. It is always 'by the Spirit' that each sanctified and sanctifying activity is exercised."[38]

It's precisely because we aren't endowed with a reservoir of strength that we need to pray daily for the Spirit's enabling work in us. Holiness requires continual effort on our part and continual nourishing and strengthening by the Spirit. Unless you plan to pray, however, and set aside a specific time to do it, you'll find that you won't carry out your good intentions. If you don't already have this practice, why not stop and make your plan now? I also find it helpful to write down on paper (for my eyes only) the specific sins I need help to deal with and the specific virtues of Christian character in which, as far as I can tell, I most need to grow.

GOOD NEWS THAT ISN'T GOOD ENOUGH?

Proclaim the gospel to the whole creation.

(MARK 16:15)

We've loaded down the gospel of the grace of God in Christ with a lot of "oughts": *I ought to be more committed, more disciplined, more obedient.* When we think or teach this way, we're substituting duty and obligation for a loving response to God's grace.

As one pastor expressed it, we often don't make the gospel "good enough."[39] We preach grace to the non-Christian and duty to the Christian. As Richard Gilbert has written, "It sometimes seems that there is plenty of grace for you if you are not a Christian, but when you become a Christian then there are all sorts of laws you must obey and you feel like you were better off before you were converted."[40] Even our terminology betrays the way we dichotomize the Christian life into "grace" and "works" compartments. We speak of the gift of salvation and the cost of discipleship. The "cost of discipleship" isn't necessarily an unbiblical expression, but the connotation we build into it is. We often convey the idea that God's grace barely gets us inside the kingdom's door; after that, it's all our own blood, sweat, and tears.

I firmly believe in and seek to practice commitment, discipline, and obedience. I'm thoroughly committed to submission to the lordship of Jesus Christ in every area of life. And I believe in and seek to practice other commitments that flow out of that basic commitment. I'm committed to my wife "until death do us part." I'm committed to integrity and fairness in business relationships. I'm committed to seek to act in love toward everyone. But I'm committed in these areas out of a grateful response to God's grace, not to try to earn God's blessings.

Transforming Grace

CLEAN CONSCIENCE

Blessed is the man against whom the Lord will not count his sin.

(ROMANS 4:8)

God has given each of us a conscience, a moral compass within our hearts, bearing witness to His Law. In sinful or self-righteous people (those whose dominant characteristics are either obvious sin or obvious self-righteousness), the conscience is to some degree "hardened." But in a growing Christian the conscience becomes more and more sensitive to violations of God's Law. As a result, our consciences continually indict us, accusing us not only of particular sins, but, more important, of our overall sinfulness. We recognize that specific sins are simply the expressions of our still-wicked hearts. Our sinfulness is very real to us, and we find it difficult to believe God would no longer remember each offense.

It's here that I find it helpful to visualize the Old Testament scapegoat carrying away the people's sins that have been laid on its head. This is an accurate picture of what Jesus did with my sin.

In fact, Christ's work on my behalf is greater still. "How much more will the blood of Christ, who through the eternal Spirit offered himself without blemish to God, purify our conscience from dead works to serve the living God" (Hebrews 9:14). Only the blood of Christ can cleanse our consciences and quiet their accusations against us. To experience this cleansing subjectively we must agree with our consciences in true penitence, then by faith appropriate the reality of His cleansing blood. The burden of uncanceled guilt ceases.

Do you believe that the sin you're now so painfully and shamefully aware of will never be counted against you? If by faith you see Jesus as your scapegoat, you'll subjectively experience the reality of that wonderful truth and be freed from a guilty conscience to serve the living God.

The Gospel for Real Life

HOW HONEST?

Lying lips are an abomination to the LORD.

(PROVERBS 12:22)

On Christmas Eve, our doorbell rang. Answering it, I found a little four-year-old neighbor girl holding out a plate of cookies. "My mommy sent you some cookies," she said with a big smile. I thanked her and put them down someplace — and promptly forgot about them for we were just leaving for a church service. A few days later as I was walking out to my car, the little girl came down the sidewalk on her tricycle and asked how I liked the cookies. "Oh, they were fine," I said, though I hadn't even tasted them.

As I drove away, I began thinking about this. I had lied. Why? Because it was expedient; it saved me embarrassment and the little girl's disappointment (though mostly I was concerned about myself). Sure, it was of little or no consequence. But God says without qualification that He detests lying.

Thinking further, I realized this wasn't an isolated instance. The Holy Spirit reminded me of other occasions of exaggeration or manipulating a story's facts just a bit. I had to face the fact that I wasn't quite as honest as I'd considered myself to be. God taught me a valuable, though humbling, lesson.

As I've told the story of the cookies to some audiences, I've gotten a troubled reaction from a few people. Some sincere Christians think I may be nit-picking. But consider Daniel. The record states that his enemies could find no corruption in him (Daniel 6:4). It seems clear they would have seized upon any inconsistency, regardless of how small or insignificant, to bring Daniel into disrepute. But they could find none. Daniel had evidently mastered this matter of absolute integrity. We should have the same goal.

The Fruitful Life

THE SIN OF SELF-SUFFICIENCY

My mighty rock, my refuge is God.
(PSALM 62:7)

I believe one of the chief characteristics of our sinful nature is an attitude of independence toward God. Even when we know and agree that we're dependent on Him, we tend out of habit to act independently. Undoubtedly, one of the reasons God allows us to fall before temptation so often is to teach us experientially that we really are dependent on Him to enable us to grow in holiness.

One of the best ways, apart from those painful experiences of failure, to learn dependence is to develop the discipline of prayer. This forces us in a tangible way to acknowledge our dependence on the Holy Spirit. Whatever else we may say about prayer, it is a recognition of our own helplessness and absolute dependence on God.

It's this admission of helplessness and dependence that is so repugnant to our sinful spirit of self-sufficiency. If we're prone by temperament to be disciplined, it's more difficult to acknowledge that we're dependent on Christ and His Spirit instead of on our self-discipline.

To become holy is to become like the Lord Jesus, and He Himself said, "By myself I can do nothing" (John 5:30, NIV). He was completely dependent on the Father, and He freely and willingly acknowledged it. His dependence was not reluctant, but wholehearted — even enthusiastic — because He knew that we're created to be dependent on God.

Dependence is not simply one of a list of several disciplines. Rather, it gives life and vitality to all of them. Just as the principle of life that makes the seed grow gives fruition to all of the farmers' efforts, so the enabling of the Holy Spirit within us gives fruition to our disciplines. Dependence on the Holy Spirit should permeate them all.

The Discipline of Grace

A Prayer on a Basement Floor

Present your bodies as a living sacrifice, holy and acceptable to God.
(Romans 12:1)

Most of my understanding of scriptural truths has come gradually through personal study and the teaching of pastors and other capable teachers. On a few rare occasions the Lord has been pleased to enlighten my understanding of some aspect of His truth in a rather sudden fashion. This was the case in my understanding of the sovereign grace of God. I'd been a confirmed legalist, and I dutifully sought to live the Christian life that way. But suddenly one day, I understood God's grace in an entirely new way.

I was spending a half day with God, seated in a basement room with a cold, hard tile floor. As my understanding of God's grace was enlightened, Romans 12:1 came to mind: "Therefore, I urge you, brothers, in view of God's mercy, to offer your bodies as living sacrifices, holy and pleasing to God — this is your spiritual act of worship" (NIV). I fell on my knees on that cold, hard floor and said something like this to God: "Lord, I have presented my body to You as a living sacrifice before, but I've never understood as I do now Your mercy and Your grace. And in view of my deeper understanding of Your grace, I now present myself to You in a new and deeper way. I give myself wholly to You without any reservation."

Now, more than thirty years later, I still build on the commitment I made in the basement room that morning. But more than that, I still seek to grow in my understanding of God's grace because I know that only my growing understanding of His grace will make the commitment stick through thick and thin.

Transforming Grace

REMOVED

Behold, the Lamb of God, who takes away the sin of the world!
(JOHN 1:29)

Expiation is another seldom-used and little-understood theological word. You can readily see its spelling similarity to *propitiation*. In fact, the two words are often confused, though significantly different in meaning.

Propitiation addresses God's wrath. It is the work of Christ saving us from that wrath by absorbing it in His own person as our substitute. Expiation, which basically means "removal," accompanies propitiation and speaks of Christ's work in removing or putting away our sin. Such is the symbolism of the two goats used on the Day of Atonement (Leviticus 16:20-22). The first goat represented Christ's work of propitiation as it was killed and its blood sprinkled on the mercy seat. The second goat represented Christ's work of expiation in removing or blotting out the sins that were against us. The object of propitiation is God's wrath; the object of expiation is our sin, which must be removed from His presence.

The two goats together constituted one offering, and both represent the work of Christ on our behalf. It would have been a blasphemous affront to a holy God to send one goat away into the desert without first sacrificing the goat whose blood symbolized the blood of Christ that alone propitiates the wrath of God.

Do you see how the work of Christ is infinitely greater than the greatest depth of your sin? The work of Christ is finished. Nothing more remains to be done. God's wrath has been propitiated. Our sins have been removed. The question is, will we appreciate it, not only at our initial moment of salvation but for our day-to-day acceptance with God? Only as we do this will we truly begin to appreciate the glory of the cross and the unsearchable riches of Christ.

The Gospel for Real Life

COMMIT YOURSELF TO GOD

Commit your way to the LORD.
(PSALM 37:5)

When Paul turned his attention from his masterful exposition of the gospel in Romans chapters 1–11 to practical issues of Christian living, the first thing he did was call for commitment: "Therefore, I urge you, brothers, in view of God's mercy, to offer your bodies as living sacrifices, holy and pleasing to God — this is your spiritual act of worship" (Romans 12:1, NIV).

As we look at Paul's call to commitment, we can see one obvious difference between the commitment of the devoted athlete and the commitment Paul called for. The athlete's commitment is to himself or herself or perhaps to the team. The commitment Paul urged upon us is to God. Commit yourself to God. Offer your body to Him as a living sacrifice, holy and pleasing to Him.

When we commit ourselves to the pursuit of holiness, we need to ensure that our commitment is actually to God, not simply to a holy lifestyle or a set of moral values. The people of my parent's generation were generally honest, chaste, sober, and thrifty. They were committed to those values, but they were not necessarily committed to God. Many of them were outstanding moralists and even church people, but they were not committed to God. They were committed to their values, not to God.

As believers we need to be careful that we don't make a similar mistake. We can be committed to a set of Christian values or to a lifestyle of discipleship without being committed to God Himself. But Paul said to offer yourselves to God, and in doing that commit yourselves to the pursuit of holiness in order to please Him.

The Discipline of Grace

HOLY AND ASSURED

All who are led by the Spirit of God are sons of God.
(ROMANS 8:14)

Holiness is necessary for our assurance of salvation — not at the moment of salvation, but over the course of our lives. True faith will always show itself by its fruits. "If anyone is in Christ, he is a new creation" (2 Corinthians 5:17).

I recall a young man, a fairly new Christian, whose father was visiting him. He hadn't seen his father for several years and not since he'd become a Christian. He was eager to share his newfound faith with his dad, and we prayed together that he might be an effective witness to his father.

Afterward I asked him how it had gone with his witness. He told me his dad claimed to have trusted Christ as his Savior when he "went forward" at age ten in an evangelistic meeting. I asked the young man, "In all the years you were growing up, did you ever see any evidence your father was a Christian?" His answer was "No." What reason have we to put confidence in that man's salvation? He was almost sixty and had never once given his son any evidence that he was a Christian.

The only safe evidence that we're in Christ is a holy life. John said everyone who has within him the hope of eternal life purifies himself just as Christ is pure (1 John 3:3). If we know nothing of holiness, we may flatter ourselves that we're Christians, but we don't have the Holy Spirit dwelling within us.

Everyone who professes to be a Christian should ask himself, "Is there evidence of practical holiness in my life? Do I desire and strive after holiness? Do I grieve over my lack of it and earnestly seek God's help to be holy?"

The Pursuit of Holiness

DECISIVE DEDICATION

Present yourselves to God.

(ROMANS 6:13)

How did the apostle Paul approach the subject of commitment and discipline? Paul's letter to the Romans is the foundation for the Bible's teaching on salvation; in it, the teaching of justification by faith in Jesus Christ alone is set forth most cogently and completely. However, Paul wrote the letter to people who were already believers. He referred to them as those "who are loved by God and called to be saints." He thanked God that their "faith is proclaimed in all the world," and he longed "that we may be mutually encouraged by each other's faith" (Romans 1:7-8,12). Clearly he was writing to believers.

He wrote to help them understand more fully the salvation they already possessed. He spent eleven chapters going through the gospel, showing that salvation is entirely by God's grace through faith in Jesus Christ, then dealing with various questions his teaching on the grace of God would raise.

Then he asked for their response: a total commitment of themselves to God. He urged them, "Present your bodies as a living sacrifice, holy and acceptable to God" (12:1).

Paul made a strong appeal. Charles B. Williams' translation interprets the phrase "offer your bodies" as "make a decisive dedication [*footnote:* once-for-all offer] of your bodies." The phrase "living sacrifice" connotes the idea of a "perpetual sacrifice never to be neglected or recalled"[41] and a "constant dedication."[42] So Paul called for a decisive, once-for-all dedication that is to be constantly reaffirmed and kindled afresh. You cannot ask for any higher level of commitment than that.

Transforming Grace

SET FREE

You were ransomed.
(1 PETER 1:18)

We associate the word *ransom* with kidnapping, but this hasn't always been its primary association. Centuries ago, ransom was the payment given an enemy country to secure the release of prisoners of war. In Bible times a ransom was the price paid to gain freedom for a slave. To pay a ransom was to purchase back someone from captivity or slavery.

Jesus said, "The Son of Man did not come to be served, but to serve, and to give his life as a *ransom* for many" (Matthew 20:28, NIV). To fully understand His meaning we must examine the related word *redeem*, which means to buy back or release someone from slavery or captivity by paying a ransom. Redemption, then, is the action to secure release; while ransom is the price paid to effect the action.

Jesus said He would give His life as "a ransom for many" (Mark 10:45). Clearly His life was considered as a ransom payment. Just what was the captivity from which the "many" are ransomed? Hebrews 9:15 tells us that Jesus "died as a ransom to set them free from the sins committed under the first covenant" (NIV). And what does it mean to be set free from sins committed under the first covenant?

Paul's answer: "Christ redeemed us from the curse of the law by becoming a curse for us" (Galatians 3:13). To be set free from the sins committed under the first covenant and to be redeemed from the curse of the Law are essentially synonymous expressions. Christ shed His blood and gave His life as a ransom to redeem us from this curse. As a captive held in chains is set free when the ransom is paid, so all who trust in Christ are set free from the condemnation and curse of the Law.

The Gospel for Real Life

SIN AND SELF-ESTEEM

Make every effort to supplement your faith with virtue.

(2 PETER 1:5)

We should not seek holiness in order to feel good about ourselves, to blend in with our Christian peer group, or to avoid the sense of shame and guilt that follows the committing of persistent sin. Far too often our concern with sin arises from how it makes us feel. Sinful habits, sometimes called "besetting sins," cause us to feel defeated, and we don't like to be defeated in anything, whether it's a game of Ping-Pong or our struggle with sin.

I once spoke at a retreat on the importance of putting on Christlike character while at the same time seeking to put off sinful habits. After my message, four or five people came to me asking for personal help in dealing with some particular sin in their lives, but no one came asking for help in putting on any Christlike virtues. As I pondered the possible reason for this, I realized that sinful habits make us feel guilty and defeated. The absence of Christlike character usually doesn't have a similar effect, so there's less motivation to seek change in our lives.

We need to work at ensuring that our commitment to holiness is a commitment to God, not to our own self-esteem. Frederick W. Faber, a nineteenth-century British writer, showed great insight into this tendency (I've paraphrased his words for clarity): "When we sin we are more vexed at the lowering of our self-esteem than we are grieved at God's dishonor. We are surprised and irritated at our own lack of self-control in subjecting ourselves to unworthy habits. . . . The first cause of this is self-love, which is unable to stand the disappointment of not seeing ourselves in time of trial come out beautiful, erect, and admirable."[43]

The Discipline of Grace

THE LURE OF GRACE

Present your bodies as a living sacrifice.

(ROMANS 12:1)

What consideration did Paul bring forward as the basis or motivation for making the total commitment he asked for in Romans 12:1? He did not appeal to a sense of duty but to the mercy of God ("by the mercies of God"). He asked for a response based not on obligation but on heartfelt gratitude.

Now, the fact is, we do have a duty and obligation to God. He's the Sovereign Ruler of this world, and in that capacity He has laid down "precepts to be kept diligently" (Psalm 119:4). He motivates us to obedience, not on the basis of His sovereign rule but on the basis of His mercy to us in Jesus Christ.

Martin Luther wrote on Romans 12:1, "A lawdriver insists with threats and penalties; a preacher of grace lures and incites with divine goodness and compassion shown to us; for he wants no unwilling works and reluctant services, he wants joyful and delightful services of God."[44]

I was asked to speak on the Lordship of Jesus Christ at a conference. I knew the intended objective was to challenge the audience to submit to Christ's lordship in the affairs of their everyday lives. But I began the message by speaking on God's goodness. After I'd spent fifteen or twenty minutes on the goodness of God, then I began to talk about the lordship of Christ in our lives. Why did I develop the message in that fashion? Because submission to the lordship of Jesus Christ should be in response to the love and mercy of God. In view of God's mercy, Paul urged the Roman believers to offer their bodies as living sacrifices. We must respond with a similar motivation to His lordship in our lives today.

Transforming Grace

UNSWERVING LOYALTY

A friend loves at all times, and a brother is born for adversity.

(PROVERBS 17:17)

The faithful person is not only honest and dependable but also loyal. The issue of loyalty arises most often in connection with our friends. The word has come to have a connotation of sticking with someone through thick and thin. There's no such person as a fair-weather friend. If a person's loyalty doesn't ensure his faithfulness to another in times of stress, he really isn't a friend—he's simply using the other person to satisfy his own social needs.

Jonathan provides probably the Bible's best illustration of loyalty. His friendship with David almost cost him his life at the hands of his own father. Amazingly, Jonathan realized that his loyalty to David would, in the end, cost him the throne of Israel. Such faithfulness is frequently a costly virtue. Only the Holy Spirit can enable us to pay that price.

We must avoid, however, a so-called "blind loyalty" that refuses to admit a friend's mistakes or faults. Proverbs 27:6 tells us, "Faithful are the wounds of a friend; profuse are the kisses of an enemy." Only the truly faithful friend cares enough about us to undertake the often thankless task of pointing out where we're wrong. None of us enjoys being confronted with our faults, so we often make it difficult for our friends to do so. As a result, most of us are more concerned about speaking agreeableness to each other than about speaking the truth. This is not loyalty. Loyalty speaks the truth in faithfulness but also in love. Loyalty says, "I care enough about you that I will not allow you to continue unchecked in your wrong action or sinful attitude that will ultimately be harmful to you."

The Fruitful Life

WHY THE CURSE?

Be careful to obey all these words that I command you.

(DEUTERONOMY 12:28)

Why was it necessary for Christ to give His life as a ransom to redeem us from the curse of the Law? Why are we under a curse from which we need to be redeemed? In Galatians 3:10, Paul wrote, "All who rely on works of the law are under a curse; for it is written, 'Cursed be everyone who does not abide by all things written in the Book of the Law, and do them.'" Mankind was under a curse because we had not perfectly obeyed the Law of God — either in Adam or as individuals.

The curse falls on everyone who does not continue to do *everything* written in the Law. This is an impossibly exacting standard. No college demands a perfect 4.0 GPA for graduation. If it did, only a scant few would graduate. But Paul tells us this is what the Law of God demands.

Some may react strongly to the rigorous demand of the Law for absolutely perfect obedience. Why isn't 90 or 95 percent obedience good enough? Why does God insist on 100 percent? After all, even highway patrolmen usually allow a five- to ten-mile-per-hour violation of the speed limit before ticketing us.

In the final analysis, we should seek no justification from God for the exactness of His Law. After all, God is God. He is the Creator who brought the whole universe into existence by His spoken command. He is the One on whom each of us depends for life and breath. He is the One who has the absolute right to establish the rules of the game, the laws by which we are to live. And He's the One who has the right to attach sanctions to those laws for breaking them.

The Gospel for Real Life

LOSING GOD

Cursed shall you be when you come in,
and cursed shall you be when you go out.

(DEUTERONOMY 28:19)

What are the effects of the curse? According to George Smeaton, the worst effect "is the loss of God, or the absence and complete withdrawal of God from a human soul."[45] I'm sure many people think they would be happy to lose Him. But remember that as Jesus hung on the cross bearing the curse in our place, He cried in anguish, "My God, my God, why have you forsaken me?" (Matthew 27:46).

In Deuteronomy 28, Moses listed God's promised blessings for Israel's obedience of God's Law (verses 1-14) and His curses for disobedience (verses 15-68). The threatened curses were horrible beyond anything imaginable. For example, it includes a siege so severe that women would be driven to cannibalize their own children.

These promised blessings and threatened curses were only temporal in nature, having to do with the nation of Israel in the Promised Land. Then consider that the severity of these threatened curses only begins to picture the unimaginable agony of being under God's curse for all eternity.

Above all, when we think the curse for violating God's Law is too severe, it's because we don't understand God or the nature of sin. God is transcendent in His majesty and sovereign in His authority. Every sin, be it ever so small in our eyes, is an assault on that authority. In effect we're saying, "I don't care what You say; I'll do as I please." Furthermore, God has commanded us to be holy as He is holy. Therefore, each sin is an insult to His character. It's as if we're telling God, "I don't want to be like You." Think what a rebellious affront it would be for a child to say that to his parent.

The Gospel for Real Life

NO EXCEPTIONS

You, O God, have heard my vows.

(PSALM 61:5)

Commitment to the pursuit of holiness is, first of all, a commitment to God to pursue a way of life that is pleasing to Him. It is commitment to a life of obedience. Such a commitment must allow for no exceptions, no secret sins we want to hold onto, no sinful habits we're unwilling to give up. *We must make it our aim not to sin.*

This doesn't mean we can arrive at sinless perfection in this life, for even our best deeds are stained with sin. But it does mean that our firm intention must be not to sin willfully. Commitment to a life of holiness without exception is a requirement for consistently making the right choices. There's no point in praying for God's help in the face of temptation if we haven't made a commitment to obedience without exception.

The psalmist said, "I have sworn an oath and confirmed it, to keep your righteous rules" (Psalm 119:106). He felt so strongly about his commitment to obedience that he took an oath that he would follow God's righteous laws. An oath, in this context, is a solemn calling on God to witness that the person sincerely intends to do what he or she says. It's a declaration or promise to fulfill a pledge, a commitment of the highest level. The psalmist not only took an oath but confirmed it. He wanted to make his commitment as strong as he possibly could.

The Puritan pastor and writer Stephen Charnock commented on this verse: "Frequently renew settled and holy resolutions. A soldier unresolved to fight may easily be defeated. . . . The weakness of our graces, the strength of our temptations, and the diligence of our spiritual enemies, require strong resolutions."[46]

The Discipline of Grace

KNOWING OUR MOTIVES

The LORD looks on the heart.

(1 SAMUEL 16:7)

Our motivation for commitment, discipline, and obedience is as important to God as our performance, perhaps even more so. As Ernest F. Kevan wrote, "The Law's demands are inward, touching motive and desire, and are not concerned solely with outward action." [47]

David said, "The LORD searches all hearts and understands every plan and thought" (1 Chronicles 28:9). The apostle Paul echoed the importance of motives when he wrote that, at the Lord's coming, He "will bring to light the things now hidden in darkness and will disclose the purposes of the heart" (1 Corinthians 4:5).

To be acceptable to God, our motives must spring from a love for Him and a desire to glorify Him. Obedience performed from a legalistic motive — from fear of consequences or to gain favor with God — is not pleasing to Him. Abraham Booth (1734–1806), an English pastor and author, wrote, "To constitute a work truly good, it must be done from a right principle, performed by a right rule, and intended for a right end." [48] Booth defined a right principle as our love for God. He defined the right rule as God's revealed will in Scripture. The right end — the right goal — is the glory of God.

Our good works are not truly good unless they're motivated by a love for God and a desire to glorify Him. But we cannot have such a Godward motivation if we think we must earn God's favor by our obedience or if we fear we may forfeit His favor by disobedience. Such a works-oriented motivation is essentially self-serving, prompted more by what we think we gain or lose than by a grateful response to the grace He has already given us through Jesus Christ.

Transforming Grace

CONTENTMENT

I have learned in whatever situation I am to be content.

(PHILIPPIANS 4:11)

There's a place for legitimate discontentment. All of us should, to some degree, be discontent with our spiritual growth. If we aren't, we will stop growing. There's also what we might call a prophetic discontentment with injustice and other evils in society, coupled with a desire to see positive change. But there's also a sinful discontentment that negatively affects our relationship with God. It can easily lead to resentment or bitterness toward God or other people.

Whatever situation tempts us to be discontent, and however severe it may be, we need to recognize that discontentment is sin. We're so used to responding to difficult circumstances with anxiety, frustration, or discontentment that we consider them normal reactions to the varying vicissitudes of life. But that just points out the subtleness and acceptability of these sins. When we fail to recognize these responses to our circumstances as sin, we're responding no differently from unbelievers who never factor God into their situations. We're back to our ungodliness as the root cause of our sins.

The truth of David's words in Psalm 139:16 — "In your book were written, every one of them, the days that were formed for me, when as yet there was none of them" — can help us (and does help me) deal with the circumstances that tempt us to be discontent.

Whatever your circumstances, and however difficult they may be, the truth is that God has ordained all our days — with all their ups and downs, blessings and disappointments — as part of His overall plan for your life. God does nothing, or allows nothing, without a purpose. And His purposes, however mysterious and inscrutable they may be to us, are always for His glory and our ultimate good.

Respectable Sins

FROM CURSE TO CHRIST

The law was our guardian until Christ came.

(GALATIANS 3:24)

The primary purpose of the Law is not to curse us but to lead us to Christ (Galatians 3:24). God does not take pleasure in the death of the wicked (Ezekiel 18:23). Rather, "Christ redeemed us from the curse of the law by becoming a curse for us" (Galatians 3:13). The language is emphatic. Christ literally *became* a curse in our place as our substitute. He experienced the full fury of the curse that we should have experienced. It's true He did it *for* us, but He did so by doing it *in our place* as our appointed substitute.

Here we see the importance of our legal union with Christ. As our God-appointed legal representative, He was legally qualified to endure the curse in our place as our substitute. There's no adequate analogy for this union in human experience. One person may pay a financial debt for someone else, but no one can serve a prison sentence as a substitute for another. In human jurisprudence, a moral debt such as a prison sentence can be served only by the person who incurred it.

Many people who deny the substitutionary nature of Christ's atonement claim that it's unjust for an innocent person to suffer in place of the guilty. That's true in a human legal system, but it's God who established the curse for breaking His Law and who ordained the remedy for the curse. Human analogies and principles, though often helpful in illustrating scriptural truths, should never be used to refute Scripture.

Above all, we should accept this wonderful truth that Jesus bore the curse in our place and paid our ransom price, not because it seems reasonable by any human standards but because God in His Word has declared it to be so.

The Gospel for Real Life

WHAT IS YOUR INTENTION?

I appeal to you . . . to present your bodies as a living sacrifice,
holy and acceptable to God.

(ROMANS 12:1)

How do we respond to the challenge to commitment — to present our
bodies as living sacrifices; to, as it were, take an oath to obey God's righteous laws; to resolve to allow no exceptions to our obedience? I suspect
all of us think first of the impossibility of totally keeping such a commitment. And we're reluctant to make a commitment we know we won't keep.
But the question still persists: Are we willing to make that our aim, our
goal in life? Are we willing to commit ourselves to a goal of obedience
without exception? Such a commitment is necessary if we are to make
progress in the pursuit of holiness.

In his classic work *A Serious Call to a Devout and Holy Life,* William
Law commented on why a particular sin was so common: "Now the
reason . . . is this, it is because men have not so much as the intention to
please God in all their actions."[49] How about us today? Is it our intention
to please God in all our actions? That's the commitment Paul called on us
to make when he urged us to offer our bodies as living sacrifices to God.

The intention to please God in all our actions is the key to commitment to a life of holiness. If we don't make such a commitment to obedience without exception, we'll constantly find ourselves making exceptions.
We'll have a "just one more time" syndrome in our lives. But the truth is,
the "one more time" manner of thinking undermines our commitment.
Every time we give in to a temptation, even though it may seem small and
insignificant to us, we make it easier to give in the next time.

The Discipline of Grace

GRACE AND A GRATEFUL HEART

You know the grace of our Lord Jesus Christ.

(2 CORINTHIANS 8:9)

Living under the grace of God instead of under a sense of duty frees us from a self-serving motivation. It frees us to obey God and serve Him as a loving and thankful response to Him for our salvation and for blessings already guaranteed to us by His grace. Consequently, a heartfelt grasp of God's grace — far from creating an indifferent or careless attitude in us — will actually provide us the only motivation that is pleasing to Him. Only when we're thoroughly convinced that the Christian life is entirely of grace are we able to serve Him out of a grateful and loving heart.

I knew a man who was a strict tither, giving exactly 10 percent of his income to God's work: never one penny less and, as far as I know, never one penny more. I asked him why he did this. He replied, "I'd be afraid not to." I knew this man fairly well, and I suspect his motivation was mixed. He did somewhat enjoy giving his 10 percent, but his basic motivation was a fear of the consequences if he did not tithe. He was not motivated to tithe from a joyful and grateful heart.

By contrast, the apostle Paul appealed to Christ's grace as a motivation to give: "For you know the grace of our Lord Jesus Christ, that though he was rich, yet for your sake he became poor, so that you by his poverty might become rich" (2 Corinthians 8:9). Paul wasn't "laying a guilt trip" on the Corinthian believers. Rather, he wanted them not only to give generously but to give from a sense of gratitude for God's grace — as a cheerful, loving response to what God had already given them in Christ.

Transforming Grace

WHO WAS PAID?

> *Christ Jesus . . . gave himself as a ransom for all.*
>
> (1 TIMOTHY 2:5-6)

If Christ paid our ransom price, to whom was it paid? Some have thought it was paid to Satan, who holds unbelievers captive, but this cannot possibly be true. If it were, there would be a sense in which Satan was victorious over Christ. If we think of the ransom in terms of money, Satan would be "laughing all the way to the bank." The better answer is obviously that the ransom was paid to God acting in His capacity as Judge. It was God's justice that Jesus satisfied, His cup of wrath that Jesus emptied, and His curse that Jesus bore as He paid our ransom price.

Once again, a human analogy of biblical truth ultimately breaks down when pressed to every detail. In human experience a ransom is paid to an adversary—a kidnapper, an opposing army, or a slaveholder. But God both demanded the ransom price and paid it in the death of His Son. In human experience we also recognize a distinction between the ransom price paid and the redeemer who pays it. Jesus, however, was both redeemer and ransom as He laid down His life in our place.

We should never cease to be amazed that the One who established the Law and determined its curse should Himself ransom us from it by bearing that curse in our place.

O, what wondrous love; O, what infinite wisdom! Our glorious God devised such a plan that satisfies His justice and upholds His Law while at the same time providing a complete redemption for us from the curse of His Law. Surely we need to say often the words of Jonah when he cried out from the belly of the fish, "Salvation comes from the LORD" (Jonah 2:9, NIV).

The Gospel for Real Life

GROWING IN FAITHFULNESS

> *Be faithful unto death.*
> (REVELATION 2:10)

For growing in faithfulness, the first step is to acknowledge the biblical standard. Faithfulness entails absolute honesty, utter dependability, and unswerving loyalty. It's to be like Daniel: neither corrupt nor negligent. Develop convictions consistent with this standard based on the Word of God, and plan to memorize one or more verses on the topic of faithfulness.

Second, evaluate your life with the aid of the Holy Spirit and perhaps a spouse or close friend. Do you seek to be scrupulously honest? Can others depend on you even when it's costly? Will you stick by your friend when he's in difficulty, and confront him in love when he's wrong?

Where you see a specific need in your life for faithfulness, make that both a matter of prayer for the aid of the Holy Spirit and the object of concrete actions on your part. Remember that your working and His working are coextensive. You cannot become a faithful person merely by trying. There's a divine dimension. But it's also true that you won't become a faithful person without trying. This is something *we* must do, even though it's at the same time the fruit of the Spirit.

Consider the reward for faithfulness. In the parable of the talents, the master replied, "Well done, good and faithful servant! You have been faithful with a few things; I will put you in charge of many things. Come and share your master's happiness!" (Matthew 25:21, NIV). The faithfulness here is in our relation to God — but faithfulness to God includes faithfulness to one another. God requires that we be faithful in all our earthly relationships. Only if we seek to grow in the grace of faithfulness toward one another will we have any hope of hearing Him say, "Well done, good and faithful servant."

The Fruitful Life

THE INCREASING PULL

The one who sows to his own flesh will from the flesh reap corruption.

(GALATIANS 6:8)

Sin has a tendency to exert an ever-increasing power on us if it isn't resisted on every occasion. Paul wrote in Romans 6:19, "Just as you once presented your members as slaves to impurity and to lawlessness leading to more lawlessness, so now present your members as slaves to righteousness leading to sanctification." Notice the phrase "lawlessness leading to more lawlessness." Paul was referring to sin's tendency to exert a greater and greater pull on us as we give in to each temptation.

It doesn't matter whether the sin to which we're tempted is seemingly small or large. In either case, the principle works: Saying yes to any temptation weakens our commitment to resist sin.

Just as we need to make a commitment not to sin willfully, so we need to make a commitment to put on or clothe ourselves with the positive virtues of Christian character. Remember that Paul said, "Clothe yourselves with compassion, kindness, humility, gentleness and patience" (Colossians 3:12, NIV). There are many of these positive character traits that we're to seek after. What is our intention regarding them? If we want to be like Christ in His character, we must commit ourselves to putting on His virtues.

It's not enough to stop cheating on our income tax returns; we must also learn to share with those in need. It's not enough to avoid being bitter against those who have wronged us; we need to forgive as God has forgiven us. It's not enough to pray that God will enable us to deal with a volatile temper; we must also ask Him to help us put on compassion and kindness.

The Discipline of Grace

COMPELLED BY CHRIST'S LOVE

The love of Christ controls us.

(2 CORINTHIANS 5:14)

In 2 Corinthians 5:14-15, Paul said, "For Christ's love compels us, because we are convinced that one died for all, and therefore all died. And he died for all, that those who live should no longer live for themselves but for him who died for them and was raised again" (NIV).

Christ's love compels us to live no longer for ourselves but for Him who died for us and was raised again. We're to live no longer for ourselves but for Him. We make His will the rule of our lives and His glory the goal for which we live. But what is the wellspring of this commitment? What motivating principle will cause a person to live no longer for himself but for God?

Paul said the love of Christ compels us to make this kind of commitment and to carry it out daily. *Compel* is a strong word and often has a negative association with force or coercion. But here its meaning is positive. Charles Hodge wrote that the love of Christ "coerces, or presses, and therefore impels. It is the governing influence which controls the life."[50] It's not a fear of consequences or expectation of reward that motivates Paul. Rather, the love of Christ manifested in dying for him is the driving force of his life.

The Williams New Testament translates the first phrase of 2 Corinthians 5:14 in this manner: "For the love of Christ continuously constrains me." Christ's love is the constant wellspring of Paul's motivation every day. Paul never lost sight of, never forgot, never took for granted the death of Christ for him. And as he reflected on this infinite love manifested in Christ's death, he was compelled to live for the One who died for him and rose again.

Transforming Grace

RELEASED AND ADOPTED

Sin reigned in death.
(ROMANS 5:21)

Think of a man sitting on death row, convicted of heinous crimes. All legal appeals to spare him have been exhausted. His impending execution looms nearer every day.

Suddenly the cell door is flung open. The judge who sentenced this man to die stands there with a full pardon in his hand. Moreover, the judge has now adopted him into his family as his own son, to be taken in and provided with all the love and care the judge lavishes on his own children.

We truly did live on God's eternal "death row." "For the wages of sin is death" (Romans 6:23) — physical and eternal death. As believers we know that we have been delivered from eternal death. That's not the final word, however, for "we wait eagerly for adoption as sons, the redemption of our bodies" (Romans 8:23). Our redemption and our adoption into God's family will reach ultimate fulfillment at the Resurrection, when we receive our immortal bodies and dwell forever in the immediate presence of the Lord.

But think again of the pardoned and adopted murderer. Would you want to be a member of that family as they brought this killer into their home? Would you lie fearfully in your bed at night, wondering if you might be his next victim?

Again we reach the limitations of human illustrations. The judge who pardoned and adopted this murderer cannot change this man's heart. But God can and does change our hearts. He promises to take away our hearts of stone that are spiritually dead and unresponsive to Him and give us hearts of flesh that are spiritually alive and responsive to Him (Ezekiel 36:26). We no longer have the heart of a criminal. This, too, is part of our redemption that Jesus secured for us.

The Gospel for Real Life

IN EVERYTHING

> *Walk in a manner worthy of the Lord, fully pleasing to him.*
> (COLOSSIANS 1:10)

We should commit ourselves to doing everything we do, not in the way that might seem to best accomplish our personal objective, but in the way that will be most pleasing to God.

This principle applies to the way a student approaches his or her studies, to the way we do our shopping and buying, to the way we compete in games and athletics, to the way we decorate our houses and keep our lawns, and even to the way we drive.

The city where I live attracts a lot of visitors in the summer, and the road I used to drive to our office is frequently crowded at that time with tourists. Being unfamiliar with the city and sometimes unsure of their directions, tourists often tend to drive more slowly than we locals. It's easy in such a situation to become impatient with them and to show that impatience in the way we drive. Sometimes, after I'd "whipped around" someone while driving to work, I found myself hoping that person didn't see me turning into the driveway of a Christian organization.

But God knows I'm a Christian and that I work for a Christian organization. If I would be ashamed to have a tourist identify my impatient driving with a Christian, how much more should I be ashamed before God. After all, He's the one I've committed myself to, to seek to please in all my thoughts and words and actions. So our commitment to pursue holiness must embrace every area of life and must include both the significant and the seemingly insignificant things we do. It must be a commitment both to put off the way of life of the old self and to put on the virtues of the new self.

The Discipline of Grace

THE HOLY EXAMPLE OF CHRIST

He committed no sin.
(1 PETER 2:22)

Christ's life is meant to be an example of holiness for us. Peter told us that Christ left an example for us to follow in His steps (1 Peter 2:21); he spoke particularly of Christ's suffering without retaliation, but in the following verse he said also that Christ committed no sin. Paul urged us to be imitators of God (Ephesians 5:1) and also said, "Follow my example, as I follow the example of Christ" (1 Corinthians 11:1, NIV).

Clearly, the sinless, holy life of Jesus Christ is meant to be an example for us. Consider then His statement, "I always do what pleases Him." Do we dare take that as our personal goal in life? Are we truly willing to scrutinize all our activities, all our goals and plans, and all our impulsive actions in light of this statement: "I'm doing this to please God"? If we ask that honestly, we'll begin to squirm a bit.

In the words of nineteenth-century Scottish theologian John Brown, "Holiness does not consist in mystic speculations, enthusiastic fervours, or uncommanded austerities; it consists in thinking as God thinks, and willing as God wills."[51] Neither does holiness mean, as is so often thought, adhering to a list of "dos and don'ts," mostly don'ts. When Christ came into the world, He said, "I have come to do your will, O God" (Hebrews 10:7). This is the example we're to follow. In all our thoughts, actions, in every part of our character, the ruling principle that motivates and guides us should be the desire to follow Christ in doing the will of the Father. This is the high road we must follow in the pursuit of holiness.

The Pursuit of Holiness

MOTIVATING REVERENCE

The fear of the LORD is clean.
(PSALM 19:9)

I find myself motivated to obedience by a deep sense of reverence for God. When Joseph was tempted to immorality by Potiphar's wife, his response was, "How then could I do such a wicked thing and sin against God?" (Genesis 39:9, NIV). He didn't calculate the possible wrath of Potiphar or the forfeiture of God's blessing, but was motivated by reverence for God. He obeyed a sovereign, holy God, even though God had allowed him to be sold into slavery by his own brothers.

Paul wrote in 2 Corinthians 7:1, "Since we have these promises, dear friends, let us purify ourselves from everything that contaminates body and spirit, perfecting holiness out of reverence for God" (NIV). These promises he mentioned were God's promises to be our Father and to make us His sons and daughters (6:18). Philip Hughes commented on this passage, "The logical consequence of possessing such promises is that Christ's followers should make a complete break with every form of unhealthy compromise."[52] Here again, promises come before duty, and duty flows out of a heartfelt response to the promises of God.

Paul then wrote that we should bring "holiness to completion in the fear of God" (2 Corinthians 7:1). This fear is a sense of profound awe, respect, and devotion. It's a recognition of God's intrinsic worthiness, the infinite majesty of His being, and the infinite perfection of His character. Because of who He is and what He is, God is infinitely worthy of my most diligent and loving obedience, even if I never receive a single blessing from His hand. The fact is, of course, I've received innumerable blessings from Him. But His worthiness is intrinsic within Himself; it is not conditioned on the number of blessings you or I receive from Him.

Transforming Grace

OUR ONLY SAFE RESPONSE

You have received the Spirit of adoption as sons.

(ROMANS 8:15)

Paul told us that God sent His Son "to redeem those under law, that we might receive the full rights of sons" (Galatians 4:4-5, NIV).

This "full rights of sons" is a reference to the status of sons who have become full-grown young adults. We've not only been redeemed from a cell on death row but also brought into God's family as fully adopted sons, with all the privileges included in that status.

All this is set against the dark background of the curse of the Law for any disobedience, which, of course, affects us all. Just as the diamonds on a jeweler's counter shine more brilliantly when set upon a dark velvet pad, so Christ's redemptive work shines more brilliantly when contrasted with our sin and the consequent curse that was upon us.

The fact is, however, that even as believers we continue to sin even though we are no longer under its dominion. And when we sin — and even our best deeds are stained with sin — we do that which apart from Christ would call down God's curse upon us. Our consciences know that, and they will continually bring accusations against us. Our only safe response is to plead guilty to those accusations without trying to minimize them.

Having done that, we must go back to the gospel and remind ourselves that the curse of the Law no longer has a claim against us. And then in grateful response to what God has done for us in Christ, we set ourselves to put to death by the power of the Spirit those very sins of which our consciences condemn us. Only in this way can we continually glory in the cross and enjoy the unsearchable riches of Christ.

The Gospel for Real Life

SPECIFIC COMMITMENTS

Daniel resolved that he would not defile himself.
(DANIEL 1:8)

In addition to an overall commitment to pursue holiness in every area of life, I find it helpful to make specific commitments in areas where we're particularly vulnerable to sin. There's great value in identifying those areas — either in what we do (for example, gossip) or in what we fail to do (such as loving our wives as Christ loved the church) — and then making specific commitments of obedience to God in those areas.

I urge you to list any areas of temptation wherein you need to make this specific commitment. Do you need to make a covenant with your eyes about what you look at (Job 31:1), or with your mouth about what you say, or with your mind about what you think? Is there a particular temptation or sinful practice that arises in your work environment that needs a commitment to fortify you against it? Write these commitments down on paper, for your eyes only, so you can review them and pray over them daily.

Perhaps there's a particular area in your marriage or in your relationship with your children, your parents, a friend, or an associate at work where you aren't demonstrating the Spirit's fruit of love, patience, or kindness. Do you need to make a commitment that, in dependence on the Holy Spirit to enable you, you'll seek to display that particular "fruit" toward that individual? If so, I urge you to make such a commitment. You may find the need to make several commitments — sins to put off or avoid and Christlike traits to put on. If you don't commit yourself to the pursuit of holiness in these specific areas of your life, you'll find a tendency to vacillate in the face of these temptations.

The Discipline of Grace

GROWING IN GRACE

But grow in the grace and knowledge of our Lord and Savior Jesus Christ.

(2 PETER 3:18)

The term *growing in grace* is most often used to indicate growth in Christian character. While I think that usage has merit, a more accurate meaning is to continually grow in our understanding of God's grace, especially as it applies to us personally, to become progressively more aware of our own continued spiritual bankruptcy and the unmerited, unearned, and undeserved favor of God. May we all grow in grace in this sense.

As we grow in grace this way, we will grow in our motivation to obey God out of a sense of gratitude and reverence to Him. Our obedience will always be imperfect in performance in this life. We will never perfectly obey Him until we are made perfect by Him. In the same way, our motives will never be consistently pure; there will frequently be some "merit points" mentality mixed in with our genuine love and reverence for God.

So don't be discouraged if you realize your motives have been largely merit-oriented. Just begin now to move toward grace motives. Begin to think daily about the implications of the grace of God in your life. Memorize and meditate frequently on such Scripture passages as Romans 12:1 and 2 Corinthians 5:14-15. Pray about the aspects of truth in those passages and ask God to motivate you by His mercy and love. When you recognize merit-oriented motives at work in you, renounce them and cast yourself completely on the grace of God and the merit of Jesus Christ. As you grow in grace in this way, you will indeed discover that His love compels you to live — not for yourself, but for Him who died for you and was raised again.

Transforming Grace

TREATING OTHERS GENTLY

Learn from me, for I am gentle.

(MATTHEW 11:29)

A profile of gentleness as it should appear in our lives will first include actively seeking to make others feel at ease, or "restful," in our presence. We should not be so strongly opinionated or dogmatic that others are afraid to express their opinions in our presence. Instead, we should be sensitive to others' opinions and ideas. We should also avoid displaying our commitment to Christian discipleship in such a way as to make others feel guilty, taking care not to break the bruised reed of the hurting Christian or snuff out the smoldering wick of the immature Christian.

Second, gentleness will demonstrate respect for the personal dignity of the other person. Where necessary, it will seek to change a wrong opinion or attitude by persuasion and kindness, not by domination or intimidation. It will studiously avoid coercion by threatening, either directly or indirectly (as Paul, for example, avoided it in his appeal to the Corinthians).

Gentleness will also avoid blunt and abrupt speech, instead seeking to answer everyone with sensitivity and respect, ready to show consideration toward all. Gentle Christians do not feel they have the liberty to "say what I think and let the chips fall where they may." Instead they're sensitive to the reactions and feelings of others. When gentle Christians find it necessary to wound with words, they also seek to bind up those wounds with words of consolation and encouragement.

Finally, gentle Christians will not degrade or belittle or gossip about the brother or sister who falls into some sin. Instead they will grieve for him or her and pray for that person's repentance. If it's appropriate to become personally involved, they'll seek to restore the person gently (Galatians 6:1), aware that they too are subject to temptation.

The Fruitful Life

FULFILLED IN THE FAMILY

You were dead.

(EPHESIANS 2:1)

In the story of redemption, deliverance from the penal curse of the Law is the major part of the story, but not the whole story. Peter told us, "You were ransomed from the futile ways inherited from your forefathers" (1 Peter 1:18). Without Christ we lived in futility and emptiness. Regardless of whether it was a decent life or a wicked life judged on a human scale of morality, it was a vain, futile, empty life.

We find a good description of this emptiness in Ephesians 2:1-3, where Paul described us as having followed the ways of the world and of Satan, and of having continually gratified the cravings of our sinful natures. Christ's ransom, then, secured for us redemption not only from the Law's curse but also from bondage to sin. These two aspects of redemption always go together: Redemption from the curse infallibly secures redemption from the bondage.

Paul addressed this absolute connection when he wrote that Jesus Christ "gave himself for us to redeem us from all wickedness and to purify for himself a people that are his very own, eager to do what is good" (Titus 2:14, NIV). The design of Christ's redemptive work goes beyond salvation from God's everlasting curse. Its purpose is to redeem us from sin to Himself, to be a people desiring to please Him.

Regarding this absolute connection between redemption from the guilt and consequent curse of sin and the release from the dominion or reign of sin in our lives, noted New Testament scholar Leon Morris wrote, "It is wrong to separate the legal status, gained by complete discharge of the law against us, from the resultant life. The only redemption Paul knew was one in which they lived as those who had been adopted into the family of God."[53]

The Gospel for Real Life

Any Room for Grace?

> *By the mercies of God . . . present your bodies as a*
> *living sacrifice, holy and acceptable to God.*
>
> (Romans 12:1)

Some may ask, "Who can possibly keep a commitment to pursue holiness without exception for even some 'small' sins? If there are no exceptions, is there any place for grace? Is God really this strict?"

Yes, God really is this strict because He cannot compromise His holiness the least bit. His goal is to conform us to the likeness of His Son, and Jesus was completely without sin, though tempted in every way that we are (Hebrews 4:15). No, we cannot, or perhaps will not, keep our commitments to God perfectly, but that should at least be our aim. In a battle, some soldiers will always be hit, but each one makes it his aim not to be hit. A lesser aim would be the height of folly for the soldier, and it's just as dangerous for us in our battle with sin.

Is there any place for grace? Most assuredly; in fact, in Romans 12:1, Paul based his call for such decisive commitment on God's mercy or grace. John Calvin commented on this verse as follows: "Paul's entreaty teaches us that men will never worship God with a sincere heart, or be roused to fear and obey Him with sufficient zeal, until they properly understand how much they are indebted to His mercy."[54]

So we see once again the relationship of grace and discipline. A loving response to God's grace and mercy is the only motive acceptable to God for the commitment Paul called for. And the continual reminding of ourselves of His grace and mercy provides the only enduring motivation to sustain such a commitment and keep it from becoming oppressive. That's why we must preach the gospel to ourselves every day.

The Discipline of Grace

A Dangerous Statement

The love of Christ controls us.
(2 Corinthians 5:14)

One issue believers frequently struggle with is the relationship between living by grace and obedience to God's commands. When I state that nothing you ever do or don't do will make God love you any more or any less, and that He accepts you strictly by His grace through the merit of Jesus Christ alone, such unqualified statements sound exceedingly dangerous — leaving me open to the charge of saying in effect that God doesn't care whether or not you sin.

But consider the alternative: "God loves you if you're obedient and doesn't love you if you're disobedient. Since God's love is conditioned on obedience, and you're never perfectly obedient, God never loves you perfectly or accepts you completely." Such a bald description puts the issue into focus.

Since we're saved by grace and accepted by God continuously by grace, are we to conclude that He doesn't care whether we sin? To use Paul's strong exclamation in Romans 6:2, "By no means!" Such a conclusion flies in the face of all the ethical commands in Scripture. Such a conclusion also ignores the very clear relationship Jesus insisted on between love for Him and obedience to His commands.

Our love for God, expressed through obedience to Him, is to be a response to His love, not a means of trying to earn it. "We love because he first loved us" (1 John 4:19). Jesus said that love for God and love for one another essentially sum up all His commands (Matthew 22:36-40). Both our love for others and our love for God are prompted by His love for us.

Transforming Grace

GOD'S HATRED

> *The LORD tests the righteous, but his soul hates the wicked.*
>
> (PSALM 11:5)

Reconciliation by definition assumes a previous state of alienation and hostility caused by the offensive actions of one or both parties. Our sin has separated us from God (Isaiah 59:2) and caused us to be "God's enemies" (Romans 5:10, NIV), those hated by God. *Does God actually hate people?* Yes, the psalmist wrote, "You hate all who do wrong" (Psalm 5:5, NIV). So when Paul described us as God's enemies, he was describing not our sinful hatred of God but rather His righteous hatred of us because of our sin.

It's difficult for us to conceive of God's holy hatred toward people. But this is simply His just and holy revulsion against sin and His holy antagonism toward those who rebel against Him.

This is why God's act of reconciling us to Himself through Christ is so amazing. We were powerless to do anything to help ourselves (Romans 5:6); nor would we even want to, left to ourselves. As Paul wrote in Romans 8:7, "The sinful mind is hostile to God" (NIV). In our natural state, not one of us would want to be reconciled to God.

The gospel's good news is that God Himself took the initiative by sending His Son to die in our place to satisfy His justice and absorb His wrath. He didn't wait for a change of heart on our part. He made the first move. Indeed, He did more: He did all that was necessary to secure our reconciliation, including our change of heart. Though He is the One offended by our sin, He is the One who makes amends to Himself through Christ's death. "God was reconciling the world to himself in Christ, not counting men's sins against them" (2 Corinthians 5:19, NIV).

The Gospel for Real Life

How Thankful Are You?

I will give thanks to the LORD with my whole heart;
I will recount all of your wonderful deeds.

(PSALM 9:1)

Most of us acknowledge that everything we have comes from God, but how often do we stop to give thanks to Him? At the end of a workday, do you take time to say, "Thank You, heavenly Father, for giving me the skill, ability, and health to do my work today"? Do you ever physically or mentally go through your house and say to God, "Everything in the house and the food in the cupboard and the car (or cars) in the driveway are gifts from You. Thank You for Your gracious and generous provision"? When you give thanks at mealtime, is it routine and perfunctory, or is it a heartfelt expression of your gratitude to God for His continual provision of all your physical needs?

Taking for granted all the temporal provisions and spiritual blessings that God has so richly bestowed on us, and so failing to continually give Him thanks, is one of our "acceptable" sins. In fact, far too many Christians wouldn't think of it as sin. Yet Paul, in his description of a Spirit-filled person, said we're to be "giving thanks always and for everything to God" (Ephesians 5:20). Note the words *always* and *everything*. That means our whole lives should be ones of continually giving thanks.

Giving thanks to God for both His temporal and spiritual blessings in our lives is not just a nice thing to do — it's the moral will of God. Failure to give Him the thanks due Him is sin. It may seem like a benign sin to us because it doesn't harm anyone else. But it's an affront and insult to the One who created us and sustains us every second of our lives.

Respectable Sins

GROUNDED IN MERCY

He saved us . . . according to his own mercy.

(TITUS 3:5)

It was in view of God's mercy that Paul urged us to commit our bodies as living sacrifices, holy and pleasing to God (Romans 12:1). Undoubtedly Paul had in mind the mercy of God as he had displayed it in the preceding chapters of Romans. He could have been thinking of the righteousness of God that comes to us by faith, of justification freely by His grace through the redemption that's in Christ Jesus, or of God presenting Jesus as a propitiation for our sins that turns aside God's just and holy wrath from us.

No doubt Paul's mind would once again have dwelt on that wonderful statement in Romans 4:8: "Blessed is the man whose sin the Lord will never count against him" (NIV). He would have thought of how we now have peace with God, having been justified through faith, and that we now stand before Him in grace every day. He would have rejoiced in our deliverance from sin's dominion through our union with Christ in His death. He would have exulted again to know there's "no condemnation for those who are in Christ Jesus" (Romans 8:1). He would have relished again the promises of future glory and the assurance that nothing can separate us from God's love in Christ Jesus.

In short, Paul would have had in mind the gospel of Jesus Christ in all its wonderfulness when he wrote of the mercy of God.

This mercy is the ground for our commitment to pursue holiness. Such a commitment as Paul called for would indeed be legalistic and oppressive if it were not grounded in love. And the only way Paul would stir up our love is to remind us of God's love for us, revealed through His mercy and His grace.

The Discipline of Grace

TRUSTED STANDARDS

If you love me, you will keep my commandments.

(JOHN 14:15)

A loving obedience to the commands of God is one clear evidence that we're living by grace. Anyone who thinks, *Since God's love is not conditioned on my obedience, I'm free to live as I please,* is not living by grace, nor does he understand grace. What he perceives as grace is really a caricature.

Jesus said that if we love Him, we'll obey His commands. The term *command* suggests clear direction. We're told what to do or not do. We are not left in doubt how we're to live. The commands in the Bible provide a clear set of moral standards.

In the popular philosophy of situation ethics, actions are morally evaluated in terms of a "loving" response to the situation at hand rather than by application of moral absolutes. Situation ethics knows no external, objective standard of behavior; it responds to what seems right at the moment. But Scripture says, "The heart is deceitful above all things and beyond cure" (Jeremiah 17:9, NIV). Anything can be made to "seem right."

Through "Christianized" situation ethics, all kinds of sinful actions have been committed in the name of "love." Christians have engaged in illicit sexual intimacy on the pretense that they were acting in love toward a lonely or hurting person. Recently I heard of a man who allegedly conspired to have his incurably ill wife murdered because "she would be happier with Jesus." This is the type of trap even Christians fall into when we don't let the commands of God give definition to love. God's commands provide us this objective standard and, when obeyed, keep us from falling into situation ethics.

Transforming Grace

Everything Necessary

God . . . through Christ reconciled us to himself.

(2 Corinthians 5:18)

Total reconciliation demands a total effort by the offending party to make amends. When Jesus satisfied God's justice and propitiated God's wrath, He did all that was required to remove the enmity of God toward us. By His death He bridged the vast gulf of divine alienation between us and objectively restored us to a position of friendship and favor with God. But it was God, the offended party, who sent His Son to reconcile us to Himself. "When we were God's enemies, we were reconciled to him through the death of his Son" (Romans 5:10, niv).

This historical, objective work of reconciliation by Christ has to be personally received by each of us. That's why Paul wrote, "We implore you on behalf of Christ, *be reconciled to God*" (2 Corinthians 5:20).

This is a most amazing passage of Scripture. Having objectively secured reconciliation for us, Christ now appeals to us through His gospel messengers to "be reconciled to God" — to receive His work of reconciliation. We ourselves should have been on our faces before God, imploring Him to be reconciled to us. Instead, we see God reconciling us to Himself through the death of His Son, then appealing to us to receive that reconciliation. What pure grace and mercy on God's part!

To add to our amazement, we know that, left to ourselves, we would never even want to be reconciled to God. According to Paul, we were so blinded by Satan that we could not even see the light of the gospel and receive it (2 Corinthians 4:4). Therefore God sends His Holy Spirit to open our hearts to understand and receive the message of reconciliation (Acts 16:14). O, what wondrous love, what matchless grace, that God would do everything necessary to reconcile us to Himself!

The Gospel for Real Life

GRACE PROVIDED

You are . . . under grace.

(ROMANS 6:14)

Romans 12:1 and 6:13 are parallel passages; in both, Paul called on us to offer our bodies to God in the pursuit of holiness. But the context of Romans 6:13 — "Present yourselves to God as those who have been brought from death to life, and your members to God as instruments for righteousness" — is the assurance of God's enablement to carry out that commitment. In verse 11 we're urged to count ourselves dead to the dominion of sin and alive to the enabling power of God. In verse 14, Paul assured us that sin shall not be our master since we "are not under law but under grace." God not only asks us to commit ourselves to the pursuit of holiness, but provides the grace to enable us to do it.

In this setting, *grace* refers to God's divine enablement through the power of His Spirit. So whether it's viewed as God's undeserved favor as we would understand it in Romans 12:1, or as God's divine enablement as we should understand it in the context of Romans 6:13, grace is the basis for our commitment to the pursuit of holiness.

An all-out, unreserved, nothing-held-back commitment to the pursuit of holiness may be exhausting, but it will not be oppressive if it's grounded in grace. But to be grounded in grace, it must be continually referred back to the gospel. So don't just preach the gospel to yourself every day merely to experience the cleansing of your conscience. You certainly need to do so for that reason. But as you do, reaffirm your commitment to God as a response of love and gratitude. And do so in reliance on His Spirit that by His grace He will enable you to carry out your commitment.

The Discipline of Grace

SELF-CONTROL

God gave us a spirit . . . of power and love and self-control.
(2 TIMOTHY 1:7)

Self-control is the governing of one's desires. D. G. Kehl described it as "the ability to avoid excesses, to stay within reasonable bounds."[55] George Bethune called it "the healthful regulation of our desires and appetites, preventing their excess."[56]

But self-control involves a wider range of watchfulness than merely control of bodily appetites and desires. We also must exercise self-control of thoughts, emotions, and speech. Self-control says yes to what we should do as well as no to what we shouldn't. For example, I seldom want to study the Bible when I first begin. There are too many other things that are mentally much easier, such as reading the newspaper, a magazine, or a good Christian book. A necessary expression of self-control, then, is to set myself down with Bible and notebook and tell myself, "Get with it!" This may not sound very spiritual, but neither does Paul's exclamation, "I beat my body and make it my slave" (1 Corinthians 9:27).

Self-control is necessary because we're at war with our own sinful desires. James described those desires as dragging us away and enticing us into sin (1:14). Peter said they war against our souls (1 Peter 2:11). Paul spoke of them as deceitful (Ephesians 4:22). What makes these sinful desires so dangerous is that they dwell within our own heart. External temptations wouldn't be nearly so dangerous if they did not find this ally of desire right within us.

Self-control is an essential character trait of the godly person that enables obedience to the words of the Lord Jesus, "If anyone would come after me, he must deny himself and take up his cross daily and follow me" (Luke 9:23, NIV).

The Fruitful Life

WORDS OF AUTHORITY

*We ... pray for you, asking that you may be filled
with the knowledge of his will.*

(COLOSSIANS 1:9)

"Do not be foolish, but understand what the will of the Lord is"
(Ephesians 5:17). This is not God's particular will for us in some issue of
personal guidance but rather His moral will — as used, for example, in
1 Thessalonians 4:3: "For this is the will of God, your sanctification: that
you abstain from sexual immorality."

A few verses before Ephesians 5:17, Paul told us to "try to discern
what is pleasing to the Lord" (verse 10). To understand what the Lord's
will is and to find out what pleases the Lord are essentially the same; both
expressions refer to the specific directions given in the ethical commands
of Scripture. These verses themselves are also commands. That is, we're
commanded to know and understand the commands contained in
Scripture. Quite obviously, we're to seek to know God's will in order to
obey it. As my first Bible study leader said many years ago, "The Bible
wasn't given just to increase your knowledge, but to guide your conduct."

A command, however, is more than a set of directions. The word
command carries the idea of authority. The most basic meaning of the
word is "to direct with authority." A command does not just give guidance
that one may accept or reject; a command implies that the one giving it
has the authority to require obedience and the intention of doing so. This
is true of the commands of God. As the Sovereign God of the universe, He
has the authority to require obedience, and He does insist that we obey
Him.

Transforming Grace

A PERMANENT CHANGE

We have now received reconciliation.

(ROMANS 5:11)

When a wayward youth is later reconciled with his or her parents, there's always the possibility the youth will revert to the former rebellious state. He or she would again be alienated from the parents. It would be a self-inflicted alienation, to be sure, but nevertheless a real one. In fact, the parents' displeasure might even be stronger the second time around. This points to a significant difference between a reconciliation between human beings and our reconciliation to God.

Our reconciliation to God is permanent and eternal. Because Christ accomplished it for us, there's no possibility it can ever be undone. Though we continue, even as believers, to do those things that in themselves deserve God's displeasure, we can never revert to a state of divine alienation. For the sake of Christ, God will always accept us. And even when God deems it necessary to discipline us for persistent disobedience, He always does so out of love to restore us to the way of obedience (Hebrews 12:4-11).

This reconciliation does — in fact, it must — affect the way we live. The very nature of our salvation guarantees that we will not continue in an absolute state of sin and rebellion against God. He not only saves us from sin's guilt and consequent alienation; He also delivers us from sin's reign and continues to work to progressively free us from sin's activity in our lives. However, in the midst of God's work and our struggle with indwelling sin, we must always keep in mind that our status of favor and friendship with God is always, and ever will be, based on the objective work of Christ for us as our representative and substitute. We have been forever reconciled to God through the death of His Son.

The Gospel for Real Life

Sanctification by Consensus

Do not be foolish, but understand what the will of the Lord is.

(Ephesians 5:17)

In many evangelical circles it seems that we have morality by consensus. We may not be doing what society around us is doing, but neither are we living according to biblical standards. Instead we live according to the standard of conduct of Christians around us. We not only have morality by consensus; we have sanctification by consensus. We expect to become holy by osmosis, by the absorption of the ethical values of our Christian peer group.

If we're going to make progress in the pursuit of holiness, we must aim to live according to the precepts of Scripture — not according to the culture, even Christian culture, around us. But how can we do this if we don't know what those precepts are? It isn't sufficient for us to hear one or two thirty-minute sermons a week. We must be exposed to the Scriptures on a daily basis if we hope to live under their authority.

To pursue holiness, one of the disciplines we must become skilled in is the development of Bible-based convictions. A conviction is a determinative belief: something you believe so strongly that it affects the way you live. Someone has observed that a belief is what you hold, but a conviction is what holds you. You may live contrary to what you believe, but you cannot live contrary to your convictions. (This doesn't mean you never *act* contrary to your convictions, but that you do not consistently violate them.) So the discipline we're talking about is the development of *convictions*, not mere beliefs. Convictions, of course, can be good or bad, so we want to make sure our convictions are Bible-based, that they are derived from our personal interaction with the Scriptures.

The Discipline of Grace

REQUEST OR COMMAND?

You are my friends if you do what I command you.

(JOHN 15:14)

Under the reign of grace, is the moral will of God (considered as a whole) a request or a command? The word *request* connotes desire; whereas the word *command* connotes authority to require. Response to a desire is optional; response to a command is not.

So when Jesus said we love Him by obeying His commands, was He using the word *command* as we ordinarily understand it, or was He using it as an expression of God's desire? In the realm of grace, does the moral will of God express the desire of God as to how He would like us to live, or does it express the requirement of God as to how we are to live?

Some people readily say God desires that we be holy, but God does not require that we be holy. They maintain that under grace we have been freed, not only from the curse and condemnation resulting from breaking the law but also from the requirements of the law as a rule of life. They believe that to insist on obedience as a requirement for a Christian is to teach legalism instead of grace. In other words, to assign the concept of requirement to the will of God is legalism, but to assign the concept of desire to it is grace.

I believe such a view is a misunderstanding of grace. God's grace does not change the fundamental character of God's moral Law. Rather, the grace of God provides for the forgiveness and acceptance of those who have broken the law. The good news of the gospel is that God has removed the guilt we incur by breaking His Law and has bestowed on us the righteousness of Christ, who perfectly kept His Law. Legalism does not consist in yielding obedience to the law. Rather, it is to seek justification and good standing with God through the merit of works done in obedience to the law — instead of by faith in Christ.

Transforming Grace

FAITH AND HOLINESS

By faith Abraham obeyed.

(HEBREWS 11:8)

Obedience to the revealed will of God is often just as much a step of faith as claiming a promise from God. In fact, one of the more intriguing thoughts from the book of Hebrews is the way the writer appears to use obedience and faith interchangeably. He spoke of the Old Testament Hebrews who would never enter God's rest because they disobeyed (3:18). Yet they were not able to enter because of their unbelief (3:19). This interchange of unbelief and disobedience also occurs later in the book (4:2,6).

The heroes of faith in Hebrews 11 were said to be "still living by faith when they died" (11:13, NIV). But the element of obedience — responding to the will of God — was just as prominent in their lives as was claiming the promises of God. They obeyed by faith. And since obedience is the pathway to holiness — a holy life being essentially an obedient life — we may say that no one will become holy apart from a life of faith.

Faith enables us to claim the promises of God, but it also enables us to obey the commands of God. Faith enables us to obey when obedience is costly or seems unreasonable to the natural mind.

The path of obedience in the pursuit of holiness is often contrary to human reason. If we don't have conviction in the necessity of obeying the revealed will of God as well as confidence in the promises of God, we'll never persevere in this difficult pursuit. We must have conviction that seeking holiness is God's will for us — regardless of how arduous and painful the seeking may be. And we must be confident that the pursuit of holiness results in God's approval and blessing, even when circumstances make it appear otherwise.

The Pursuit of Holiness

THE PRIMARY ISSUE

Christ . . . offered himself without blemish to God.
(HEBREWS 9:14)

From different points of view, look at Christ's work for us: He perfectly obeyed the Law of God. He satisfied the justice of God. He exhausted the wrath of God. He removed our sins from the presence of God. He redeemed us from the curse of God. He reconciled us to God.

One thing is readily apparent: Every work of Christ is *directed toward God*. It's God's Law that was obeyed, His justice that was satisfied, His wrath that was propitiated, His holy presence from which our sins were removed, His curse from which we were redeemed, and alienation from His divine presence that has been reconciled.

This Godward focus tells us that the integrity of God's moral government and the upholding of His honor and glory are the primary issues in our salvation. It's true that God's love for sinful people such as you and me is the wellspring of our salvation, but this love could be shown only in such a way that the glory of His holiness and the honor of His Law would be magnified. Jesus in His sinless life and sin-bearing death did just that. *Hallelujah, what a Savior!*

As we contemplate the glory of the cross, we see that not only is our deepest need of salvation met, but it was met in the way that brings the most glory to God Himself. At the cross both God's Law and God's grace are most brilliantly displayed, and His justice and mercy both glorified. It's also at the cross where we're most humbled, where we admit to God and ourselves that absolutely nothing we do can earn or merit our salvation. As someone has well said, "We bring nothing to our salvation except our sin that made it necessary."

The Gospel for Real Life

ONLY TWO OPTIONS

Through your precepts I get understanding;
therefore I hate every false way.
(PSALM 119:104)

In Romans 12:1, Paul made a strong appeal for us to commit ourselves to live holy lives pleasing to God. In the following verse, he begins telling us how to carry this out: "Do not be conformed to this world, but be transformed by the renewal of your mind, that by testing you may discern what is the will of God, what is good and acceptable and perfect" (Romans 12:2).

Paul established a contrast between conforming (or being conformed) to the pattern of this world and being transformed by the renewal of one's mind. He assumed only two alternatives. Our convictions and values will come either from society around us (the world), or as our minds are renewed by the Word of God. There is no third option.

The writer of Psalm 1 stated this truth in a similar fashion: "Blessed is the man who walks not in the counsel of the wicked, nor stands in the way of sinners, nor sits in the seat of scoffers; but his delight is in the law of the LORD, and on his law he meditates day and night" (Psalm 1:1-2). The psalmist envisioned two groups of people. One group is drawn more and more under the controlling influence of wicked people, until at last they themselves begin to negatively influence others. The second group is those who delight in God's Law and meditate on it, thinking about it continually. The psalmist presented a contrast between two diametrically opposing influences: the pervasive influence of sinful society or the life-changing influence of the Law of God. There's no neutral sphere of influence. We're being influenced by the forces of sinful society, or we're being influenced by the Word of God.

The Discipline of Grace

THE WHITE SIGNS ARE STILL THERE

If anyone loves me, he will keep my word.

(JOHN 14:23)

Although God, through Christ, is our Savior and heavenly Father, He's also still the supreme Ruler and moral Governor of His creation. A king's sons and daughters, even though they're his children, are still under obligation to obey the laws of his realm. They are no more exempt from the laws than any other citizen. They're subject to these laws even though they love their father, agree with his laws, and freely and willingly obey them.

We as God's children are still subject to the laws of His realm. In response to His grace, we should obey in a loving and grateful way. And because God has written His Law on our hearts, we'll usually be in agreement with His Law written in His Word. But we're still to regard God's Law as commands to be obeyed, not merely as expressions of His desires.

Along our highways we have white speed limit signs and yellow speed advisory signs. The speed limit signs declare the law; the speed advisory signs are there to caution you. You can be fined for exceeding the posted speed limit because you've broken the law. You won't be fined for exceeding the advisory speed because you haven't broken any law.

The Law of God is like the white speed limit signs. It's the declared law of the realm. We've broken that law many times, but Christ has paid our "fine" (which is death) for us. But His payment did not abolish the Law; it did not, so to speak, change His speed limit signs to caution signs. God's Law hasn't become merely optional or advisory.

Transforming Grace

RIGHT WITH GOD

No one does good, not even one.

(ROMANS 3:12)

In a recent runaway bestseller, the author stated, "There is only one question which really matters: Why do bad things happen to good people? All other theological conversation is intellectually diverting."[57]

Setting aside the issue of whether *only one* question really matters, the Bible tells us that in light of eternity, the *most important* question we all face is how a sinful man or woman can come into a right relationship with an infinitely holy and just God. After all, Jesus said, "What good is it for a man to gain the whole world, yet forfeit his soul?" (Mark 8:36, NIV). Suppose a person lives his entire life experiencing nothing but prosperity and happiness, yet dies without a right relationship with God. What has he gained? Actually, he has lost everything.

Because God Himself is perfectly righteous and cannot look with favor on any unrighteousness, the only way we can have a right relationship with Him is to be perfectly righteous, as He is. But that's our problem, for, as Paul wrote, "There is no one righteous, not even one" (Romans 3:10, NIV).

What are we to do? Try harder? That won't help because, as Paul observed, "No one will be declared righteous in [God's] sight by observing the law; rather, through the law we become conscious of sin" (Romans 3:20, NIV). Regardless of how hard we try, we'll never attain the perfect righteousness God will accept.

So the question remains: How may we attain a right relationship with God? Happily, Paul answered it. After describing our predicament in Romans 3:20, he announced that God has provided a solution: "The righteousness of God has been manifested apart from the law . . . the righteousness of God through faith in Jesus Christ for all who believe" (verses 21-22).

The Gospel for Real Life

WORSHIPPING GOD

Worship the LORD in the splendor of holiness.

(1 CHRONICLES 16:29)

Another essential part of our practice of devotion to God is worship. By *worship* I mean the specific act of ascribing to God the glory, majesty, honor, and worthiness which are His. Revelation 4:8-11 and 5:9-14 give us clear illustrations of the worship that goes on in heaven and should be emulated by us here on earth. I almost always begin my daily quiet time with a period of worship. Before beginning my Bible reading for the day, I take a few minutes to reflect upon one of the attributes of God or to meditate upon a passage about His majesty and holiness, and then ascribe to Him the glory and honor due to Him.

I find it helpful to assume a kneeling position as a physical acknowledgment of my reverence, awe, and adoration of God. Worship is a matter of the heart, not of one's physical position; nevertheless, the Scriptures do frequently portray bowing the knee as a sign of homage and adoration. David said, "In reverence will I bow down toward your holy temple" (Psalm 5:7, NIV). The writer of Psalm 95 said, "Come, let us bow down in worship, let us kneel before the LORD our Maker" (verse 6, NIV). And we know that one day every knee shall bow before Jesus as a sign of homage to His Lordship (Philippians 2:10).

Obviously, it's not always possible to bow before God in our times of worship. God understands this and surely allows for it. But when we can do so, I strongly recommend bowing before God, not only as a sign of reverence to Him but also for what it does in helping us prepare our minds to worship God in a manner acceptable to Him.

The Fruitful Life

AN EVERYDAY DELIGHT

When I think on my ways, I turn my feet to your testimonies.

(PSALM 119:59)

We believers are being influenced by both society and the Word of God. We can think of these two opposing influences as representing the two extremes of a continuum — sinful society at one end and the Word of God at the other.

All believers are somewhere on that continuum, partially influenced by sinful society and partially influenced by the Word of God. What determines whether we're moving toward one end or the other? Psalm 1 gives us the answer: our attitude toward the Word of God and the time we spend thinking about it.

The person who's living toward the "God's Word" end of the continuum is described first of all as one whose "delight" is in the Law of God (Psalm 1:2). Like Paul, this person has determined that God's Law is "holy and righteous and good" (Romans 7:12). He or she sees that God's Law is not onerous or burdensome but is given to help us please God and live productive and satisfying lives — "like a tree planted by streams of water that yields its fruit in its season, and its leaf does not wither. In all that he does, he prospers" (Psalm 1:3). One who delights in the Law of God sees the Bible not as a book of difficult rules but as the Word of our heavenly Father, the God of all grace.

This person "mediates" on God's law "day and night" (Psalm 1:2). In Scripture, the word *meditate* means to think about a truth with a view to its meaning and application to one's life. It includes reflection on one's own life to determine what conformity, or lack of it, there is between the scriptural truth and one's character or conduct.

The Discipline of Grace

FULFILLING THE LAW

Love is the fulfilling of the law.
(ROMANS 13:10)

The fundamental character of God's Law has not changed from Old Testament to New Testament. What *has* changed is our reason for obedience, our motive. Under a sense of legalism, obedience is done with a view to meriting salvation or God's blessing on our lives. Under grace, obedience is a loving response to salvation already provided in Christ and the assurance that, having provided salvation, God will also, through Christ, provide all else that we need.

There's no question that obedience to God's commands prompted by fear or merit-seeking is not true obedience. The only obedience acceptable to God is impelled by love because "love is the fulfilling of the law" (Romans 13:10). In a profound way, love and obedience are bound together: "If anyone loves me, he will keep my word, and my Father will love him, and we will come to him and make our home with him" (John 14:23).

God's Law as revealed in His Word prescribes our duty, but love provides the correct motive for obedience. We obey God's Law, not to *be* loved but because we *are* loved in Christ.

I readily acknowledge that it's indeed difficult to keep in our minds and hearts the commandment nature of God's will without falling into the trap of legalism. Samuel Bolton recognized this difficulty when he wrote, "It is a hard lesson to live above the law, and yet to walk according to the law. But this is the lesson a Christian has to learn, to walk in the law in respect of duty, but to live above it in respect of comfort, neither expecting favour from the law in respect of his obedience nor fearing harsh treatment from the law in respect of his failing."[58]

p.322

Transforming Grace

Through Open Doors

The righteousness of the blameless keeps his way straight.

(Proverbs 11:5)

Martin Luther at first thought "the righteousness of God" which Paul mentioned in Romans 3:21 was the righteousness God required of us in perfectly fulfilling His Law. Because Luther realized more and more he could not possibly measure up to that impossible demand, he grew increasingly angry with God. At one time he had exclaimed, "Love God? I hate him."[59] Eventually he came to realize that the righteousness of God was that which *God* provided for us. "Thereupon I felt myself reborn and to have gone through open doors into paradise."[60]

What then is this righteousness from God that Paul announced to us, and over which Martin Luther struggled? It's a righteousness that God both requires and provides for us. It's the righteousness that He requires because it must fully satisfy the utmost demands of His Law, both in its precepts and penalty. For although this righteousness is apart from Law as far as we're concerned, it is not apart from Law as far as God is concerned. Rather it must be a righteousness that both perfectly fulfills the righteous requirements of His Law and satisfies the demands of His justice toward those who have broken His Law.

This righteousness from God, then, is nothing less than the perfect righteousness of Jesus Christ, who, through His sinless life and His death in obedience to the Father's will, perfectly fulfilled the Law of God in both its precepts and its penalty. In other words, this righteousness that God both requires and provides embraces *all* the work of Christ — how He perfectly obeyed God's law, satisfied God's justice, exhausted God's wrath, removed our sins from God's presence, redeemed us from God's curse, and reconciled us to our Creator.

The Gospel for Real Life

CHOOSING OUR MENTAL DIRECTION

On his law he meditates day and night.

(PSALM 1:2)

If we want to live under the influence of God's Word, our minds must be steeped in the Scriptures. We must constantly turn our minds to His Word, continually pondering the meaning and application of its truths to our lives. This may seem unrealistic and unattainable in our busy age when our minds need to be occupied with the various responsibilities we all have. How can we meditate on Scripture when we have to think about our work all day long?

We should not think of the concept of *continually* as meaning every moment, but rather *consistently* and *habitually*. When you can think about anything you want, what do you think about? Is it your problems or a mental argument with someone else? Do you allow your mind to drift into the wasteland of impure thoughts? Or do you begin to meditate on Scripture?

Thinking is our most constant activity. Our thoughts are our constant occupation. We're never without them. But we can choose the direction and content of those thoughts.

Meditation on Scripture is a discipline. We must commit ourselves to be proactive. We must memorize key passages (or carry them on cards) so we can think about them. We must be alert for those times during the day when we can turn our minds to the Word of God, and then we must do it. Even the practice of daily Bible reading is insufficient if we go the rest of the day without meditating on some truths of Scripture. We must choose to meditate instead of thinking about other things or listening to the radio or watching television. We simply have to decide what we want our minds to be influenced by, and take steps accordingly.

The Discipline of Grace

OUR FAILURES AND GOD'S SOVEREIGNTY

It is the purpose of the LORD that will stand.

(PROVERBS 19:21)

God's sovereignty doesn't do away with our duty to act responsibly and prudently on all occasions. But does our failure to act as we should frustrate God's sovereign plan? The Scriptures never indicate that God is frustrated to any degree by our failures. In His infinite wisdom, God's sovereign plan includes even our sins.

When Mordecai asked Queen Esther to intercede with King Xerxes on behalf of the Jews, she demurred with the explanation that she could not enter the king's presence unbidden, under threat of death (Esther 4:10-11). Mordecai sent word back to her, "If you keep silent at this time, relief and deliverance will rise for the Jews from another place" (Esther 4:14). God was not limited to Esther's response. His options for bringing about deliverance for the Jews were as infinite as His wisdom and power. He literally did not need Esther's cooperation. But He chose to use her. Mordecai's closing argument to Esther — "And who knows whether you have not come to the kingdom for such a time as this?" — assumes that God uses people and means to accomplish His sovereign purpose. As subsequent events proved, God had indeed raised up Esther to accomplish His purpose. But He could just as easily have raised up someone else or used an altogether different means.

God usually works through ordinary events (as opposed to miracles) and the voluntary actions of people. But He always provides the necessary means and guides them by His unseen hand. He is sovereign, and He cannot be frustrated by our failure to act or by our actions, which in themselves are sinful. We must always remember, however, that God still holds us accountable for the very sins that He uses to accomplish His purpose.

Is God Really in Control?

THE LAW IS FOR GRACE

I came not to call the righteous, but sinners.
(MATTHEW 9:13)

Ironically, the Law of God, viewed as commands to be obeyed, should actually promote living by grace. When we view God's commands as optional — or think that as God's children we are no longer under the law as a moral requirement — we subtly slip into a works mentality. If obedience to God's Law is optional, then in our minds we begin to accumulate merit or extra points. "After all, I don't *have* to obey, so I must gain some merit by voluntary obedience."

But the person who knows he's required to obey God's commands, even as a child of God, will see more and more how far short he comes in obedience. And if that person understands the biblical concept of grace, he'll be driven more and more into the arms of the Savior and His merit alone.

Evangelist D. L. Moody is reported to have said something to this effect: "You've got to get people lost before you can get them saved." He was saying that only those who recognize they are lost will turn to the Savior. The Lord Jesus stated the same principle: "For I came not to call the righteous, but sinners" (Matthew 9:13).

This principle applies to us even as believers living under grace. We need to be reminded that we are still sinners. The best way to do this is to take seriously the commands of God as a required rule of life. We'll be continually reminded that we really are spiritually bankrupt — even as believers. And as redeemed sinners in a perpetual state of bankruptcy, we'll come to appreciate more each day the superabounding grace of God.

Transforming Grace

JUSTIFICATION

We hold that one is justified by faith apart from works of the law.

(ROMANS 3:28)

Justification is one of Paul's major themes in both Romans and Galatians. The word occurs (usually as the verb *justify*) about forty times in the New Testament, mostly in Paul's writings.

A helpful approach to understanding its meaning is to look at Romans 3:20, where Paul wrote, "By works of the law no human being will be justified in his sight." To justify is to declare righteous. Justification is God's declaration that we are righteous before Him.

For us, justification means that God has forgiven all our sins and accepts us as righteous in His sight. How can this be? How can God accept us as righteous when our very best deeds fall so far short of the righteous demands of His Law? The answer lies in our federal or legal union with Christ. Because we're united by faith to Him who is perfectly righteous, God accepts us as perfectly righteous. God does not resort to some kind of legal fiction, calling something righteous that is not. Rather, He declares us righteous on the basis of the real accomplished righteousness of Christ, imputed to us because of our union with Him.

The apostle Paul expressed it very succinctly in my favorite verse of Scripture, 2 Corinthians 5:21: "God made him who had no sin to be sin for us, so that in him [through union with him] we might become the righteousness of God" (NIV). That is, God took our sin and imputed (charged) it to Christ, and took His righteousness and imputed (credited) it to us. To put it in a very contemporary form, God treated Christ as we deserved to be treated so that He might treat us as Christ deserved to be treated.

The Gospel for Real Life

OUR COMPLETE AUTHORITY

Scripture cannot be broken.

(JOHN 10:35)

In thinking about Scripture and its application to our lives, we need to be sure we're thinking *God's* truth, not our own opinions. This means, first of all, that we must be absolutely convinced the Bible is God's Word — that what Scripture says, God says. We need to approach the Bible with the deep, settled conviction that it accurately expresses the mind of God and the will of God as to how we are to live.

Ambivalence on this point can be fatal to the pursuit of holiness, for, after all, only God is the final authority on what constitutes holy living. If the Bible is not the complete, authoritative Word of God, then there is no absolute moral truth, and we are left to our own opinions.

The Bible, however, consistently affirms that it is indeed the very Word of God. The apostle Paul said, "All Scripture is God-breathed" (2 Timothy 3:16, NIV). The apostle Peter said that "men spoke from God as they were carried along by the Holy Spirit" (2 Peter 1:21).

We may not understand how the Holy Spirit moved upon the minds of those who wrote the Scriptures or how He spoke through the mouths of such men as David so that what they wrote or said was exactly what He wanted them to say, but this is what the Bible consistently affirms. If this is a new thought to you, or if you have some doubts about this, I urge you to make this issue a matter of prayerful, humble study. Ask God to remove any doubts you might have and give you a settled conviction that the Bible is indeed God's Word, that it is complete and authoritative, and that it is absolute truth.

The Discipline of Grace

Law and Love Indistinguishable

> *The whole law is fulfilled in one word:*
> *"You shall love your neighbor as yourself."*
> (Galatians 5:14)

Some people maintain that the "law of love" has replaced even the moral commands of Jesus and that our only rule is to "love our neighbor as ourself." They quote Paul: "The one who loves another has fulfilled the law. For the commandments, 'You shall not commit adultery, You shall not murder, You shall not steal, You shall not covet,' and any other commandment, are summed up in this word: 'You shall love your neighbor as yourself.' Love does no wrong to a neighbor; therefore love is the fulfilling of the law" (Romans 13:8-10).

Some people understand Paul to say that the New Testament principle of love has replaced the Old Testament principle of law. Whereas the Jewish nation in the Old Testament lived under a number of specific moral laws, the church in the New Testament has "come of age" and now lives by the higher principle of love. Since love must be voluntary and cannot be compelled, so the thinking goes, love and law are mutually exclusive.

But if we realize the moral law is a transcript — a written reproduction — of the moral character of God and that "God is love" (1 John 4:8), we see that we cannot distinguish between law and love. Both express the character of God. They're two sides of the same coin.

For example, Paul said in Romans 13:10, "Love does no wrong to its neighbor" (NIV). If we didn't also have the commandments (which Paul quoted in verse 9) against such things as adultery, stealing, and murder, how would we know what it means to harm one's neighbor?

Love provides the motive for obeying the commands of the Law, but the Law provides specific direction for exercising love.

Transforming Grace

PAUL'S BONE

We have been justified by faith.
(ROMANS 5:1)

Paul announced in Romans 3:22, "The righteousness of God *through faith* in Jesus Christ for all who *believe*." It's through faith in Christ that we experience God's justifying act and enter into a right relationship with Him.

We're justified because of our union with Christ, and we're justified through faith — both statements are true because it's through faith that we're united to Christ so that His life becomes our life, His death our death, and His righteousness our righteousness. All the objective work of Christ for us is applied to us and received by us through faith in Him.

When it comes to justification through faith, Paul was like a dog with a bone. He wouldn't let go. He kept hammering away on the truth that justification is through faith, not works. "We hold that one is justified by faith apart from works of the law," he said in Romans 3:28, then went on to devote the entire fourth chapter of Romans to this truth.

Or consider Galatians 2:16: "We know that a person is not justified by works of the law but through faith in Jesus Christ, so we also have believed in Christ Jesus, in order to be justified by faith in Christ and not by works of the law, because by works of the law no one will be justified."

Notice Paul's repetition of the word *justified*. I often jokingly say that Paul's work wouldn't get past my editor because editors by nature are highly allergic to frequent use of the same word. But Paul wanted to be sure the Galatian believers didn't miss his point: We're justified by faith in Christ and not by observing the Law — the same message he developed more fully in Romans 3–4.

The Gospel for Real Life

HEARING GOD WITH HUMILITY

Open my eyes, that I may behold wondrous things out of your law.

(PSALM 119:18)

It isn't enough to believe that all Scripture is from God. We need to strive to understand it as best we can. We need to approach the Bible each day with a spirit of deep humility, recognizing that our understanding of spiritual truth is at best incomplete and to some extent inaccurate. No Christian or body of Christians has a corner on all of truth.

Jesus once said, "I praise you, Father, Lord of heaven and earth, because you have hidden these things from the wise and learned, and revealed them to *little children*" (Luke 10:21, NIV). However knowledgeable about Scripture we may be, we need to approach it each day as little children, asking the Holy Spirit to teach us. Regardless of how much we already understand, there's still an infinite storehouse of understanding of the mind of God waiting for us in Scripture. My own experience is that the more I learn and understand of Scripture, the more I see how little I understand of all that God has revealed to us in His Word. So as you read or study the Bible, don't do so just to buttress your own opinions or favorite doctrines. Rather, ask the Holy Spirit to teach you.

God may indeed confirm your convictions more deeply as you see them aligned with the teaching of Scripture. He'll also very likely make you aware of areas of your life where you aren't fully obedient to His revealed will, or He may cause you to see in a different light some doctrinal position you've assumed. So we should approach the Scriptures in humility and expect the Spirit to humble us even further as we continue being taught by Him from His Word.

The Discipline of Grace

GRACE AND FREEDOM

> *For freedom Christ has set us free; stand firm therefore,*
> *and do not submit again to a yoke of slavery.*
>
> (GALATIANS 5:1)

It's difficult for us today to appreciate the struggle the newly emerging Gentile churches had with the Jewish "law-keepers" in Paul's day. We must seek to understand what Paul meant by *freedom* (in Galatians 5:1) in the context of the issue he was contending against. Otherwise, we may interpret Paul as saying more than he actually said.

In the history of the United States, a famous patriot cried out, "Give me liberty, or give me death!" Because we know he uttered this in the context of the American Revolution, we readily understand he was speaking specifically of liberty from the rule of the British monarch. He was not crying out for liberty from all civil law, but from what he considered the tyranny of unjust laws.

In the United States, we say we live in a "free country." We understand that freedom to be political freedom: the right to have a say in our government. But we all recognize we are not free to disobey the laws of our state or nation. We are not free, for example, to drive on the left side of the highway.

When we stop to think about it, there's no such thing as unqualified freedom. Such "freedom" would not be freedom; it would be anarchy. It would be everyone doing what is right in his own eyes; and given our sinful nature, it would be total chaos.

In the same manner, Paul did not call for freedom in an absolute sense, but freedom from the bondage of the Jewish law system, which was abolished by Christ in His death.

Transforming Grace

FAITH EXPLORED

The righteous shall live by faith.

(ROMANS 1:17)

Since faith is so essential to our being justified, we need to explore it more fully.

Note the four italicized verbs in Romans 10:13-15: "For 'everyone who calls on the name of the Lord will be saved.' How then will they *call* on him in whom they have not believed? And how are they to *believe* in him of whom they have never heard? And how are they to *hear* without someone preaching? And how are they to *preach* unless they are sent?" These four words, taken in reverse order, help us understand the nature of faith.

First, someone *preaches* a message. In light of Acts 8:4, we should understand *preach* to cover every instance of sharing the gospel, to an individual or an audience. What is preached? Romans 10:17 says, "The message is heard through the word of Christ" (NIV). The message is obviously the gospel of Christ.

As someone shares the gospel, a person *hears* it. Faith involves hearing and understanding the gospel. Faith must have content. It's not a leap in the dark, hoping all will turn out well.

Then the person must *believe* that the gospel message is true and applicable to his or her situation. Paul wrote of "believing in" the One of whom they've heard. Faith's object is not the mere content of the message, but the One the message is about.

Finally, as we believe in Jesus, we *call* on Him — embracing and trusting in Him alone for our salvation. Scripture uses several words for this, such as *receive* (John 1:12), *believe in* (John 3:16), and *trust* (Romans 4:5). The Puritans had a quaint expression for it. They spoke of *closing* with Christ, using that word the way we use it to refer to closing on a home.

The Gospel for Real Life

DILIGENCE IN RECEIVING GOD'S WORD

Be attentive, that you may gain insight.

(PROVERBS 4:1)

We need to approach the Scriptures with an attitude of mental discipline. We need both discipline and dependence in the pursuit of holiness, and the same is true in our study of the Scriptures.

There are many Bible study methods and approaches, but common to all of them is an attitude of dependent diligence that's well expressed in Proverbs 2:1-5: "If you receive my words and treasure up my commandments with you, making your ear attentive to wisdom and inclining your heart to understanding; yes, if you call out for insight and raise your voice for understanding, if you seek it like silver and search for it as for hidden treasures, then you will understand the fear of the LORD and find the knowledge of God." The thought of searching the Scriptures with the same intensity that one would search for hidden treasures suggests the value we should place on Scripture's teaching. We see this value expressed also in Proverbs 7:2: "Keep my teaching as the apple of your eye."

We also see in Proverbs 2:1 that there must be a spirit of humility in approaching Scripture, as expressed by the opening phrase "if you receive my words." This attitude is in contrast with the attitude of the foolish, who "would have none of my counsel and despised all my reproof" (Proverbs 1:30).

The question we must ask ourselves is this: What value do we place upon the Word of God? Do we search it as if we were seeking for hidden treasures, or do we read it and study it only because we know it is something we should do?

The Discipline of Grace

MORAL SUPERIORITY

We have sinned against you. Even I and my father's house have sinned.

(NEHEMIAH 1:6)

Of all our subtle, "acceptable" sins, the pride of moral superiority may be the most common, second only to the sin of ungodliness. Although it's so prevalent, it's difficult to recognize because we all practice it to some degree. In fact, we seem to get a perverse enjoyment out of discussing how awful society around us is becoming. When we do that, we're guilty of the pride of moral superiority.

How, then, can we guard against this sin of self-righteousness? First, by seeking an attitude of humility. If we're morally upright, it's only because God's grace has prevailed in us. No one is morally upright by nature. Rather, we all have to say with David, "Surely I was sinful at birth, sinful from the time my mother conceived me" (Psalm 51:5, NIV). We ought to feel deeply grateful that God by His grace has kept us from, or perhaps rescued us from, the lifestyle of those who practice the flagrant sins we condemn.

We can also identify ourselves before God with the sinful society we live in. Ezra the scribe was a godly man who lived an exemplary life. Yet when he became aware of a deep sin among the people, he identified himself with it, though he himself was not guilty. Consider his prayer: "O my God, I am ashamed and blush to lift my face to you, my God, for *our* iniquities have risen higher than our heads, and *our* guilt has mounted up to the heavens" (Ezra 9:6). He included himself in this confession of guilt. As we in our day see the increasing moral degradation of our society, we need to adopt Ezra's attitude.

Respectable Sins

FREEDOM OR CHAOS?

The precepts of the LORD are right, rejoicing the heart.
(PSALM 19:8)

My son visited a country in which automobile drivers are undisciplined and "free spirited." He saw cars stopped at a railroad crossing for a passing train. Instead of lining up behind one another to cross in their proper turn, several cars lined up across the entire road. Each driver wanted to be first to cross when the crossing guard was raised. But when the train had passed, cars were also lined up completely across the road on the other side of the tracks. "Freedom" quickly turned to chaos!

That kind of thing happens in a much more serious way when we insist on unqualified freedom from God's Law. We have indeed been set free from the bondage and curse that results from breaking the law. And we've been called to freedom from works as a means of obtaining any merit with God. But we haven't been called to freedom from the Law as an expression of God's will for our daily living.

Paul said, "For I delight in the law of God, in my inner being," and "I myself serve the law of God with my mind" (Romans 7:22,25). A few verses earlier he had characterized God's Law as "holy and righteous and good" (verse 12). It seems inconceivable that Paul would want to be free, or urge others to be free, from what was holy, righteous, and good — that in which he himself delighted.

God's Law is not opposed to grace, nor is it an enemy of grace. Neither is the Law of God opposed to us as we seek to live by grace. Out of a grateful response to God's grace, we seek to understand His will and to obey Him, not to be blessed but because we have been blessed.

Transforming Grace

Renunciation and Reliance

We also have believed in Christ Jesus, in order to be justified
by faith in Christ and not by works of the law.

(Galatians 2:16)

I like to say that exercising faith involves renunciation and reliance. Trusting in Christ necessarily involves renouncing any trust in our own good works, whatever form they might take. (See, for example, Romans 4:4-5; 10:1-4; Galatians 2:15-16; Ephesians 2:8-9.) Then we must rely entirely on Christ's perfect righteousness. Paul spoke of "the man who does not work but trusts God who justifies the wicked" (Romans 4:5, NIV). There's an absolute antithesis between trusting, even to the smallest degree, in our own works of goodness and trusting or relying entirely on Christ's righteousness for our justification.

This complete renunciation of any confidence in our own goodness and total reliance upon Christ and His work for us is well expressed in Edward Mote's hymn "The Solid Rock": "My hope is built on nothing less than Jesus' blood and righteousness; no merit of my own I claim,[61] but wholly lean on Jesus' name."

As we come empty-handed to Christ, claiming no merit of our own but clinging by faith to His blood and righteousness, we are justified. We pass immediately from a state of condemnation and spiritual death to a state of pardon, acceptance, and the sure hope of eternal life. Our sins are blotted out, and we are "clothed" with the righteousness of Jesus Christ. In our standing before God, we'll never be more righteous, even in heaven, than we were the day we trusted Christ, or than we are now. Obviously in our daily experience we fall far short of the perfect righteousness God requires. But because He has imputed to us the perfect righteousness of His Son, He now sees us as being just as righteous as Christ Himself.

The Gospel for Real Life

DESPERATE FOR UNDERSTANDING

Blessed are you, O LORD; teach me your statutes!

(PSALM 119:12)

Along with an attitude of diligence in approaching God's Word, we also need an attitude of dependence, as is expressed in Proverbs 2:3: "Call out for insight and raise your voice for understanding." This is an almost-desperate sense of dependence, an attitude far different from a more usual perfunctory prayer for God to teach us as we begin our weekly Bible study.

Do we really believe we're dependent on the Holy Spirit to enlighten our understanding, or do we actually depend on our own intellectual ability in our study of Scripture? I suspect that many of us, while giving lip service to dependence on the Spirit, actually depend on our own intellect.

It's difficult to maintain an attitude of both diligence and dependence, but we must do this if we want to learn from the Holy Spirit. He does not reward either indolence or sinful self-confidence. He does bless diligence when it's pursued in a sincere attitude of dependence on Him. What we're talking about here is not just acquiring more knowledge of biblical truth, but rather developing Bible-based convictions by which we are to live.

Unfortunately, too many Christians seem to approach Bible study in the same way they would approach more academic subjects. When we do this, we're more apt to become proud over our "superior" knowledge of biblical truth than humbled over our lack of obedience to what Scripture teaches. We should pray for knowledge of truth that will change our lives rather than simply inform our minds. We need to pray with the psalmist, "Teach me, O LORD, the way of your statutes; and I will keep it to the end" (Psalm 119:33).

The Discipline of Grace

IN CHRIST, NOT IN US

> *He who sanctifies and those who are sanctified all have one source.*
>
> (HEBREWS 2:11)

Arthur W. Pink has identified a key issue in living by grace: "The great mistake made by most of the Lord's people is in hoping to discover in themselves that which is to be found in Christ alone."[62]

All Christians recognize that we're justified — declared righteous — solely on the basis of the righteousness of Christ imputed to us by God through faith (Romans 3:21-25). But few of us fully recognize that we're also sanctified through faith in Christ. Sanctification, or holiness (the two words are virtually interchangeable), is essentially conformity to the moral character of God. We normally think of sanctification as progressive, as an inner change of our character whereby we are conformed more and more to the likeness of Christ. That's certainly a major part of sanctification, but not all of it.

Scripture speaks of both a holiness we already possess in Christ before God and a holiness in which we're to grow more and more. The first is the result of the work of Christ *for* us; the second is the result of the work of the Holy Spirit *in* us. The first is perfect and complete and is ours the moment we trust Christ; the second is progressive and incomplete as long as we're in this life.

The objective holiness we have in Christ and the subjective holiness produced by the Holy Spirit are both gifts of God's grace and are both appropriated by faith. And the perfect holiness we have in Christ is the reason we can appear daily before a perfectly holy God when even our best deeds are stained and polluted.

Transforming Grace

THAT POINT IN TIME

I would remind you, brothers, of the gospel . . .
which you received, in which you stand.

(1 CORINTHIANS 15:1)

In Romans 5:1, Paul spoke of our justification in the past tense: "We have been justified." Justification is a point-in-time experience that occurs the moment we trust in Christ as Savior. I realize the precise moment is not identifiable to many people who grew up in Christian homes and whose faith in Christ was a growing experience. If such is your situation, I would ask: Are you trusting in Christ as your Savior today? If so, there was a time, known only to God, when you were declared righteous before Him. You can have confidence in this fact.

This point-in-time event has eternal ongoing benefit for us. In Romans 5:2, Paul wrote that through Christ "we have also obtained access by faith into this grace in which we stand." This grace is the grace of justification, and he says we *stand* in it — now, today. By His grace we've gained the standing of justification, and we will forever remain in that status. It can never change. For the remainder of our lives and throughout eternity we'll stand before God justified, declared righteous in His sight because He has given to us the righteousness of Christ.

There was a point in time when we trusted in Christ and were by faith united to Him so that His death became our death, His obedience our obedience, His righteousness our righteousness. If this is true of you, then you have an answer to the most important question you could ever ask: How can I, a sinful human being, come into a right relation-ship with a holy and just God? You stand before God today and are forevermore declared righteous by Him. You now possess that right relationship with God.

The Gospel for Real Life

THE DISCIPLINE OF SCRIPTURE MEMORY

Let the word of Christ dwell in you richly.

(COLOSSIANS 3:16)

To influence our minds with the Word of God, there's simply no better way than through the discipline of Scripture memorization. I know it requires work and is sometimes discouraging when we can't recall accurately a verse we've worked hard to memorize. The truth is, however, all forms of discipline require work and are often discouraging. But the person who perseveres in any discipline, despite the hard work and discouraging times, reaps the reward the discipline is intended to produce.

The example of Jesus' use of Scripture when He was tempted by the Devil in the wilderness is often used as a challenge to us to memorize Scripture. Three times He was tempted, and three times He answered Satan's temptation by resorting to the Scriptures, saying, "It is written" (Matthew 4:1-11). It's obvious He had memorized these Old Testament commands that He effectively used to thwart Satan's assaults. But it should also be apparent to us that Jesus knew more than a few isolated verses of the Mosaic Law. Rather, His mind was steeped in the Scriptures. If you and I are going to be holy as He is holy, our minds must also be filled with Scripture.

Christ's use of specific Scriptures to thwart Satan's temptations should be instructive to us. He brought particular passages from the Old Testament to bear on the particular temptations He faced. So I encourage you to memorize Scriptures that deal with the particular temptations to which you are especially vulnerable. (I again encourage you to identify specific temptations to which you are vulnerable, list them on a private prayer page, and make specific commitments regarding these areas of vulnerability.) Then ask the Holy Spirit to bring these passages to your mind at times of temptation.

The Discipline of Grace

CHRIST OUR HOLINESS

He has perfected for all time those who are being sanctified.
(HEBREWS 10:14)

Paul wrote, "And because of [God] you are in Christ Jesus, who became to us wisdom from God, righteousness and sanctification and redemption" (1 Corinthians 1:30). God Himself chose us to be in Christ — who has become our righteousness, sanctification, and redemption.

That Christ is our righteousness is an accepted and well-understood truth and the basis for our justification. But Christ is also our sanctification, or holiness. This fact is not as well understood. All Christians look to Christ alone for their justification, but not nearly as many also look to Him for their perfect holiness before God. The blessed truth, though, is that all believers are sanctified in Christ, even as we are justified in Christ.

Hebrews 10:10,14 help us see this objective aspect of sanctification — the holiness we have in Christ alone. Verse 10 says that by the will of God "we have been sanctified through the offering of the body of Jesus Christ once for all." Note that "we have been sanctified" speaks of a completed work. The emphasis here is on the holiness we have in Christ through His once-for-all sacrifice.

Verse 14, on the other hand, says, "by a single offering [Christ] has perfected for all time those who are being sanctified." This verse mentions "being sanctified" — the continuing work of the Holy Spirit in progressive sanctification. This verse also refers to our completed, objective sanctification in Christ when it speaks of those He has "perfected for all time." So, in one aspect of sanctification you're already holy because Christ's holiness is imputed to you; you've been made perfect forever. In another aspect, you're *being made holy* day by day through the work of the Holy Spirit imparting Christ's life to you.

Transforming Grace

A PRESENT REALITY

Now if we have died with Christ, we believe that we will also live with him.

(ROMANS 6:8)

Unfortunately, many believers do not live as if justification is a permanent state. They've divorced their hope of eternal life from their relationship with God today. They expect to "put on" Christ's robe of righteousness only at death. Meanwhile, in this life they draw their sense of God's acceptance from their most recent performance of Christian duties or their avoidance of certain sins. Their "robe of righteousness" for daily living isn't from Christ, but one they've stitched together by their own performance.

By contrast, the apostle Paul lived in a continuous state of conscious justification. In Galatians 2:20 he wrote, "The life I *now* live in the flesh I live by faith in the Son of God, who loved me and gave himself for me." In the context, Paul was speaking of his faith in Christ for justification. But this was not simply a past event. Rather, he was speaking of his present daily experience of living in a state of justification. As George Smeaton wrote, "Obviously, this is not the language of faith for attaining justification, but the language of a man already justified, and glorying in a sense of acceptance and the experience of grace." [63]

For Paul, justification was not only a point-in-time event that occurred in the past, but a present reality in which he rejoiced every day. Paul did what we should do. He renounced any confidence in his own performance or, for that matter, any dismay over his lack of performance. Instead, by faith he looked to Jesus Christ and His righteousness for his sense of being in right standing with God today, tomorrow, and throughout eternity.

The Gospel for Real Life

OBEDIENCE APPLIED

My mother and my brothers are those who hear the word of God and do it.
(LUKE 8:21)

Bringing ourselves under the transforming influence of the Word of God means much more than just acquiring knowledge about the contents of Scripture. In fact, the mere acquisition of Bible facts or doctrinal truth without application to one's life can lead to spiritual pride. As Paul said, "Knowledge puffs up, but love builds up" (1 Corinthians 8:1, NIV). By contrast Paul also spoke of "the knowledge of the truth that leads to godliness" (Titus 1:1, NIV).

What is the difference between these two concepts of Bible knowledge? In the first instance the Corinthians were using their knowledge in a selfish and prideful way. They were "looking down their noses" at people with different convictions from theirs. On the other hand, the knowledge leading to godliness is knowledge of the Scriptures that is being applied to one's life and results in godly behavior.

One of the banes of present-day evangelical Christianity is the way we sit every week under the teaching of God's Word, or even have private devotions and perhaps participate in a Bible study group, without a serious intent to obey the truth we learn. The indictment of the Jewish people God made to Ezekiel could well be said of us today: "My people come to you, as they usually do, and sit before you to listen to your words, but they do not put them into practice" (Ezekiel 33:31, NIV).

Our tendency seems to be to equate knowledge of the truth, and even agreement with it, with obedience to it. James said when we do this we deceive ourselves (James 1:22). This is especially true when we focus on the more scandalous sins "out there" in society to the neglect of the more "refined" sins we commit.

The Discipline of Grace

DON'T INTERPRET; LEARN!

Remember the whole way that the LORD your God has led you . . .
that he might humble you.

(DEUTERONOMY 8:2)

Because God's wisdom is infinite and His ways inscrutable to us, we should also be very careful in seeking to interpret the ways of God in His providence, especially in particular events. Additionally, we need to be cautious of others who offer themselves as interpreters about the why and wherefore of all that is happening. Be wary of those who say, "God let this happen so you could learn such and such a lesson." The fact is, we don't know what God is doing through a particular set of circumstances or events.

This doesn't mean we shouldn't seek to learn from God's providence as well as His revealed will in Scripture. Quite the contrary. The psalmist learned God's decrees experientially through affliction (Psalm 119:71). The people of Israel also learned through God's adverse providence in their lives: "And he humbled you and let you hunger and fed you with manna, which you did not know, nor did your fathers know, that he might make you know that man does not live by bread alone, but man lives by every word that comes from the mouth of the LORD" (Deuteronomy 8:3). God taught the nation through His divine providence — through putting them in a situation where they could not simply go to the cupboard for their daily bread — that they were utterly dependent upon Him. God was leading the nation into a land where material provision would be "naturally" plentiful (Deuteronomy 8:7-9). He knew they would be tempted by the pride of their own hearts to say, "My power and the might of my hand have gotten me this wealth" (verse 17). So before they entered the land, God taught them about their dependence on His divine providence.

Is God Really in Control?

HIS HOLINESS IS OUR HOLINESS

God has not called us for impurity, but in holiness.
(1 THESSALONIANS 4:7)

Holiness should be an objective for your daily life. But to live by grace, you must never, never look to the work of the Holy Spirit in you as the basis for your relationship with God. You must always look outside of yourself to Christ. You will never be holy enough through your own efforts to come before God. You are holy only through Christ.

Two parallel passages in Paul's letters to the Ephesians and Colossians should encourage all of us: "He chose us in him before the foundation of the world, that we should be holy and blameless before him" (Ephesians 1:4). "And you, who once were alienated and hostile in mind, doing evil deeds, he has now reconciled in his body of flesh by his death, in order to present you holy and blameless and above reproach before him" (Colossians 1:21-22).

The common teaching in both passages is that we are holy and blameless in God's sight. It seems like a paradox to state that we are holy in God's sight. How can we who are not only guilty but morally filthy possibly be holy in the sight of One whose gaze penetrates our very hearts, who knows our every motive and thought as well as our words and actions? The answer is that because of our union with Christ, God sees *His* holiness as *our* holiness. Arthur Pink said, "In the person of Christ God beholds a holiness which abides His closest scrutiny, yea, which rejoices and satisfies His heart; and whatever Christ is before God, He is for His people."[64]

Transforming Grace

THE WAR'S OVER

May the God of peace be with you.

(ROMANS 15:33)

Paul said, "Since we have been justified through faith, we have peace with God through our Lord Jesus Christ" (Romans 5:1, NIV). This is an objective peace. The war is over. The alienation and divine displeasure toward us because of our sin have been removed. We're no longer objects of wrath. We have peace with God whether we realize it or not. However, to the extent that we understand and believe the truth regarding justification, we'll experience a subjective peace within our souls. We'll know that we've been brought from a state of condemnation and the prospect of eternal judgment into a state of forgiveness and favor with God.

I well remember the night I trusted Christ as an eighteen-year-old. Outwardly I was a model teenager but not a Christian, though I knew the gospel message. One night alone in my bed I asked Christ to be my Savior. Immediately I had peace in my soul, brought to me by the Holy Spirit. But that experiential peace was possible only because Christ had made peace with God for me through His death on the cross.

There's nothing you will ever do that makes you acceptable to God. You must be accepted for Christ's sake, not only when you believe but for all of your life.

Take some time to prayerfully ask yourself some questions: Do I have a right relationship with God based on the imputed righteousness of Christ? Am I trusting in Christ alone for my salvation, or am I to some degree relying on my own morality and religious duties? If I know I'm justified through faith in Christ, do I enjoy the reality of it in my daily experience, or do I look to my own performance for acceptance with God?

The Gospel for Real Life

REAL-LIFE APPLICATION

For the word of God is living and active.
(HEBREWS 4:12)

We cannot develop Bible-based convictions merely by storing up Bible knowledge, or even by Bible study or Scripture memorization. We come closer as we meditate on Scripture consistently. But convictions are really developed when we begin applying Scripture's teachings to real-life situations.

My wife and I recently went shopping for a coffee table. We had agreed on the style we wanted and quickly found one at a price within our range. I'm the type of person who's ready to buy as soon as I find what I like, but my wife is a "shopper." She likes to look at everything in the store. Sure enough, she soon came upon her "dream" coffee table, a rather uncommon design that she'd dreamed about for years but never thought she would own. As you might guess, it was more expensive.

I started talking about being good stewards of the money God has given us, but God started "talking" to me (through His Spirit's convicting work) about husbands loving their wives as Christ loved the church (Ephesians 5:25). I realized one of the concrete ways I was to love my wife was to be more sensitive to her dreams and desires. In that situation God desired that I learn more about what it means for husbands to love their wives than about stewarding His resources. But the point of my story is this: I knew Ephesians 5:25. I believed it, had memorized it, and meditated on it. But through the application of it in a real-life situation, I deepened my conviction about it. Since that incident, I've found that I'm more sensitive to what it means practically to love my wife as Christ loved the church in a sacrificial, self-giving way.

The Discipline of Grace

ACCEPTED IN THE BELOVED

> *I glorified you on earth, having accomplished*
> *the work that you gave me to do.*
>
> (JOHN 17:4)

Many Christians grew up in homes where parental acceptance was largely based on academic, athletic, musical, or perhaps some other standard of achievement. Often they never quite felt as if they measured up to expectations, regardless of how successful they were. Then they transfer that sense of inadequacy to their relationship with God. They continually wonder: *Is God pleased with me? Is He smiling on me with Fatherly favor?*

The answer to that question is an unqualified yes. God is smiling on you with Fatherly favor. He is pleased with you because He sees you as holy and without blemish in Christ. Do you want to talk about performance? Then consider that Jesus could say matter-of-factly and without any pretentiousness, "I *always* do the things that are pleasing to him" (John 8:29).

When our Father looks at us, He does not see our miserable performance. Instead, He sees the perfect performance of Jesus. And because of the perfect holiness of Jesus, He sees us as holy and without blemish.

I like the translation of Ephesians 1:6 in the King James Version: "To the praise of the glory of his grace, wherein he hath made us *accepted in the beloved.*" Or to be more direct, God has made us acceptable to Himself through our union with Christ. You will never be accepted in yourself. You can never, to use a figure of speech, "scrub yourself clean."

We never reach the point where we can look inside ourselves to find the holiness we need to stand before a holy God. But God in His grace has provided a perfect holiness in the person of His Son. Through our union with Him we have been made holy.

Transforming Grace

ONLY GARBAGE

I myself have reason for confidence in the flesh.
(PHILIPPIANS 3:4)

In Philippians 3:4-8, Paul spoke of the loss of his religious credentials as he'd earlier spoken of the loss of a ship's cargo (in Acts 27:10,22, the only other place in the New Testament where *loss* is used).

Paul had viewed all of his religious past as something to be grateful for and nothing to be ashamed of. Even in persecuting the church he thought he was working for God. Yet there came a time when he "threw it all overboard": "Whatever gain I had, I counted as loss for the sake of Christ. Indeed, I count everything as loss because of the surpassing worth of knowing Christ Jesus my Lord" (Philippians 3:7-8).

Paul learned that any confidence in one's own religious attainments in the issue of salvation is not only useless but downright dangerous, for those very things could keep him from eternal salvation.

Here, however, the analogy to losing a ship's cargo ends. A ship's crew (especially the captain) would throw the cargo overboard with deep regret because doing so meant great financial loss. For Paul, however, there was no regret whatsoever. In fact he spoke of his "cargo" of religious background and attainments as rubbish: "I have suffered the loss of all things and count them as rubbish, in order that I may gain Christ" (Philippians 3:8). Probably a more accurate and descriptive word for *rubbish* here is *garbage* — table scraps or the kind of stuff you put down your garbage disposal.

Paul had come to the conclusion that his religious background was something to be deliberately dumped. Why? Because he'd discovered something far more valuable: the righteousness that comes from God through faith in Jesus Christ (Philippians 3:9).

The Gospel for Real Life

THE GREAT EXCHANGE

Christ is the end of the law for righteousness to everyone who believes.

(ROMANS 10:4)

Like his fellow Jews, Paul sought to establish his own righteousness through keeping the Law (Romans 10:3-4). But there came a time, possibly during his three days of blindness and fasting in Damascus (Acts 9:7-9), when he realized his efforts to become righteous through law-keeping were going nowhere. They kept him from the only means of salvation God has provided. As he realized more clearly the perfect righteousness God has provided through His Son, Jesus Christ, he saw his own efforts to be righteous as no more than garbage to be dumped overboard.

Paul made what I call his "great exchange" — his own righteousness for the perfect righteousness of Christ. He not only threw his own righteousness overboard, but he regarded it as mere garbage compared to the surpassing greatness of knowing Christ as his Savior and being credited with His righteousness. He exchanged the garbage of his goodness for the unsearchable riches of Christ.

Of course, Paul could make his great exchange only because God had already made *the* great exchange described in 2 Corinthians 5:21: "God made him who had no sin to be sin for us, so that in him [that is, through union with Christ] we might become the righteousness of God." God laid our sin upon Christ that He might lay Christ's righteousness upon us.

Note the subtle wording. Paul exchanged his righteousness through keeping the Law for Christ's righteousness that comes by faith. Yet in 2 Corinthians 5:21, God exchanges our sin for Christ's righteousness. Our own efforts at righteousness are, at bottom, only sin because they fail to measure up to the perfect righteousness required by God's Law. They're only scraps to be thrown out as garbage.

The Gospel for Real Life

ANY ROOM FOR GRACE?

Grow in the grace and knowledge of our Lord and Savior Jesus Christ.
(2 PETER 3:18)

As we practice the disciplines necessary to develop Bible-based convictions — diligent but dependent Bible study, Scripture memorization, continual meditation, and applying Scripture to real-life situations — is there any room for grace? What happens if I stumble in Scripture memorization, for example?

First of all, God does not love us any less. His love for us is based solely on the fact that we're in union with His Son. Christ's righteousness has become our righteousness. Our sins were laid upon Him, and the penalty for them was fully paid by Him on the cross. Daily His blood cleanses us from all sin. God's grace, His unmerited favor, is never conditioned on our performance but always on the unchanging merit of our Lord Jesus Christ.

Our progress in the pursuit of holiness, however, is conditioned on our practice of the disciplines God has given us. It's true that we're transformed increasingly into the likeness of Christ by the Spirit. It's also true that one of the chief means — in fact, probably *the* chief means — He uses is the renewing of our minds. And Paul was quite emphatic in Romans 12:2 about submitting ourselves to the transforming influence of God's Word by which our minds are renewed.

Therefore, we may say that our acceptance by God the Father is based solely on His grace to us through Christ. His favor is never earned by what we do nor forfeited by what we don't do. But we may say with equal emphasis that our progress in pursuing holiness is significantly conditioned on our use of God-appointed disciplines. And they have been appointed by God and initiated by God.

The Discipline of Grace

EXPERIENTIAL SANCTIFICATION

Jesus Christ . . . gave himself for us . . .
to purify for himself a people for his own.

(TITUS 2:13-14)

Holiness or sanctification is an actual conformity within us to the likeness of Christ begun at the time of our salvation and completed when
we're made perfect in His presence. This process of gradually conforming
us to the likeness of Christ begins at the very moment of our salvation
when the Holy Spirit comes to dwell within us and to actually give us a
new life in Christ. We call this gradual process progressive sanctification,
or growing in holiness, because it truly is a growth process.

The holiness we have in Christ is purely objective, outside of ourselves.
It's Christ's perfect holiness imputed to us because of our union with Him,
and it affects our standing before God. God is pleased with us because He
is pleased with Christ. Progressive sanctification is subjective or experiential and is the work of the Holy Spirit within us imparting to us the life and
power of Christ, enabling us to respond in obedience to Him.

Both aspects of sanctification are gifts of God's grace. We deserve
neither our holy standing before God nor the Spirit's sanctifying work in
our lives. Both come to us by His grace because of the merit of Jesus Christ.

Progressive sanctification begins in us with an instantaneous act
of God at the time of our salvation. God always gives justification and
this initial imparting of sanctification at the same time. The author of
Hebrews described this truth in this way: "'This is the covenant that I will
make with them after those days, declares the Lord: I will put my laws on
their hearts, and write them on their minds,' then he adds, 'I will remember their sins and their lawless deeds no more'" (Hebrews 10:16-17).

Transforming Grace

GARBAGE OR LEFTOVERS?

> *This is not your own doing; it is the gift of God.*
> (EPHESIANS 2:8)

I believe that human morality, rather than flagrant sin, is the greatest obstacle to the gospel today. If you ask the average law-abiding person why he expects to go to heaven, the answer will be some form of "because I've been good." And the more religious a person is, the more difficult it is to realize his or her need for the righteousness of Christ.

Have you renounced any confidence in your own religious experience and trusted solely in Christ's blood and righteousness? Perhaps you grew up in a highly moral and religious family. You've always been good and essentially blameless in the eyes of other people. That's nothing to be ashamed of. But if your hope of eternal life is based on that goodness, your religion has actually become dangerous to you. It will keep you from heaven.

Or you may think your sin is too great to be forgiven. But the blood of Christ can indeed cleanse us from all sin.

All of us have a natural drift toward a performance-based relationship with God. We know we're saved by grace through faith — not by works (Ephesians 2:8-9), but we somehow get the idea that we earn blessings by our works. After throwing overboard our works as a means to salvation, we want to drag them back on board as a means of maintaining favor with God. Instead of seeing our own righteousness as table scraps to be dumped, we see it as leftovers to be used later to earn answers to prayer.

We need to remind ourselves every day that God's blessings and answers to prayer come to us not on the basis of our works, but on the basis of the infinite merit of Jesus Christ.

The Gospel for Real Life

SELFISH INTERESTS

Let each of us please his neighbor for his good, to build him up.

(ROMANS 15:2)

Selfishness is so easy to see in someone else but so difficult to recognize in ourselves. Moreover, there are degrees of selfishness as well as degrees of subtlety in expressing it. One person's selfishness may be crass and obvious, while ours will likely be more delicate and refined.

Several areas of selfishness may be observed in believers. One of them is selfishness with our interests. Paul wrote in Philippians 2:4, "Let each of you look not only to his own interests, but also to the interests of others." In using the word *interests*, Paul was undoubtedly referring to the concerns and needs of other people, but I'm going to use it in a narrow sense to mean subjects we're interested in.

What are our interests? At this stage of our lives, my wife and I are interested in our grandchildren. We like to talk about them and show pictures of them to our friends. The problem is that our friends like to do the same. So when we're with them, whose grandchildren will we talk about? The answer, of course, is both if we and our friends are sensitive to the interests of each other. But if one or both couples are not sensitive, the conversation is apt to be one-sided, or else we find ourselves waiting for our turn to share instead of showing a genuine interest in the other couple's grandchildren.

A good test of the degree of selfishness in our interests would be to reflect on the conversation after you've been with someone (or with another couple). Ask yourself how much time you spent talking about your interests compared to listening to the other person.

Respectable Sins

Pressing On

> *My zeal consumes me.*
>
> (Psalm 119:139)

If God's favor comes to us only on the basis of Christ's merits, is there any place in the Christian life for the spiritual disciplines, obedience to God, and sacrificial service to Him?

Absolutely! There's no doubt Paul was just as diligent and zealous, probably more so, after he trusted Christ as he was before. We have only to read his own words: "One thing I do: forgetting what lies behind and straining forward to what lies ahead, I press on toward the goal for the prize of the upward call of God in Christ Jesus" (Philippians 3:13-14).

Note the intense expressions Paul used: "straining forward" and "press on." The first is a graphic picture of a runner straining nerve and muscle to cross the finish line. The phrase "press on" has the idea of vigorous pursuit.

There's a direct correlation between faith in the righteousness of Christ and zeal in the cause of Christ. The more a person counts as loss his own righteousness and lays hold by faith of the righteousness of Christ, the more he'll be motivated to live and work for Christ.

Let me ask you two questions: Are you trusting in the righteousness of Christ alone as the basis of your right standing with God, or are you still depending on your religious performance, even to a small degree? And if you've clearly trusted in Christ alone for your salvation, are you still clinging to the idea that you must now earn God's favor in this life by your own performance?

May we clearly see that in the unsearchable riches of Christ and in right standing with God that comes from those riches, we have both the assurance of eternal life and God's favor in this life.

The Gospel for Real Life

IGNORING GOD?

The word that you hear is not mine but the Father's who sent me.

(JOHN 14:24)

Everything I've taught about the disciplines of Bible study, Scripture memorization, continual meditation, and application of Scripture in daily life has been based on Scripture. I have not developed man-made theories about Christian growth. All I've done is point out what the Scriptures say about these disciplines. And what Scripture says, God says. If we ignore these disciplines, we're ignoring God.

We must always remember, though, that practicing these disciplines does not earn us any favor with God. It's helpful to distinguish between a *meritorious* cause of God's blessing and an *instrumental* cause. The meritorious cause is always the merit of Christ. We can never add to what He has already done to procure God's blessing on our lives. The instrumental cause, however, is the means or avenues God has ordained to use. God has clearly set forth certain disciplines for us to practice in pursuing holiness. As we practice them, God will use them in our lives, not because we've earned His blessing but because we've followed His ordained path of blessing.

We also need to keep in mind that the imperative in Romans 12:2 to be transformed immediately follows the imperative of verse 1 — to offer our bodies as living sacrifices, holy and pleasing to Him. Both exhortations are based on the mercy of God. The discipline of developing Bible-based convictions, then, should be a response to God's mercy and grace to us through Christ. If we truly desire to live by grace, we'll want to respond to that grace by seeking to live lives that are pleasing to God. And we simply cannot do that if we do not practice the disciplines necessary to develop Bible-based convictions.

The Discipline of Grace

A COMPLETE SUIT

*You were sanctified, you were justified
in the name of the Lord Jesus Christ.*

(1 CORINTHIANS 6:11)

Sanctification and justification are both gifts from God and expressions of His grace. Though they're each distinct aspects of salvation, they can never be separated. God never grants justification without also giving sanctification at the same time.

I think of justification and sanctification as being like the jacket and pants of a suit. They always come together. A friend once wanted to give me a suit. He took me to a clothing store, and I walked out with a jacket and matching pants — a complete suit. Neither the jacket nor the pants alone would have been sufficient. I needed both to have what my friend wanted to give me.

Sometimes we think of salvation as more like a sports coat and a pair of slacks. We think God gives us the sports coat of justification by His grace, but we must "buy" the slacks of sanctification by our own efforts. But salvation is like a suit. It always comes with the jacket of justification and the pants of sanctification. God never gives one without the other because both are necessary to have the complete suit of salvation.

Sanctification in us begins as an instantaneous act of the Holy Spirit and is carried forward by His continued action in our lives. This instantaneous act is described in a number of ways in Scripture. It is called the "renewal of the Holy Spirit" (Titus 3:5), making us alive with Christ when we were dead in transgressions and sins (Ephesians 2:1-5). It results in the new creation Paul referred to in 2 Corinthians 5:17: "Therefore, if anyone is in Christ, he is a new creation. The old has passed away; behold, the new has come."

Transforming Grace

How Do We Get Faith?

And as many as were appointed to eternal life believed.

(Acts 13:48)

If there's any one truth Paul seems to feel strongly about, it's the absolute antithesis between justification by faith and justification by keeping the Law. This is why faith must involve a complete renunciation of trust in one's own goodness (keeping the Law), as well as a total reliance on Jesus Christ and His righteousness.

The question then arises: How do we get faith? Does it come simply as an intellectual response to the gospel message? Or do those of us who share the gospel with others need to master the art of persuasion or learn the technique of "closing the sale"? How does one get faith?

The short answer is that faith is the gift of God. It has to be. There's an old adage that "a man convinced against his will is of the same opinion still." Have you ever tried to convince someone to change his mind when that person didn't want to change? You may marshal well-documented reasons and unassailable facts, but unless that person is receptive to you, he will not change. He just mentally "digs in his heels." Now if this is true in the ordinary affairs of life, how much more is it true in the spiritual realm?

God does not believe for us, but through His Spirit He creates spiritual life in us so that we can believe. Faith is a gift of God. It's part of the whole salvation package that God gives to us through the work of Christ for us and the work of the Holy Spirit in us. It's not our contribution, so to speak, to God's great plan of salvation. God does it all. Faith is part of the unsearchable riches of Christ.

GUIDING YOUR CONDUCT

Your word is a lamp to my feet and a light to my path.
(PSALM 119:105)

A defining moment in my life occurred very quietly one evening in the first Bible study group I attended. The leader of the study said to us, "The Bible wasn't given just to increase your knowledge but to guide your conduct." As obvious as that truth is to me now, at the time it was brand new. It was as if someone had turned on a light in my mind. I saw clearly what I'd been completely oblivious to before.

It wasn't that I was living what we would consider a sinful lifestyle. Quite the opposite was true. I'd grown up in a church setting, trusted Christ as my Savior, read the Bible every day, and even memorized a few Bible verses. But the idea of applying Scripture to specific situations in my daily life had never occurred to me. That night I prayed a simple prayer: "God, starting tonight I want You to use the Bible to guide my conduct." My whole approach to the Word of God changed overnight, and the Scriptures suddenly became very relevant. That was the beginning of my own personal "pursuit of holiness."

The Bible is indeed a very relevant book, giving instruction and guidance for our daily lives. In following this instruction, however, we're continually faced with a series of choices. Of course, life is a constant series of choices from the time we arise in the morning until we go to bed at night. Many of these choices have moral consequences. For example, although the route you choose to drive to work each morning is probably not morally significant, the thoughts you choose to think while you're driving are moral choices, as is the way you choose to drive.

The Discipline of Grace

A NEW HEART

If anyone is in Christ, he is a new creation.

(2 CORINTHIANS 5:17)

One of the best descriptions of this initial act of God in sanctification is found in Ezekiel 36:26-27 where God makes this gracious promise: "And I will give you a new heart, and a new spirit I will put within you. And I will remove the heart of stone from your flesh and give you a heart of flesh. And I will put my Spirit within you, and cause you to walk in my statutes and be careful to obey my rules."

Note the changes God brings about in our inner being when He saves us. He gives us a *new* heart and puts a *new* spirit within us — a spirit that loves righteousness and hates sin. He puts His own Spirit within us and *causes* us to follow His decrees and obey His law. God gives us a growing desire to obey Him. We no longer have an aversion to the commands of God, even though we may not always obey them. Instead of being irksome to us, they have now become agreeable to us.

David said in Psalm 40:8, "I delight to do your will, O my God." Why did David have this delight? It was because, as the remainder of the verse says, "Your law is within my heart." David found a law written in his own heart corresponding to the law written in God's Word. There was an agreeableness between the spiritual nature within him and the objective law of God external to him.

It's that way with a person who's a new creation in Christ. There's a basic though imperfect correspondence between the law written in a believer's heart and the law written in Scripture.

Transforming Grace

OUR UNDERLYING HOSTILITY

> *No one understands.*
> (ROMANS 3:11)

It's difficult for decent, upright Americans to accept that they're by nature hostile to God, that we cannot please Him. This is because they've confused general American morality, plus a dose of church attendance, with obedience to God's Law. Most have never been seriously confronted with the exceedingly high standard of God's eternal Law. When they are, they typically reveal their underlying hostility to it.

Paul's writings are filled with dismal descriptions of our spiritual condition before we became believers. He said, for example, "You were dead in the trespasses and sins in which you once walked" (Ephesians 2:1-2). He's speaking, of course, about spiritual death. We were totally unresponsive to the God of Scripture. We may have been religious, but we were still dead.

Spiritually dead people cannot receive and embrace the gospel. As Paul said in 1 Corinthians 2:14, "The man without the Spirit does not accept the things that come from the Spirit of God, for they are foolishness to him, and he cannot understand them, because they are spiritually discerned" (NIV). Does this mean unbelievers cannot understand the facts of the gospel? No—it means they cannot sense their own need of it and embrace it. As long as we were spiritually dead, we could not just "decide" to believe the gospel and trust in Jesus Christ.

In our spiritual deadness, we were "following the course of this world" (Ephesians 2:2). *World* is often used in the Bible for the sum total of human society in opposition to God. The world's attitude toward God varies from indifference to hostility, but the bottom line is, "No one seeks for God" (Romans 3:11). This is the world we followed. We were spiritually dead, enmeshed in a culture totally opposed to God.

The Gospel for Real Life

ONE CHOICE AT A TIME

I have set before you life and death, blessing and curse.
Therefore choose life.

(DEUTERONOMY 30:19)

The practice of putting off sinful attitudes and actions and putting on Christlike character involves a constant series of choices. We choose in every situation which direction we'll go. Through these choices we develop Christlike habits of living. Habits are developed by repetition, and it's in the arena of moral choices that we develop spiritual habit patterns.

We see this in Romans 6:19: "Just as you used to offer the parts of your body in slavery to impurity and to ever-increasing wickedness, so now offer them in slavery to righteousness leading to holiness" (NIV). The more the Roman believers sinned, the more they were inclined to sin. They were continually deepening their habit patterns of sin simply through their practice of making sinful choices.

What was true of them can be just as true of us today. Sin tends to cloud our reason, dull our consciences, stimulate our sinful desires, and weaken our wills. Because of this, each sin we commit reinforces the habit of sinning and makes it easier to give in to that temptation the next time.

Paul wanted the Roman believers, and us today, to turn in the other direction and develop habits of godly living: "So now offer [the parts of your body] in slavery to righteousness leading to holiness" (Romans 6:19, NIV). Righteousness in this passage refers to the ethical righteousness — the right conduct — we're to practice every day. Whereas *righteousness* in this verse refers to our conduct, *holiness* refers to our character. So it's through righteous actions that we develop holy character. Holiness of character is developed one choice at a time as we choose to act righteously in each and every situation and circumstance we encounter during the day.

The Discipline of Grace

THE HOSTILITY GONE

All this is from God.
(2 CORINTHIANS 5:18)

One reason we don't appreciate the grace of God more is that we either don't understand or don't appreciate the radical dimension of the instantaneous act of sanctification which God gives at salvation. If we had a moral lifestyle before conversion, we find it difficult to accept Paul's description of our attitude toward God: "The mind that is set on the flesh is hostile to God, for it does not submit to God's law; indeed, it cannot. Those who are in the flesh cannot please God" (Romans 8:7-8). We don't think of our former attitude as being hostile to God's Law.

But human morality and submission to God's Law are entirely different in principle, though they may appear similar in outward appearance. Human morality arises out of culture and family training and is based on what is proper and expected in society. It has nothing to do with God except to the extent that godly people have influenced that society. Submission to God's Law arises out of a love for God and a grateful response to His grace, and is based on a delight in His Law as revealed in Scripture. When society's standards vary from Scripture, we then see the true nature of human morality: It's just as hostile to God's Law as is the attitude of the most hardened sinner.

Sanctification changes our attitude. Instead of being hostile to God's Law, we begin to delight in it (Romans 7:22). We find that "his commandments are not burdensome" (1 John 5:3), but rather are "holy and righteous and good" (Romans 7:12). This radical and dramatic change in our attitude toward God's commands is a gift of His grace, brought about solely by the mighty working of His Spirit within us.

Transforming Grace

GOD'S SOVEREIGNTY

Our God is in the heavens; he does all that he pleases.

(PSALM 115:3)

Confidence in God's sovereignty in all that affects us is crucial to our trusting Him. If there's a single event in all the universe that can occur outside of God's control, then we cannot trust Him. His love may be infinite, but if His power is limited and His purpose can be thwarted, we cannot trust Him. You may entrust to me your most valuable possessions; I may love you and my aim to honor your trust may be sincere. But if I don't have the power or ability to guard your valuables, you cannot truly entrust them to me.

Paul, however, said we can entrust our most valuable possession to the Lord: "I know whom I have believed, and am convinced that he is able to guard what I have entrusted to him for that day" (2 Timothy 1:12, NIV). "But," someone says, "Paul is speaking there of eternal life. It's our problems in this life that make me wonder about God's sovereignty."

It should be evident, however, that God's sovereignty does not begin at death. His sovereign direction in our lives even precedes our births. God rules as surely on earth as He does in heaven. He permits, for reasons known only to Himself, people to act contrary to and in defiance of His revealed will. But He never permits them to act contrary to His sovereign will.

Our plans can succeed only when they are consistent with God's purpose, and no plan can succeed against Him (Proverbs 16:9; 19:21; 21:30). No one can straighten what He makes crooked or make crooked what He has made straight (Ecclesiastes 7:13). No one can say, "I'll do this or that," and have it happen if it is not part of God's sovereign will (James 4:15).

Trusting God

BLIND SLAVES

You . . . were once slaves of sin.
(ROMANS 6:17)

Before we became believers, Paul said we were "following the prince of the power of the air" (Ephesians 2:2). This "prince" is Satan, the Devil. We don't like to think we were followers of the Devil, but that's what the Bible says.

This doesn't mean we were as wicked as we could be; after all, as Paul said elsewhere, "Satan himself masquerades as an angel of light" (2 Corinthians 11:14). What it does mean is that Satan blinded us to the gospel: "The god of this age has blinded the minds of unbelievers, so that they cannot see the light of the gospel of the glory of Christ, who is the image of God" (2 Corinthians 4:4). But God "rescued us from the dominion of darkness [Satan's kingdom] and brought us into the kingdom of the Son he loves" (Colossians 1:13).

Before God delivered us, we were Satan's captives. We could not see the light of the gospel. This inability was spiritual, not mental. We were spiritually blind, unable to recognize our need of the Savior or to see God's gracious provision of Him.

Paul also said that "we all once lived in the passions of our flesh, carrying out the desires of the body and the mind, and were by nature children of wrath" (Ephesians 2:3). And more specifically: "The mind that is set on the flesh is hostile to God, for it does not submit to God's law; indeed, it cannot. Those who are in the flesh cannot please God" (Romans 8:7-8). Note the absolute negatives Paul used.

We were under the dominion of Satan, and slaves of our own sinful natures. And apart from a supernatural work of God in our lives, we were helpless to do anything about our condition.

The Gospel for Real Life

OUT OF THE TOMB

Awake, O sleeper, and arise from the dead.

(EPHESIANS 5:14)

Paul was fond of painting an absolutely dismal picture of our condition, then saying, "But here's God's remedy." He did it in Ephesians 2:1-5, where he said that although we were dead in our transgressions and sins, God "made us alive together with Christ." It's God who gives us spiritual life. We couldn't make ourselves spiritually alive any more than a dead person can make himself alive.

When Lazarus lay dead in the tomb, he could not decide to come to life again. He could not even respond to Jesus' call, "Lazarus, come out," unless with that call Jesus gave him life (John 11:1-44). Lazarus's condition, as he lay dead in the tomb, is a picture of our spiritual predicament. We can hear the gospel a hundred times, but unless that call is accompanied by the life-giving power of the Holy Spirit, we can no more respond to it than Lazarus could respond to a vocal call from Jesus.

I know it's difficult for us to accept the fact that we could not just decide to trust Christ in much the same way we might decide to buy more life insurance. The truth is, we did decide to trust Christ, but the reason we made that decision is that God had first made us spiritually alive. This is part of the good news. God comes to us when we're spiritually dead, when we don't even realize our condition, and gives us the spiritual ability to see our plight and to see the solution in Christ. God comes all the way, not partway, to meet us in our need. When we were dead, He made us alive in Christ. And the first act of that new life is to turn in faith to Jesus.

The Gospel for Real Life

BECOME HOLY BY OBEDIENCE

I have chosen the way of faithfulness.

(PSALM 119:30)

We do not become more holy by discipline, by dependence, by committing ourselves to God, or by developing Bible-based convictions. We become more holy by obeying the Word of God, choosing to obey His will as revealed in the Scriptures in all the various circumstances of our lives.

It's just as true, however, that the discipline, dependence, commitment, and convictions are absolutely necessary to our making the right choices. We don't make them in a vacuum. They're determined by convictions we've developed and commitments we've made. We can make the right choices only through the enabling power of the Holy Spirit. But all these principles and means of spiritual growth find ultimate fulfillment only when we obey God's commandments one choice at a time. As we do, our righteous actions lead to holy character.

I recently observed my wife making a quilt. She first made a number of one-foot "squares," each with a sewn design. The particular overall design she'd chosen, a mariner's compass, was rather intricate, with each square containing about forty narrow triangles. Each square was beautiful, a testimony to her sewing ability. But those individual squares, beautiful as they were, did not make a quilt. Only by being sewn together with a narrow strip of cloth between each row of squares did they become a quilt.

Pursuing holiness is like that. We have the quilt squares of discipline, dependence, commitment, convictions, and beholding the glory of Christ in the gospel. Each one is beautiful in and of itself. But if we just look at these principles and means of holiness individually, we still do not have the "quilt" of holiness. What joins them all together to form the "quilt of holiness" is obedience. And we obey one choice at a time.

The Discipline of Grace

OLD WAY, NEW WAY

> *We serve in the new way of the Spirit and not*
> *in the old way of the written code.*
>
> (ROMANS 7:6)

Far too many Christians still serve in the old way of the Law instead of in the new way of the Spirit:

1. Old Way: *External Code* — God's moral precepts are only an external code of conduct. New Way: *Internal Desire* — God's moral precepts are written on our hearts. The Spirit inclines our hearts and gives us a desire to obey.

2. Old Way: *Commanding* — The Law commands but gives no enabling power for obedience. New Way: *Enabling* — The Spirit enables us to obey the Law's commands.

3. Old Way: *Hostility* — Before our conversion, the commands of the Law actually provoked and incited us to sin. New Way: *Delight* — By removing our hostility and writing the Law on our hearts, the Spirit causes us to delight in God's Law.

4. Old Way: *Fear* — The Law produces a legalistic response to God. We try to obey because of fear of punishment for disobedience or to win favor with God. New Way: *Gratitude* — The Spirit, by showing us God's grace, produces a response of love and gratitude. We obey out of gratitude for favor already given.

5. Old Way: *Working* — We perform in order to be accepted by God. Since our performance is always imperfect, we never feel completely accepted by Him. We're always working from a position of weakness, feeling we never quite make it. New Way: *Relying* — The Spirit bears witness with our spirit that we're accepted by God through the merit of Christ. By relying solely on His perfect righteousness, we feel accepted by Him. We work from a position of strength because we've been accepted through Jesus, and through Him, we've "made it."

Transforming Grace

THE STARK CONTRAST

> *The old has passed away; behold, the new has come.*
> (2 CORINTHIANS 5:17)

Probably no other passage suggests more starkly the contrast between living by grace and living by works than Romans 7:6: "But now we are released from the law, having died to that which held us captive, so that we serve in the new way of the Spirit and not in the old way of the written code."

The new way of the Spirit is not a less rigorous ethic than the old way of the written code. The difference doesn't lie in the content of God's moral will. Since that's a reflection of the holy character of God, it cannot change. Rather, the difference lies in the reason for obeying and the ability to obey.

Are you seeking to build and maintain your relationship with God on the basis of "keeping the Law" — on the basis of your personal performance — or on the basis of the merit of Jesus Christ? Do you view God's moral precepts as a source of bondage and condemnation for failure to obey them, or do you sense the Spirit producing within you an inclination and desire to obey out of gratitude and love? Do you try to obey by your own sheer will and determination, or do you rely on the Spirit daily for His power to enable your obedience?

Do you feel God has set before you an impossible code of conduct you cannot keep, or do you view Him as your divine heavenly Father who has accepted you and loves you on the basis of the merit of Christ? For acceptance with God, are you willing to rely solely on the finished perfect work of Jesus instead of your own pitifully imperfect performance?

Transforming Grace

AN OPENED HEART

> *God . . . has shone in our hearts.*
>
> (2 CORINTHIANS 4:6)

In Jesus' conversation with Nicodemus the Pharisee (John 3:1-21, NIV), we see the necessity of the Spirit's work to give us faith. Jesus said emphatically,[65] "No one can see the kingdom of God unless he is born again" (verse 3). He said, "No one can enter the kingdom of God unless he is born of water and the Spirit" (verse 5). And He compared the Spirit's life-giving action with the sovereign and mysterious action of the wind (verses 7-8).

Notice that Jesus spoke not of permission to enter the kingdom but of *inability* to enter it apart from a new birth: "No one *can* . . . " We *cannot*—we don't have the ability to—enter the kingdom unless the Spirit of God gives us life through the new birth. We're born again, then, by a sovereign, monergistic (that is, the Spirit working alone) act of the Holy Spirit. Then, as a result of that new birth, we exercise the faith given to us and enter the kingdom of God.

In this light we better understand a Scripture such as Acts 16:14: "One who heard us was a woman named Lydia, from the city of Thyatira, a seller of purple goods, who was a worshiper of God. *The Lord opened her heart* to pay attention to what was said by Paul."

What does it mean that the Lord opened Lydia's heart? It means He made her spiritually alive, that she was born again. It means He removed the Satan-induced blindness from her mind so she could understand and embrace the gospel. It means He delivered her from the kingdom of darkness, where she'd been held captive, so she could respond in faith. Note the sequence: She could not respond to Paul's message until God first opened her heart.

The Gospel for Real Life

TRAIN IN THE RIGHT DIRECTION

The mature . . . have their powers of discernment trained by constant practice to distinguish good from evil.

(HEBREWS 5:14)

Paul exhorted Timothy, "Train yourself for godliness" (1 Timothy 4:7). Though godliness is a broader concept than holiness, holiness is a major part of it, so training ourselves to be godly certainly includes training in holiness.

This training requires exercise. In fact, the King James Version translates this phrase, "Exercise thyself . . . unto godliness." How do we exercise ourselves in the spiritual realm? Through the choices we make. When we make wrong choices, we train ourselves in the wrong direction — like the false teachers Peter described, who had "hearts trained in greed" (2 Peter 2:14).

God wants us to train ourselves in the right direction through making right choices. Frankly, this is where the going gets tough. We'll agree with Scripture's teaching about some particular sin and even make a commitment of sorts to put it out of our lives. Then the temptation to indulge that sin comes once again, and we're unwilling to make the tough choice. We would like to be rid of that sin, and even pray to God to take it away, but are we willing to say no to it?

Every day we're training ourselves in one direction or the other: toward lying or truthfulness; selfishness or unselfishness; anger or forgiveness; impurity or purity; irritability or patience; covetousness or generosity; pride or humility; materialism or simplicity.

Only through making the right choice to obey God's Word will we break the habits of sin and develop habits of holiness. This is where we desperately need the Holy Spirit's power to enable us to make the right choices. So cry out to God every day for His help; cry out each time you are confronted with the choice to sin or to obey.

The Discipline of Grace

GROWING IN CHRISTLIKENESS

He has perfected for all time those who are being sanctified.

(HEBREWS 10:14)

Sanctification is the radical change God brings about in the heart of a person who trusts Jesus Christ as Savior. It's the passing from spiritual death to spiritual life, the beginning of a new creation in Christ, and the writing of God's Law in our hearts. It means a new relationship to the Law of God and a new attitude toward it. And all this is from God, a gift of His grace just as surely as is the gift of justification.

God doesn't bring us into His kingdom, then leave us on our own to grow. He continues to work in our lives to conform us more and more to the likeness of His Son. As Paul said, "He who began a good work in you will bring it to completion at the day of Jesus Christ" (Philippians 1:6). This continuing work of God is called "progressive sanctification." It differs from initial sanctification in two respects.

Initial sanctification occurs instantly at the moment of salvation when we're delivered from the kingdom of darkness and brought into the kingdom of Christ (Colossians 1:13). Progressive sanctification continues over time until we go to be with the Lord. Initial sanctification is entirely the work of God the Holy Spirit who imparts to us the very life of Christ. Progressive sanctification is also the work of the Holy Spirit, but it involves a response on our part so that we as believers are actively involved in the process.

The progressive nature of sanctification is implied throughout the New Testament epistles in all those instances where we are exhorted to grow, to change, to put off the deeds of the old man and put on Godlike character.

Transforming Grace

NOT A NEW THOUGHT

To this he called you through our gospel,
so that you may obtain the glory of our Lord Jesus Christ.

(2 THESSALONIANS 2:14)

Though the notion that the regenerating work of the Holy Spirit (the new birth) precedes and results in our faith may be new to many of our day, it is in fact the historic teaching of the church since the sixteenth-century Reformation. Consider these words of Charles Wesley, the famous Methodist hymn writer of the eighteenth century: "Long my imprisoned spirit lay fast-bound in sin and nature's night; Thine eye diffused a quick'ning ray; I woke, the dungeon flamed with light; my chains fell off, my heart was free; I rose, went forth, and followed thee."[66]

Note how Wesley saw his own heart imprisoned in sin, then the almighty work of the Spirit quickening (giving life to) him. Only then did he arise and follow Christ. What was true for Wesley is just as true for us today.

Obviously the Holy Spirit works through our human channels of evangelism. As Paul said, "Faith comes from hearing the message, and the message is heard through the word of Christ" (Romans 10:17, NIV). But our message is impotent apart from the working of the Holy Spirit, who both empowers the messenger and opens the heart of the listener — as He did in the case of Lydia in Acts 16:14: "The Lord opened her heart."

Consider Paul's words to the Thessalonian believers: "Our gospel came to you not simply with words, but also with power, with the Holy Spirit and with deep conviction" (1 Thessalonians 1:5, NIV). What resulted when Paul's message was accompanied by the powerful working of the Holy Spirit? The Thessalonians "turned to God from idols to serve the living and true God" (1:9). The Thessalonians themselves believed. They exercised faith.

The Gospel for Real Life

Living as We Please

Every athlete exercises self-control in all things.

(1 Corinthians 9:25)

We have boundaries from our Christian culture that tend to restrain us from obvious sins, but within those boundaries we pretty much live as we please. We seldom say no to our desires and emotions. A lack of self-control may well be one of our more "respectable" sins. And because we tolerate it, we become more vulnerable to other "respectable" sins. A lack of control of our tongue, for example, opens the door to all manner of defiling speech, such as sarcasm, gossip, slander, and ridicule.

What is self-control? It's a governance or prudent control of one's desires, cravings, impulses, emotions, and passions. It's saying no when we should say no. It's moderation in legitimate desires and activities, and absolute restraint in areas that are clearly sinful. It would, for example, involve moderation in watching television and absolute restraint in viewing Internet pornography.

Biblical self-control is not a product of one's own natural willpower. Some unbelievers exercise self-control in specific areas to achieve some goal. But in other areas, they may live with little or no self-control. An athlete may be strict in his diet while totally lacking in control of his temper.

Biblical self-control, however, covers every area of life and requires an unceasing conflict with the passions of the flesh that wage war against our souls (1 Peter 2:11). This self-control depends on the Spirit's influence and enablement. It requires continual exposure of our mind to the words of God and continual prayer for the Holy Spirit to give us both the desire and power to exercise self-control. We might say that self-control is not control by oneself through one's own willpower but rather control of oneself through the power of the Holy Spirit.

Respectable Sins

THE DISCIPLINE OF MORTIFICATION

Put to death therefore what is earthly in you.

(COLOSSIANS 3:5)

Making the right choices to obey God rather than our sinful desires necessarily involves the discipline of mortification. What is mortification? And what does it have to do with holiness?

The apostle Paul gave us the answer: "For if you live according to the flesh you will die, but if by the Spirit you put to death [mortify] the deeds of the body, you will live" (Romans 8:13). To make the right choices it's necessary to mortify, or put to death, the misdeeds of the body — the sinful actions we commit in thought, word, or deed. Paul was more explicit about some of these in Colossians 3:5: "Put to death therefore what is earthly in you: sexual immorality, impurity, passion, evil desire, and covetousness, which is idolatry."

As we look at Romans 8:13, one thing we clearly see is that mortification, or putting sin to death, is our responsibility. Paul said, "If *you* put to death . . ." It's our responsibility, something we must do, not something we turn over to God.

We should also note that Paul said, "For if you live according to the flesh you will die." Paul was talking about spiritual, not physical death. The opposite is also true. If we live according to the Spirit — that is, if by Him we "put to death the deeds of the body" — we shall live in the spiritual sense. Once again, as he did so frequently, Paul stressed the inextricable link between justification and sanctification. Paul clearly taught that we're saved by grace through faith (Ephesians 2:8), but he also stressed that we're to work out our salvation with fear and trembling (Philippians 2:12), that is, without presuming on the grace of God.

The Discipline of Grace

BE TRANSFORMED

Be transformed by the renewal of your mind.

(ROMANS 12:2)

The verb *be transformed* in Romans 12:2 is a command to do something. This indicates that we as believers are not passive in this transforming process. We're not like blocks of marble being transformed into a beautiful sculpture by a master sculptor. God has given us a mind and heart with which to respond to and cooperate with the Spirit as He does His work in us.

That thought leads naturally to a classic statement in Scripture of the working together of the believer and the Holy Spirit within: "Therefore, my beloved, as you have always obeyed, so now, not only as in my presence but much more in my absence, work out your own salvation with fear and trembling, for it is God who works in you, both to will and to work for his good pleasure" (Philippians 2:12-13).

Paul urged the Philippian believers to apply themselves diligently to working out their salvation. He urged them to display the evidences of salvation in their daily lives through their obedience to God's commands and through putting on the godly character traits that Paul elsewhere called the fruit of the Spirit. And, according to William Hendriksen, the tense of the verb *work out* indicates "continuous, sustained, strenuous effort."[67] Here again we see that sanctification is a process, and a process in which we, as believers, are very actively involved.

But Paul's strong exhortation to the Philippians is based on the confidence that God's Spirit is working in them, working to enlighten their understanding of His will, to stimulate in their emotions a desire to do His will, and to turn their wills so they actually obey. He gives them the enabling power so that they're able to do His will.

Transforming Grace

ENCOURAGEMENT TO PRAYER

For from him and through him and to him are all things.

(ROMANS 11:36)

The realization that faith is the gift of God should encourage us to pray with confidence for others' salvation. It means that no one, however hardened he or she may be, is beyond the regenerating, life-creating work of the Holy Spirit.

I think of some for whose salvation I pray regularly. One wants nothing to do with God. Another is happily indifferent, seeing no need of a Savior because he's a good, moral person. Others would be highly insulted to be told they need a Savior because, after all, they're both moral and religious.

What hope is there for these people? It lies only in the sovereign, mysterious work of the Holy Spirit. I pray regularly that He'll work in their hearts through the gospel message to create the faith they must have to believe in Christ.

Awareness that faith is the gift of God should also arouse a sense of profound gratitude and worship in our hearts. We could not even take advantage of God's gracious gift of salvation apart from His prior working in our hearts. But God gave us life when we were dead, gave us sight when we were blind, and gave us the faith to trust in Christ for our salvation. If we spent the rest of our lives doing nothing but saying thank-you to God, we could still never sufficiently express our gratitude for His gift of salvation, including the gift of faith by which we receive it.

Do you want to grow in your own worship of God? That growth will be directly related to your understanding of the gospel in all its fullness, including the fact that the faith by which you believed was a gift from God.

The Gospel for Real Life

SIN FOR SIN

If by the Spirit you put to death the deeds of the body, you will live.

(ROMANS 8:13)

We'll never reach the place where we don't have to contend against the flesh. But the life of a Christian should be characterized by an earnest desire and sincere effort to put to death (mortify) the sins of the body.

Although mortification is our responsibility, it can be done only through the enabling power of the Holy Spirit. Paul said, "But if *by the Spirit* you put to death the deeds of the body, you will live" (Romans 8:13). John Owen wrote, "All other ways of discipline are in vain. All other helps leave us helpless. Mortification is accomplished only 'through the Spirit' . . . No other power can accomplish it."[68]

Although the Scriptures emphasize both human discipline and dependence on the Holy Spirit, we tend to emphasize one to the neglect of the other. To some, it seems more spiritual to "just turn it all over to God" and trust Him to do the mortifying. Any mention of our responsibility is dismissed as being only "a work of the flesh."

To other people who stress discipline, it seems more responsible to "just do it." But mortification attempted only by human willpower always ends in self-righteousness or frustration. The more naturally disciplined person tends toward self-righteousness and wonders why everyone else can't be as successful in mortification as he or she is. But all that person has done is exchanged one sin for another. The problem of impure thoughts, for example, is exchanged for pride and self-righteousness. Another person who tries to mortify some particular sin by his or her own willpower fails and becomes frustrated and guilty. So pride or frustration is always the result of attempts to mortify sin that are carried on apart from utter dependence on the Spirit.

The Discipline of Grace

DESPERATELY DEPENDENT

If we live by the Spirit, let us also walk by the Spirit.

Progressive sanctification is not a partnership with the Spirit in the sense that we each — the believer and the Holy Spirit — do our respective tasks. Rather, we work as He enables us to work. His work lies behind all our work and makes our work possible.

The Holy Spirit can and does work within us apart from any conscious response on our part. We see this in the initial act of sanctification when He creates within us a new heart and a new disposition toward God and His will. He's not dependent on us to do this.

But we're dependent on Him to do our work; we cannot do anything apart from Him. In the process of sanctification there are certain things only the Spirit can do, and certain things He has given us to do. For example, only He can create in our hearts the *desire* to obey God, but He does not obey for us. We must do that, but we can do so only as He enables us.

So we must depend on the Spirit to do within us what only He can do. And we must equally depend on Him to enable us to do what He has given us to do. Whether His work or our work, we're dependent on Him.

We aren't just dependent on Him; we're *desperately* dependent. Because we so often equate Christlike character with ordinary morality, we fail to realize how impossible it is for us to attain any degree of conformity to Christ by ourselves. But if we take seriously the many Christlike character traits we're to put on, we see how impossible it is to grow in Christlikeness apart from the sanctifying influence and power of the Spirit.

Transforming Grace

WE REALLY ARE HIS CHILDREN

Behold what manner of love the Father has bestowed on us,
that we should be called children of God!

(1 JOHN 3:1, NKJV)

When used as an imperative verb, *behold* carries the strong idea of imploring someone's attention. This is how John used it in 1 John 3:1. He was saying, "Stop! Think of this! Consider this astonishing fact: God loves us so much that *we're called His children!*"

Think of it: If you've trusted in Christ as Savior, you're God's child, a son or daughter of the Creator, Sustainer, and Ruler of the universe — though our circumstances, or even our behavior, can often obscure that fact.

After John's exclamation about this, he added, "And so we are" (3:1). It's as if he was saying, "It's really true! We really *are* His children!" Why does John get so excited about a truth we often take for granted?

This truth is amazing, first of all, because of who we once were. Consider the fact that every sin you've committed was an act of rebellion against the sovereign authority of God, or, as someone has said, an act of cosmic treason. But instead of the death we deserve as punishment for such treason, we're made sons and daughters of the very King we've rebelled against! Instead of death, we get eternal life. Instead of wrath, we receive favor. Instead of eternal ruin, we're made heirs of God and coheirs with Christ. And all of this becomes ours without our doing a single thing to earn the King's favor or any attempt on our part to make restitution! His Son has done it all for us.

Do you believe that? Do you each day realize that you're a child of the heavenly King?

The Gospel for Real Life

HATING ALL SIN

> *By the Spirit . . . put to death the deeds of the body.*
> (ROMANS 8:13)

To mortify a sin means to subdue it, to deprive it of its power, to break the habit pattern we have developed of continually giving in to the temptation to that particular sin. The goal of mortification is to weaken the habits of sin so that we make the right choices.

Mortification involves dealing with all known sin in one's life. Without a purpose to obey all of God's Word, isolated attempts to mortify a particular sin are of no avail. An attitude of universal obedience in every area of life is essential. As Paul wrote to the Corinthians, "Let us cleanse ourselves from every defilement of body and spirit, bringing holiness to completion in the fear of God" (2 Corinthians 7:1). We cannot, for example, mortify impure hearts if we're unwilling to also put to death resentment. We cannot mortify a fiery temper if we aren't also seeking to put to death the pride that so often underlies it. Hating one particular sin is not enough. We must hate all sin for what it really is: an expression of rebellion against God.

A man came to me wanting help in dealing with sexual lust in his thoughts and habits. I knew, however, that he had a greater problem in interpersonal relationships. He was critical and judgmental and very vocal about it. His lust bothered him because it made him feel guilty and defeated. His judgmental spirit and critical words didn't bother him, so he was making no effort to deal with those sins. He needed to learn to mortify all sin, not just what made him feel bad about himself.

The Discipline of Grace

DIFFERING OPINIONS

> *As for the one who is weak in faith,*
> *welcome him, but not to quarrel over opinions.*
>
> (ROMANS 14:1)

The issue of differing opinions about certain practices has been around at least since the days of the apostle Paul. He devoted an entire chapter of the book Romans to this brand of legalism.

The crux of the problem is stated well by Paul in Romans 14:5: "One person esteems one day as better than another, while another esteems all days alike. Each one should be fully convinced in his own mind." People simply have different opinions about various issues. One person sees no problem in a certain practice; another person considers that practice to be sinful.

As Christians we can't seem to accept the clear biblical teaching in Romans 14 that God allows equally godly people to have differing opinions on certain matters. We universalize what we think is God's particular leading in our lives and apply it to everyone else.

When we think like that we are putting God in a box, so to speak. We're insisting that He must surely lead everyone as we believe He has led us. We refuse to allow God the freedom to deal with each of us as individuals. When we think like that, we are legalists.

We must not seek to bind the consciences of other believers with the private convictions that arise out of our personal walk with God. Even if you believe God has led you in developing those convictions, you still must not elevate them to the level of spiritual principles for everyone else to follow. The respected Puritan theologian John Owen taught that "only what God has commanded in his word should be regarded as binding; in all else there may be liberty of actions."[69]

Transforming Grace

NOW IN THE FAMILY

You . . . become partakers of the divine nature.
(2 PETER 1:4)

We've come to see that justification is the legal act by which God forgives all our sins and accepts us as righteous in His sight because of the perfect righteousness of Christ imputed (or credited) to us by God and received by us through faith.

However, we need something more than a legal standing if we're to live in the presence of God for all eternity. We need to become members of His family — and this is what has happened. God has not only justified us; He has made us family members. In theological terms this is called *adoption*. However, it isn't adoption in the sense that we use that term today. It's much more.

A son or daughter in any human family is either born to or adopted by the parents. By definition, a child can't be both. But with God we're *both* born of Him and adopted by Him. The very idea of being reborn is staggering, but that's what the Bible says: We're born again by His Spirit through His Word, the gospel (see John 3:8; 1 Peter 1:23).

John used the expression "born of God" seven times in his first letter,[70] and all seven refer to evidence of new life in Christ. To become a child of God, then, refers not only to a new relationship but also to a new life. Just as parents pass on certain physical and personality traits to their natural-born children, so traits of divine life are passed on to those born of God. Thus John could say that those born of God do what is right, love others, believe in Jesus, and cease to practice sin. These are all family traits that show up to some degree in everyone born of God.

The Gospel for Real Life

HIS WISE, LOVING, SOVEREIGN PLAN

He does according to his will . . . and none can stay his hand.

(DANIEL 4:35)

God does as He pleases, only as He pleases; He works out every event to bring about the accomplishment of His will. Such a bare unqualified statement of the sovereignty of God would terrify us if that were all we knew about God. But God is not only sovereign; He is perfect in love and infinite in wisdom. God exercises His sovereignty for His glory and the good of His people.

But how is this any more than merely an abstract statement about God to be debated by the theologians, a statement that has little relevance to our day-to-day lives? The answer is that God does have a purpose and a plan for you, and He has the power to carry out that plan. It's one thing to know that no person or circumstance can touch us outside of God's sovereign control; it's still another to realize that no person or circumstances can frustrate God's purpose for our lives.

God has an overarching purpose for all believers: to conform us to the likeness of His Son, Jesus Christ (Romans 8:29). He also has a specific purpose for each of us that is His unique, tailor-made plan for our individual life (Ephesians 2:10). And God will fulfill that purpose. As Psalm 138:8 says, "The LORD will fulfill his purpose for me." Because we know God is directing our lives to an ultimate end and because we know He is sovereignly able to orchestrate the events of our lives toward that end, we can trust Him. We can commit to Him not only the ultimate outcome of our lives, but also all the intermediate events and circumstances that will bring us to that outcome.

Trusting God

A CONSTANT FIGHT

Keep yourself pure.
(1 TIMOTHY 5:22)

Not only must there be a universal fight against sin; there must also be a constant fight against it. We must put sin to death continually, every day, as the flesh seeks to assert itself in various ways in our lives. No believer, regardless of how spiritually mature he or she may be, ever gets beyond the need to mortify the sinful deeds of the body.

John Owen wrote, "Even the choicest saints who seek to remain free from the condemning power of sin need to make it their business, as long as they live, to mortify the indwelling power of sin."[71]

To mortify sin we must focus on its true nature. So often we are troubled with a persistent sin only because it disturbs our peace and makes us feel guilty. We need to focus on it as an act of rebellion against God. Our rebellion is, of course, against the sovereign authority of God. But it is also rebellion against our heavenly Father who loved us and sent His Son to die for us. God our Father is grieved by our sins.

Genesis 6:5-6 tells us, "The LORD saw that the wickedness of man was great in the earth, and that every intention of the thoughts of his heart was only evil continually. And the LORD was sorry that he had made man on the earth, and it *grieved* him to his heart." Your sin and my sin are not only acts of rebellion; they are acts that grieve God. Think of the persistent sin patterns in your life that you've identified and are hopefully praying daily over, and remember that these are grievous to your heavenly Father. And yet, He sent His Son to die for those very sins that fill His heart with pain.

The Discipline of Grace

WHAT OTHERS THINK

Am I trying to please man?
(GALATIANS 1:10)

Often we don't enjoy our freedom in Christ because we're afraid of what others will think. We do or don't do certain things because of a fear that we'll be judged by others. But standing firm in our freedom in Christ means resisting that fear. In Galatians, Paul wrote, "Am I now seeking the approval of man, or of God? Or am I trying to please man? If I were still trying to please man, I would not be a servant of Christ" (Galatians 1:10).

I had to learn this lesson the hard way. Surprisingly soon after the death of my first wife, God brought into my life another godly lady — a single woman who had been a family friend for many years. As our friendship deepened into a romantic relationship, I became concerned about what people would think. I knew I would be violating the culturally accepted maxim of "don't make any major decisions the first year." I also sensed an inner compulsion in my spirit, which I felt was from God, to move ahead. My journal during those days records numerous times when I struggled with God over this issue. One day I wrote, "I wonder if God is pushing me along faster in this relationship than I want to go because of fear of what people will think."

I'd put God in the box of our culturally accepted norm. Surely He wouldn't do anything in my life that would be unacceptable to my friends. God was actually doing a wonderful thing, but instead of fully enjoying His work of grace, I was struggling with Him because of what people might think.

If you're going to experience the joy of your freedom in Christ, you have to decide whether you'll please God or people.

Transforming Grace

WHY SIN IS WRONG

How often they rebelled against him . . . and grieved him!
(PSALM 78:40)

The verb *mortify*, or put to death, is used eleven times in the New Testament. In nine of those instances it refers to a literal putting to death of a person; each of those is in the context of an underlying hostility toward what that person stood for. For example, in Matthew 10:21: "Children will rebel against their parents and have them put to death" (NIV). The hostility is not only toward the parents but also toward their authority. Likewise Stephen, the first Christian martyr, was put to death because of his bold, uncompromising witness for Jesus Christ (Acts 7).

Now apply that sense of hostility toward the sin you wish to mortify. See your sin for what it is and what it stands for — a rebellion against God, a breaking of His law, a despising of His authority, a grieving of His heart. This is where mortification actually begins, with a right attitude toward sin. It begins with the realization that sin is wrong, not because of what it does to me or my spouse or child or neighbor, but because it is an act of rebellion against the infinitely holy and majestic God who sent His Son to be the propitiation for my sins.

Think of an unusually persistent sin in your life — perhaps some secret lust that lies in your heart that only you know about. You say you cannot overcome it. Why not? Is it because you exalt your secret desire above the will of God? If we are to succeed in putting sin to death, we must realize that the sin we are dealing with is none other than a continual exalting of our desire over God's known will.

The Discipline of Grace

HIS FULL-GROWN CHILD

You have received the Spirit of adoption as sons.

(ROMANS 8:15)

What does it mean to be adopted as sons by God? The adoption Paul refers to is not that of an infant or small child. In Jewish culture, it would refer to the status of those who had advanced from minors to full-grown sons. And in Roman culture, wealthy couples would adopt a worthy young man to be their heir and carry on the family name.

Even the brand-new believer comes into the family of God with the full rights of an adult son. Although this new believer is a spiritual babe and needs discipling from more mature Christians, he has all the rights and privileges of a full-grown son.

A good sense of this can be seen in the prodigal son's restoration after his return from the far country (Luke 15:22-24). The father orders the servants to quickly bring the best robe, a ring, and sandals. The robe would have been a status symbol, the ring probably an indication of family authority, and the sandals a sign of sonship. This once-rebellious son is immediately restored to a position of dignity, honor, and full acceptance, and even becomes the guest of honor at a feast of celebration.

We should never lose sight of the fact that we were rebels, objects of God's wrath, and on death row. The tremendous contrast between what we once were and what we have become by His grace makes our sonship so amazing. We have been redeemed from slavery to sin and Satan, clothed with the robe of Christ's perfect righteousness, and given status as sons in the royal household.

I hope you're encouraged to live as a full-grown child of God through Jesus Christ our Lord.

The Gospel for Real Life

CONTROLLERS

Test everything; hold fast what is good.

(1 THESSALONIANS 5:21)

"Controllers" are people who aren't willing to let you live your life before God as you believe He's leading you. They have all the issues buttoned down and have cast-iron opinions about all of them. These people only know black and white. There are no gray areas to them.

They insist you live your Christian life according to their rules and their opinions. If you insist on being free to live as God wants you to live, they will try to intimidate you and manipulate you one way or another. Their primary weapons are guilt trips, rejection, or gossip.

These people must be resisted. We must not allow them to subvert the freedom we have in Christ. Paul treated the legalism in the Galatian church as heresy, and he called down a curse on its perpetrators. I'm not prepared to go that far with our present-day legalists/controllers, but I want to tell you their actions are no incidental matter. Their presence in our evangelical ranks is much more than a minor irritant, like a fly buzzing around our heads. There are spiritual casualties all over our nation today because of the effects of legalistic controllers in their lives.

Controllers have been around a long time. More than three hundred years ago, the Puritan Samuel Bolton wrote these instructive words: "Let us never surrender our judgments or our consciences to be at the disposal and opinions of others, and to be subjected to the sentences and determinations of men. . . . It is my exhortation therefore to all Christians to maintain their Christian freedom by constant watchfulness. You must not be tempted or threatened out of it; you must not be bribed or frightened from it; you must not let either force or fraud rob you of it."[72]

Transforming Grace

GOD'S FATHERLY RESPONSIBILITIES

O LORD, you are our Father.

(ISAIAH 64:8)

What does it mean in everyday life that God is our Father? Let me suggest five fatherly responsibilities that God has assumed toward His children.

God provides for us. "And my God will meet all your needs according to his glorious riches in Christ Jesus" (Philippians 4:19, NIV).

God protects us. "Are not two sparrows sold for a penny? Yet not one of them will fall to the ground apart from the will of your Father. And even the very hairs of your head are all numbered. So don't be afraid; you are worth more than many sparrows" (Matthew 10:29-31, NIV).

God encourages us. "You hear, O LORD, the desire of the afflicted; you encourage them, and you listen to their cry" (Psalm 10:17, NIV).

God comforts us. "Praise be to the God and Father of our Lord Jesus Christ, the Father of compassion and the God of all comfort, who comforts us in all our troubles, so that we can comfort those in any trouble with the comfort we ourselves have received from God" (2 Corinthians 1:3-4, NIV).

God disciplines us. "Our fathers disciplined us for a little while as they thought best; but God disciplines us for our good, that we may share in his holiness" (Hebrews 12:10, NIV).

I realize, and can testify from my own experience, that there are times when it does not seem as if God is doing any of these things. There are times when it seems as if He has forsaken us. At such times we need to lay hold of such promises as "Never will I leave you; never will I forsake you" (Hebrews 13:5, NIV). God in His own inscrutable way is always at work to fulfill His role as our perfect heavenly Father.

The Gospel for Real Life

MIGHTY, TENDERHEARTED FATHER

For in Christ Jesus you are all sons of God, through faith.

(GALATIANS 3:26)

For some the very word *father* brings up images of harshness, cruelty, abuse, unfaithfulness, or perhaps just plain indifference. I remember the words of one student: "If God is like my father, I want nothing to do with God." Happily, God is not like his father. God "is gracious and compassionate, slow to anger and rich in love" (Psalm 145:8, NIV).

Whether we have a father whom we respect and cherish or one who is worthy to be despised, we should never form our view of God from any human pattern. Rather, we should go to the Bible to get a true picture of our heavenly Father.

Note the contrasting views of God in Psalm 147:3-4: "He heals the brokenhearted and binds up their wounds. He determines the number of the stars and calls them each by name" (NIV). The same God who by His mighty power creates and sustains the stars in their courses is at the same time the tenderhearted God who heals the broken and binds up their wounds. The psalms are replete with such fatherly images of God.

As we think of this relationship to God as our heavenly Father, we must always bear one important truth in mind. We have this relationship only through Jesus Christ. It's only because of our union with Christ that we are God's children and He is our Father. That's why Paul wrote, "In him [that is, through our union with Christ] and through faith in him we may approach God with freedom and confidence" (Ephesians 3:12, NIV; see also Ephesians 2:18; Hebrews 10:19-22).

Our status as children of God is one more glorious aspect of our inexhaustible treasure in "the unsearchable riches of Christ" (Ephesians 3:8).

The Gospel for Real Life

MORTIFY YOUR SINFUL DESIRES

*Those who belong to Christ Jesus have
crucified the flesh with its passions and desires.*

(GALATIANS 5:24)

We must realize that in putting sin to death we're saying no to our own desires. Sin most often appeals to us through our desires, or what the older writers called our affections. Not all desires, of course, are sinful; we can desire to know God, to obey Him, and to serve Him. There are many good, positive desires.

The Scriptures, however, speak of "deceitful desires" (Ephesians 4:22), evil "passions" (1 Peter 1:14), and "passions of the flesh" (1 Peter 2:11). The apostle James told us, "But each person is tempted when he is lured and enticed by his own *desire*. Then *desire* when it has conceived gives birth to sin, and sin when it is fully grown brings forth death" (James 1:14-15).

It is evil desire that causes us to sin. All sin is desired, or perhaps the perceived benefits of the sin are desired, before the sin is acted upon. Satan appeals to us first of all through our desires. Eve saw "that the fruit of the tree was good for food and pleasing to the eye, and also desirable for gaining wisdom" (Genesis 3:6). Note how the concept of desire is implied in "good for food" and "pleasing to the eye," as well as explicitly mentioned in "desirable for gaining wisdom."

John Owen was very perceptive on this subject: "Sin also carries on its war by entangling the affections [desires] and drawing them into an alliance against the mind [our reason]. Grace may be enthroned in the mind, but if sin controls the affections, it has seized a fort from which it will continually assault the soul. Hence, as we shall see, mortification is chiefly directed to take place upon the affections."[73]

The Discipline of Grace

THE LURE OF INDEPENDENCE

In his hand is the life of every living thing and the breath of all mankind.

(JOB 12:10)

God's grace assumes our sinfulness, guilt, and ill-deservedness — and it also assumes our weakness and inability. Just as grace is opposed to the pride of self-righteousness, so it is also opposed to the pride of self-sufficiency. The sin of self-sufficiency goes all the way back to the Fall in the Garden of Eden.

Satan's temptation of Eve was undoubtedly complex and many faceted. That is, it included what we would now consider a number of different temptations. But one of those facets was the temptation of self-sufficiency.

Satan said to Eve, "You will be like God, knowing good and evil" (Genesis 3:5). Mankind was created to be dependent upon God — physically: "In him we live and move and have our being" (Acts 17:28); and spiritually: Jesus said, "Apart from me you can do nothing" (John 15:5). God intended our dependence on Him to be conscious and continuous, just as it was for Jesus with the Father: "The Son can do nothing of his own accord, but only what he sees the Father doing. . . . I can do nothing on my own" (John 5:19,30).

But Satan tempted Eve to assert her autonomy and self-sufficiency. As G. Ch. Aalders said, "That ideal of sovereign independence, which had been presented to her by the serpent, lured her on, 'and she took some [of the fruit] and ate it.'"[74]

Ever since the Fall, God has continually worked to cause His people to realize their utter dependence on Him. He does this through bringing us to the point of human extremity where we have no place to turn but to Him.

Transforming Grace

SEEING ANGER'S CAUSE

> *The LORD said to Cain, "Why are you angry?"*
>
> (GENESIS 4:6)

In facing up to our anger, we need to realize that no one else causes us to be angry. Someone else's words or actions may become the occasion of our anger, but the cause lies deep within us — usually our pride, selfishness, or desire to control.

We can choose how we'll respond to the sinful actions of others toward us. Consider Peter's words to slaves in the first-century churches, who often served under cruel masters. We might think they would be justified in their anger, but Peter told them, "Be subject to your masters with all respect, not only to the good and gentle but also to the unjust. For this is a gracious thing, when, mindful of God, one endures sorrows while suffering unjustly. . . . If when you do good and suffer for it you endure, this is a gracious thing in the sight of God" (1 Peter 2:18-20).

Peter's instructions to slaves are a specific application of a broader scriptural principle: In responding to any unjust treatment, we're to be "mindful of God" — to think of His will and His glory. How would God have me respond in this situation? How can I best glorify God by my response? Do I believe this difficult situation or unjust treatment is under God's sovereign control, and that in His infinite wisdom and goodness He's using these difficult circumstances to conform me more to the likeness of Christ? (See Romans 8:28; Hebrews 12:4-11.) I'm realistic enough to know that in the emotional heat of a tense situation, we won't go through a checklist of questions such as these. But we can and should develop the habit of thinking this way.

Respectable Sins

WITH NO UNCERTAINTY

Be all the more diligent to make your calling and election sure.
(2 PETER 1:10)

Life is filled with uncertainties, some major, some minor. But whether
the issue is significant or trivial — waiting for the results of a cancer
biopsy or wondering if you'll make your connecting flight — no one likes
uncertainty.

"How may we attain a right relationship with God?" is the most
important question we can ever ask. That being true, it follows that uncertainty over whether that relationship is real has to be the greatest uncertainty of all. If a cancer biopsy rates an eight or nine on our stress scale,
this question has to be off the chart.

God, however, doesn't want us to be uncertain about it. As the apostle
John said, "I write these things to you who believe in the name of the Son
of God so that *you may know that you have eternal life*" (1 John 5:13). God
wants us to *know* we have eternal life. To some people the claim to know
such a thing sounds presumptuous and arrogant. But if God *wants* us to
know it, we're only laying hold of what pleases Him when we affirm our
assurance of eternal life.

How then can I know that I have eternal life — that I've indeed come
into a right relationship with God? The Scriptures show us three means by
which God assures us that we do have eternal life: (1) the promises of His
Word, (2) the witness of the Spirit in our hearts, and (3) the transforming
work of the Spirit in our lives.

The unsearchable riches of Christ are a treasure trove of blessings
given to us. Part of that treasure is the assurance God gives that we do
have eternal life. Don't stop short of availing yourself of His riches until
you have that assurance.

The Gospel for Real Life

NEVER SATISFIED

The eye is not satisfied with seeing, nor the ear filled with hearing.

(ECCLESIASTES 1:8)

Mortification involves a struggle between what we know to be right (our convictions) and what we desire to do. This is the struggle depicted by the apostle Paul when he wrote, "For the sinful nature desires what is contrary to the Spirit, and the Spirit what is contrary to the sinful nature. They are in conflict with each other, so that you do not do what you want" (Galatians 5:17, NIV). The person who tends to overindulge in sweets will struggle between a conviction about the importance of self-control and the desire to eat that delicious, tempting dessert. The man who has developed a habit of undisciplined and wandering eyes will struggle between a conviction regarding purity and the desire to indulge a lustful look. Whatever our particular areas of vulnerability to sin are, mortification is going to involve struggle — often intense struggle — in those areas.

The ceaselessness of this struggle is suggested to us in Proverbs 27:20: "Death and Destruction are never satisfied, and neither are the eyes of man" (NIV).

Our eyes, of course, are often the gateway to our desires. But whether the appeal to our desires comes through the eye or another avenue such as the memory, our desires are never satisfied. But it is these sinful desires that must be mortified, that is, subdued and weakened in their power to entice us into sin.

It is always emotionally painful to say no to those desires, especially when they represent recurring sin patterns, because those desires run deep and strong. They cry out for fulfillment. That is why Paul used such strong language: "Put to death therefore what is earthly in you" (Colossians 3:5).

The Discipline of Grace

UTTER DEPENDENCE

Man lives by every word that comes from the mouth of the LORD.
(DEUTERONOMY 8:3)

On the first page of the notebook I use for morning devotions and prayer, I've written these words from J. A. Thompson's commentary on Deuteronomy 8:2-3: "Already during the forty years of wandering God had taught Israel utter dependence on Him for water and food. Hunger and thirst could not be satisfied by human aid but only by God. The need for such divine provision in the hour of their extremity could not but humiliate the people. . . . Without the divine word the food itself may not be available. . . . Nothing was possible without Him, and even to eat they had to await His pleasure."[75]

The fact is, I'm just as dependent on God for water and food as were the people of Israel in the desert. God provided for the Israelites through a continual daily miracle for forty years. He has provided for me and my family through His providential circumstances, also for many years. God wanted the Israelites to remember their utter dependence on Him, so He used an extremity of need and a miraculous provision to capture their attention. Still, they forgot. How much easier is it for us to forget when God is supplying our needs through ordinary, mundane ways.

It's even more difficult for us to learn our dependence on God in the spiritual realm. We can exist for months — going through the motions, perhaps even teaching Sunday school or serving as an elder or deacon — depending on nothing more than mere natural human resources.

If I'm dependent in the physical realm, how much more in the spiritual realm, where our struggle is not against flesh and blood, but against spiritual forces of evil (Ephesians 6:12)?

Transforming Grace

PROMISED FAITH

> *Everyone who calls on the name of the Lord will be saved.*
>
> (ROMANS 10:13)

We've seen that faith is the gift of God. Some may wonder whether God has truly given them this gift. But that's the wrong question. Instead we should focus on God's promises given without restriction.

Consider these gracious invitations: "Come, *everyone who thirsts,* come to the waters; and *he who has no money,* come, buy and eat! Come, buy wine and milk without money and without price" (Isaiah 55:1). "The Spirit and the Bride say, 'Come.' And let the one who hears say, 'Come.' And let the *one who is thirsty* come; let the one who desires take the water of life without price" (Revelation 22:17).

Thirst is a metaphorical description here of those who realize their need of a Savior. And "he who has no money" is a picture of one who renounces any confidence in his own good works as the way to a right relationship with God. Does this describe you? Have you realized you have no spiritual "money" with which to "buy" eternal life? If so, have you responded to these gracious invitations, coming as one who longs for that right relationship with God? God has promised that you'll drink freely of the gift of the water of life.

Look also at the gracious words of Jesus in John 6:37: "All that the Father gives me will come to me, and whoever comes to me I will never cast out." If you've truly come to Him, sincerely asking Him to be your Savior, He will not drive you away.

Don't ask, "Do I have faith?" Ask rather, "Do I believe the promises of God?" If you do, it's because God has given you the gift of faith. Let God's promises drive away doubt.

The Gospel for Real Life

THE SUFFICIENCY OF GRACE

Be strong in the Lord and in the strength of his might.
(EPHESIANS 6:10)

Before we can learn the sufficiency of God's grace, we must learn the insufficiency of ourselves. As I have said, the more we see our sinfulness, the more we appreciate grace in its basic meaning of God's undeserved favor. In a similar manner, the more we see our frailty, weakness, and dependence, the more we appreciate God's grace in its dimension of His divine assistance. Just as grace shines more brilliantly against the dark background of our sin, so it also shines more brilliantly against the background of our human weakness.

Paul said in Romans 5:20: "Where *sin* increased, grace abounded all the more." In 2 Corinthians 12, he could have just as aptly said, "But where *human weakness* increased, grace abounded all the more." That is essentially what he said in different words in verse 9: "But he said to me, 'My grace is sufficient for you, for my power is made perfect in weakness.' Therefore I will boast all the more gladly of my weaknesses, so that the power of Christ may rest upon me." On this Philip Hughes wrote, "Indeed, the abject weakness of the human instrument serves to magnify and throw into relief the perfection of the divine power in a way that any suggestion of human adequacy could never do. The greater the servant's weakness, the more conspicuous is the power of his Master's all-sufficient grace."[76]

God's power infusing our weakness is a concrete expression of His grace, coming to our aid through the ministry of His Spirit in our lives. This is the mysterious operation of the Holy Spirit on our human spirit through which He strengthens us and enables us to meet in a godly fashion whatever circumstances we encounter.

Transforming Grace

When Satan Accuses

> *The Lord rebuke you, O Satan!*
>
> (Zechariah 3:2)

Satan is our accuser; in fact, that seems to be his primary strategy toward sincere believers. This is vividly illustrated in his accusation of the high priest, Joshua, recorded in Zechariah 3:1-4. Joshua stands before the angel of the Lord, with Satan standing at his right hand to accuse him. But God rebukes Satan, takes away Joshua's filthy clothes (depicting his sin), and clothes him with rich garments (symbolizing the robe of Christ's righteousness). Perhaps Paul had this passage in mind when he wrote, "Who will bring any charge against those whom God has chosen? It is God who justifies" (Romans 8:33, NIV). God no longer allows Satan to accuse us before Him. In fact, we might say God has thrown Satan out of His heavenly courtroom.

However, though Satan can no longer accuse us before God, he accuses us to ourselves. He plants thoughts in our minds: *How could a Christian struggle with sin as much as you do?* What is our defense in such instances? It isn't to ignore or minimize sin's seriousness. Rather it's to look at the cross of Christ and see Him bearing those sins in all their severity and ugliness in His body. It's to believe that "there is now no condemnation for those who are in Christ Jesus" (Romans 8:1, NIV), because Jesus was condemned in our place as our substitute.

When you're troubled with uncertainty about your salvation, ask yourself, "Have I called on the name of the Lord? Have I come to Jesus as one who is thirsty but has no money? Have I renounced any confidence in my own goodness and relied entirely on Jesus' blood and righteousness?" If you answer yes to those questions, rely on the promises of God.

The Gospel for Real Life

GRACE FOR GLORY

My grace is sufficient for you.

(2 CORINTHIANS 12:9)

God's grace is not given to make us feel better but to glorify Him. Modern society's subtle, underlying agenda is good feelings. We want the pain to go away. We want to feel better in difficult situations. But God wants us to glorify Him in those circumstances. Good feelings may or may not come, but that's not the issue. The issue is whether we honor God by the way we respond to our circumstances. God's grace — the enabling power of the Holy Spirit — is given to help us respond in such a way.

God's grace is sufficient. The Greek verb for *is sufficient* in 2 Corinthians 12:9 is translated "will be content" in 1 Timothy 6:8: "If we have food and clothing, with these we will be content" (NIV). This helps us understand what *sufficient* means. Food and clothing refer to life's necessities, not luxuries. If we have the necessities, we're to be content, realizing they're sufficient.

So it is with God's grace in the spiritual realm. God always gives us what we need, perhaps sometimes more, but never less. The spiritual equivalent of food and clothing is simply the strength to endure in a way that honors God. Receiving that strength, we're to be content. We would like the "luxury" of having our particular thorn removed, but God often says, "Be content with the strength to endure that thorn." We can be confident He always gives that.

John Blanchard said, "So he [God] supplies perfectly measured grace to meet the needs of the godly. For daily needs there is daily grace; for sudden needs, sudden grace; for overwhelming need, overwhelming grace. God's grace is given wonderfully, but not wastefully; freely but not foolishly; bountifully but not blindly."[77]

Transforming Grace

Week 40 / THURSDAY

THE SPIRIT'S WITNESS

You did not receive the spirit of slavery to fall back into fear.

(ROMANS 8:15)

God knows our tendencies to sometimes doubt whether His promises are true for us. Therefore, He has given us another strong means of assurance, the witness of His Spirit: "The Spirit himself bears witness with our spirit that we are children of God" (Romans 8:16).

How the Holy Spirit interacts with our human spirit to give us assurance is a mystery, going beyond our investigative abilities. However, though I cannot explain it, I've certainly experienced it.

I still remember the night more than fifty years ago when I asked Jesus to be my Savior. I was a teenage church member, but had no peace about my relationship with God. The moment I asked Jesus Christ to be my Savior, my heart was flooded with peace. I had peace *with* God as a result of Jesus' work on the cross. And I had the peace *of* God — the inner witness of His Spirit that I now had eternal life.

This inner witness of the Spirit is highly personal. The Spirit tailors His witness to our particular temperament and circumstances. Each of us comes to the point of trusting in Christ from different experiences. For someone from a flagrantly sinful life, there may be a deep, penetrating assurance that his sins are forgiven, that he has been washed clean and has a new life in Christ. For the moral or religious person, there may be a sense of relief that he or she no longer has to try to earn God's favor. For me, it was a quiet sense of peace; my five-year struggle with God was over. In every case, though, it's the Spirit's application of the gospel to our lives that produces this inner witness.

The Gospel for Real Life

TWO ARE BETTER THAN ONE

Iron sharpens iron, and one man sharpens another.
(PROVERBS 27:17)

Because mortifying sins is difficult, we need the help of one or two friends to engage in the struggle with us. These friends should be believers who share our commitment to pursuing holiness and who are also willing to be mutually open with us about their own struggles. This principle is well expressed in Ecclesiastes 4:9-10: "Two are better than one, because they have a good reward for their toil. For if they fall, one will lift up his fellow. But woe to him who is alone when he falls and has not another to lift him up!"

In the battle of putting sin to death, we need the mutual support of one another. In the New Testament we're taught to admonish one another (Colossians 3:16), encourage one another (Hebrews 3:13), confess our sins to one another (James 5:16), bear one another's burdens (Galatians 6:2), and pray for one another (James 5:16).

Although this principle applies to every aspect of the Christian life, it's particularly helpful in the pursuit of holiness. We need at least one other person of like heart to pray with us, encourage us, and if necessary, admonish us. This person must be someone who's also personally involved in the struggle to mortify sin, so that he or she can enter into our struggles and not be scandalized by the nature of our deepest sins. It's said that the Puritans used to ask God for one "bosom friend" with whom they could share absolutely everything. This is the type of friend we should also pray for and seek out to help us in our struggle to mortify sin in our lives. Remember, however, it's a mutual effort. Each one should be committed to both helping and receiving help.

The Discipline of Grace

LEARNING TO TRUST

Trust in him at all times.

(PSALM 62:8)

It's difficult to believe God is in control when we're in the midst of heartache or grief. I've struggled with this many times myself. Each time I've had to decide if I would trust Him, even when my heart ached. I realized anew that we must learn to trust God one circumstance at a time.

It's not a matter of my feelings but of my will. I never feel like trusting God when adversity strikes, but I can choose to do so anyway. That act of the will must be based on belief, and belief must be based on the truth that God is sovereign. He carries out His own good purposes without ever being thwarted, and nothing is outside of His sovereign will. We must cling to this in the face of adversity and tragedy, if we're to glorify God by trusting Him.

I'll say this as gently and compassionately as I know how: Our first priority in adversity is to honor and glorify God by trusting Him. Gaining relief from our feelings of heartache or disappointment or frustration is a natural desire, and God has promised to give us grace sufficient for our trials and peace for our anxieties (2 Corinthians 12:9; Philippians 4:6-7). But just as God's will is to take precedence over our will ("Yet not as I will, but as you will" — Matthew 26:39), so God's honor is to take precedence over our feelings. We honor God by choosing to trust Him when we don't understand what He is doing or why He has allowed some adverse circumstance to occur. As we seek God's glory, we may be sure He has purposed our good and that He won't be frustrated in fulfilling that purpose.

Trusting God

DAILY GRACE

> *And he humbled you . . . and fed you with manna.*
> (DEUTERONOMY 8:3)

There's a lesson about grace in the way God distributed the manna to the Israelites in the desert:

"This is what the LORD has commanded: 'Gather of it, each one of you, as much as he can eat. . . .' And the people of Israel did so. They gathered, some more, some less. But when they measured it with an omer, whoever gathered much had nothing left over, and whoever gathered little had no lack. Each of them gathered as much as he could eat. And Moses said to them, 'Let no one leave any of it over till the morning.' But they did not listen to Moses. Some left part of it till the morning, and it bred worms and stank. And Moses was angry with them. Morning by morning they gathered it, each as much as he could eat; but when the sun grew hot, it melted" (Exodus 16:16-21).

Three times the text mentions that each person could gather as much as he needed. There was an ample supply for everyone; no one need go hungry. And God in some mysterious way saw that no one had an overabundance: Someone gathering much did not have too much; someone gathering little did not have too little. Furthermore, the gathering was to be a daily activity; they were not allowed to store up for the future.

This illustrates the way God distributes grace. There's always an ample supply; no one ever need go without. But there's only as much as we need — and even that is on a day-to-day basis. God doesn't permit us to "store up" grace. We must look to Him anew each day for a new supply. Sometimes we must look for a new supply each hour!

Transforming Grace

EMBOLDENED

All that the Father gives me will come to me,
and whoever comes to me I will never cast out.

(JOHN 6:37)

We need the inner witness of the Spirit, not only at the time we come to Christ, but throughout our Christian lives, especially in times of severe temptation and failure. Once I was on my way to speak at a conference on the pursuit of holiness. The trip itself had been one of those stressful experiences when I did not exhibit the fruit of the Spirit of love, joy, and peace to airline personnel. I felt like an utter failure (which was true). How could I possibly speak to others about pursuing holiness when I had been so unholy myself?

Arriving at my hotel room late at night, I opened my Bible to try to find some encouragement. Soon I came to a short phrase in Colossians 2:13: "He forgave us all our sins" (NIV). My heart was flooded with joy. The Spirit bore witness with my spirit that my sins of that very day were forgiven, washed away by the blood of Christ. I was emboldened with courage to speak at that conference, not because I was good enough, but because the Holy Spirit bore witness with my spirit that my sins were forgiven.

Once in a while I get discouraged about my Christian life when God gives me a glimpse of the sinfulness in my heart. At those times I'm tempted to ask, "Am I really a Christian?" When those rare occasions do occur, I go back to these promises, especially John 6:37. I know that I have come to Jesus and that He has promised me that He will not drive me away. Thus I regain and strengthen my assurance.

We have to let the promises of God drive away our doubts.

The Gospel for Real Life

OUR WEAKNESSES

When I am weak, then I am strong.
(2 CORINTHIANS 12:10)

Paul's attitude toward his weakness was vastly different from our usual response. We abhor weakness and glory in self-sufficiency and manmade accomplishments. Even Christians flock to hear a testimony from the sports superstar or the popular entertainer simply because of that person's fame and status. How many of us would make any effort to hear a man who said, "I will boast all the more gladly of my weaknesses. . . . I am content with weaknesses. . . . When I am weak, then I am strong" (2 Corinthians 12:9-10)?

I think of how I've struggled with my own weaknesses instead of delighting in them. I think of the disappointment of failing to reach important goals, of humiliations suffered that were too painful to ever share with anyone, of somewhat minor but very annoying lifetime physical infirmities. Only in the last few years have I realized what a significant contribution these have made on my walk with God and my service for Him, especially in their cumulative effect. I think I'm only beginning to understand a little the validity of Paul's statement, "When I am weak, then I am strong."

Sometimes when I'm introduced as a speaker, I cringe inwardly as the person introducing me waxes eloquent about my accomplishments. I think, *What if they knew the other side of the story? Would they all get up and leave?* Yet ironically, it is the other side of the story, the humiliations and heartaches, the failures and frustrations — not the successes and accomplishments — that have qualified me to be there to speak. Those difficult times have driven me to the Lord. I'll be honest. It wasn't that I wanted to lean on God; I had no other choice. But I'm finally learning that in weakness I find strength — His strength.

Transforming Grace

OUR NORMAL PRACTICE

No one born of God makes a practice of sinning.

(1 JOHN 3:9)

The apostle John gave us another indicator for knowing we have eternal life: "You may be sure that everyone who practices righteousness has been born of him" (1 John 2:29).

This test can be a tricky one. We might understand John to say that only those who always do what is right are born of God. Though that's certainly God's standard for us, obviously none of us measures up to it. Even John himself said, "If we claim to be without sin, we deceive ourselves and the truth is not in us" (1 John 1:8).

When John spoke of "everyone who *practices* righteousness," he was thinking of our normal *practice*, of the dominant direction of our lives.

Sometimes our obedience is marked more by desire than by performance. So we have to ask ourselves: Is my life characterized by an earnest desire and a sincere effort to obey God in all that He commands? What is my attitude toward God's Law? Do I find it to be holy, just, and good? And do I delight in it in my inner being, even though I find my sinful nature struggling against it? (See Romans 7:12,22-23.)

Accompanying our sincere desire to obey God will be a heightened sensitivity to our indwelling sin. Often it's our increased awareness of sin that causes us to doubt our salvation or to give Satan an inroad into our minds to suggest that "a Christian wouldn't sin like you do." But Satan would certainly not suggest such a thought to an unbeliever. Rather, he wants unbelievers to be complacent about their sin. So turn the tables on Satan and your own internal doubts. Ask yourself if those accusations or doubts are not really a sign that you do trust Christ.

The Gospel for Real Life

DO WE LOVE EACH OTHER?

Whoever loves has been born of God and knows God.

(1 JOHN 4:7)

The apostle John gave us yet another indicator of the Spirit's work within us in 1 John 3:14: "We know that we have passed out of death into life, because we love the brothers." Do you love other believers? Do you enjoy gathering with them to worship God?

I once became baffled while seeking to help another believer struggling with assurance. Nothing I suggested seemed to work. Then one day he told me his struggle was over. He'd come across 1 John 3:14. As he thought about that verse, he said, "I do love other believers. I rejoice to be around them and fellowship with them. I must truly be a Christian." The Holy Spirit had used that Scripture to give him assurance that he was indeed God's child.

We should ask ourselves if our love for other believers is the kind described in 1 Corinthians 13:4-7. Are we patient, kind, gracious, slow to anger, and ready to forgive? None of us can completely measure up to this standard, but do you *want* to? Do you grieve over your failures in these areas? If so, you love your brothers.

Of course, this indicator (like others) can cut both ways. Paul wrote to the Corinthians, "Examine yourselves to see whether you are in the faith; test yourselves. Do you not realize that Christ Jesus is in you — unless, of course, you fail the test?" (2 Corinthians 13:5).

We should never be afraid to examine ourselves. But when doubts arise, the solution is not to try harder to prove to ourselves that we are believers. The solution is to flee to the cross and to the righteousness of Christ, which is our only hope.

The Gospel for Real Life

FROM RAW EXPERIENCE

I know how to be brought low.

(PHILIPPIANS 4:12)

Philip Hughes said, "Every believer must learn that human weakness and divine grace go hand in hand together."[78] Paul had learned that lesson well. He said, "Therefore I will boast all the more gladly of my weaknesses, so that the power of Christ may rest upon me" (2 Corinthians 12:9).

Paul had learned that God's grace is indeed sufficient; His divine enabling through the power of the Holy Spirit would sustain him in the midst of the torments of his thorn, and in the depths of other "weaknesses, insults, hardships, persecutions, and calamities" (verse 10).

When Paul wrote these words to the Corinthians, it had been fourteen years since Paul received those surpassingly great revelations. If we assume the thorn was given to him at about the same time, and that the three instances when he pleaded for its removal occurred soon afterward, we can say that Paul had had almost fourteen years to prove the sufficiency of God's grace. Hardships, troubles, and dangers would continue unabated (2 Corinthians 11:25-28).

Paul was no ivory tower theologian. He did not write from the comfortable confines of a minister's study or a counselor's office (nor, for that matter, does any competent pastor or counselor today). Paul wrote from raw experience because he "had been there." The anguish he experienced was real anguish, and the grace he received was real grace. It was not theoretical, nor make-believe, nor merely "whistling in the dark" to keep up his courage. No, Paul experienced a very concrete expression of God's love and power as the Holy Spirit ministered comfort and encouragement to him in the midst of affliction.

Transforming Grace

BEING LIKE HIM

For those whom he foreknew he also predestined
to be conformed to the image of his Son.

(ROMANS 8:29)

The Spirit's work within us is as much a gift of God's grace as is our justi-fication and adoption as sons. But whereas justification and adoption are instantaneous and complete at once, our growth in Christlikeness is a lifelong process. Therefore, we should never look solely to our love and obedience for our assurance of salvation. At most they can demonstrate our salvation, never prove it. Ultimately our assurance must rest on the gospel and on the promises of God.

Meanwhile, we can grow in realizing how those promises point to both a glorious present and an even more glorious future. John spoke of our glorious present when he wrote, "Beloved, we are God's children now" (1 John 3:2). In the same verse he went on to speak of our even more glori-ous future: "We know that when he appears *we shall be like him*, because we shall see him as he is." Likeness to Christ is God's ultimate purpose for us and the hope we look forward to.

What does it mean to be like Jesus?

First, it means to be like Him *in spirit*, in our true inner being. This is a process that begins at conversion and will reach its ultimate fulfillment when we enter the Lord's presence at death. Paul calls this process *transfor-mation*. "And we all, with unveiled face, beholding the glory of the Lord, are being *transformed* into the same image from one degree of glory to another. For this comes from the Lord who is the Spirit" (2 Corinthians 3:18). God has predestined us to be conformed to the likeness or image of His Son, and He's now at work in us through His Spirit to bring that to pass.

The Gospel for Real Life

THE UNWORTHY APOSTLE

To me, though I am the very least of all the saints . . . grace was given.

(EPHESIANS 3:8)

Paul freely acknowledged that he received his apostleship purely as a result of God's undeserved favor. God used Paul's testimony to encourage me at a time when I most keenly felt my complete unworthiness to write on the subject of personal holiness.

So is all ministry — whether teaching a children's Sunday school class, witnessing to inmates at the local prison, or preaching to thousands of people each Sunday — performed by the grace of God by people who are unworthy to be doing it?

Harry Blamires had an incisive answer to that question: "In the upshot there is only one answer for the preacher who wonders whether he is worthy to preach the sermon he has composed or for the writer who wonders whether he is worthy to write the religious book he is working on. The answer is: Of course not. To ask yourself: Am I worthy to perform this Christian task? is really the peak of pride and presumption. For the very question carries the implication that we spend most of our time doing things we are worthy to do. We simply do not have that kind of worth."[79]

In Romans 12:6, Paul described us as "having gifts that differ according to the grace given to us." He was referring to spiritual gifts enabling believers to fulfill God-appointed ministry or service in the body of Christ. But note that Paul said these spiritual gifts are given according to God's *grace*, not according to what we deserve. The Greek word for a spiritual gift is *charisma*, which means "a gift of God's grace," whether it is the gift of eternal life as in Romans 6:23 or the gift of a spiritual ability for use in the body.

Transforming Grace

SOMETIMES FAILURE

God's kindness is meant to lead you to repentance.

(ROMANS 2:4)

As we begin to mortify a particular sin, we'll often fail more than we succeed. Then we must realize that we stand before God on the basis of His grace rather than our performance.

I realize there's a fine line between using grace as an excuse for our sin and using grace as a remedy for it. John Owen had keen insight on this: "Here then is where the deceit of sin intervenes. . . . It persuades us to dwell upon the notion of grace and diverts our attention from the influence that grace gives to achieve its proper application in holy lives. From the doctrine of assured pardon of sin, it insinuates a carelessness for sin. . . . the soul — needing frequently to return to gospel grace because of guilt — allows grace to become commonplace and ordinary. Having found a good medicine for its wound, it then takes it for granted."[80]

The way to stay on the right side of the fine line between using and abusing grace is repentance. The road to repentance is godly sorrow (2 Corinthians 7:10, NIV). Godly sorrow is developed when we focus on the true nature of sin as an offense against God rather than something that makes us feel guilty. Sin is an affront to God's holiness, it grieves His Holy Spirit, and it wounds afresh the Lord Jesus Christ. It also gratifies Satan, the archenemy of God. Dwelling on the true nature of sin leads us to godly sorrow, which in turn leads us to repentance.

Having come to repentance, we must by faith lay hold of the cleansing blood of Christ, which alone can cleanse our consciences. In fact, it is faith in Christ and the assurance of the efficacy of His cleansing blood that leads us to repentance.

The Discipline of Grace

WHEN OTHERS ABUSE

[Love] . . . is not easily angered.
(1 CORINTHIANS 13:5, NIV).

I certainly don't advocate "doormat" Christianity, letting people continually run over us or abuse us. There are times when we must stand up for what is right and just. But we should not sin in the process. We must face the fact that much, if not most, of our anger is sinful, even though it may arise from the sinful actions of others. In emphasizing our sin of anger, I do not mean to minimize the sin of those other people. But there's an old saying, "Two wrongs never make a right." The other person's sin does not make our sin of anger "right" or justifiable. Or as James wrote, "The anger of man does not produce the righteousness that God requires" (1:20).

Furthermore, I suspect that much of our anger is not a result of significant injustices or wrongs against us but is the manifestation of our own pride and selfishness. I've been embarrassed or inconvenienced or frustrated by the actions (or even the inactions) of other people, so I get angry. While there is plenty of injustice that deserves a response of righteous anger, we should not use that as an excuse to evade the reality of the sinful anger that so often arises in our hearts and may be expressed by our words or actions.

So I commend to you three principles or practices that I find so helpful: a firm belief in the sovereignty of God; a diligent pursuit of brotherly love that covers a multitude of sins and does not keep a record of wrongs; and a humble realization that, in comparison to my brother's sin against me, I am the ten-thousand-talent debtor to God (Matthew 18:21-35).

Respectable Sins

GRACE AND GIFTS

> *I give thanks to my God always for you because*
> *of the grace of God that was given you in Christ Jesus.*
>
> (1 CORINTHIANS 1:4)

In his comments on 1 Corinthians 1:4, Dr. Gordon Fee has helpful insight on the connection of grace and gifts: "The specific basis of Paul's thanksgiving in their case is God's 'grace given you in Christ Jesus.' Commonly this is viewed as a thanksgiving for grace as such, i.e., the gracious outpouring of God's mercy in Christ toward the undeserving. However, for Paul *charis* ('grace') very often is closely associated with charisma/charismata ('gift/ gifts') and in such instances refers to concrete expressions of God's gracious activity in his people. Indeed, the word 'grace' itself sometimes denoted these concrete manifestations, the 'graces' (gifts), of God's grace."[81]

Peter wrote, "As each has received a gift, use it to serve one another, as good stewards of God's varied grace" (1 Peter 4:10). Peter and Paul are saying the same thing. Our spiritual gifts and the ministries we perform are gifts of God's grace. None of us deserves the gifts he or she has been given by God's undeserved favor to us through Christ.

This means that both the most "worthy" and the most "unworthy" of Christians receive their gifts and their ministries on the same basis. The "unworthy" person surely doesn't deserve his gift, but neither does the most "worthy." They both receive them as unmerited favors from God.

In reality there is no such distinction in God's sight between "worthy" and "unworthy." In His sight, we're all totally and permanently bankrupt spiritually. Paul's statement is just as true for believers as for unbelievers: "There is no distinction: for all have sinned and fall short of the glory of God" (Romans 3:22-23).

Transforming Grace

MADE PERFECT

> *You have come . . . to the spirits of the righteous made perfect.*
>
> (HEBREWS 12:22-23)

Although the Spirit is at work in us to transform us, our sinful nature opposes Him every step of the way. We find we still struggle with indwelling sin. "For the sinful nature desires what is contrary to the Spirit, and the Spirit what is contrary to the sinful nature. They are in conflict with each other, so that you do not do what you want" (Galatians 5:17, NIV). A continuous conflict wages between two opposing forces in our hearts. When we want to do good, evil is right there with us (Romans 7:21). We struggle with pride, selfishness, impatience, a critical spirit, a sharp tongue, a lack of love, and countless expressions of our sinful natures.

We'll have this struggle as long as we live in these bodies. It's painful because we're at war within ourselves, and continually we have to say no to sinful desires. It's sometimes humiliating as sinful traits reveal themselves to our consciousness. Sometimes we soar into the heavenlies with Christ in our morning devotions, only to come crashing down with a thud before nine o'clock through some conflict with another person.

We long to be released from this warfare, and one day we will be. In Hebrews 12:22-24, a quick preview of heaven as it is now, we read of "the spirits of the righteous made perfect" (verse 23). This is a reference to believers of all ages whose spirits are now with Christ in heaven, and who are now "made perfect." The sinful nature that now clings to our spirits like dirty, wet clothes will be done away with, and our spirits will be completely conformed to the likeness of Christ. This happens immediately at death when we go directly into the presence of the Lord.

The Gospel for Real Life

From Repentance to Blessing

Blessed are those whose lawless deeds are forgiven,
and whose sins are covered.

(Romans 4:7)

David's experience is very helpful to us in the relationship of repentance and grace: "Blessed is the one whose transgression is forgiven, whose sin is covered. Blessed is the man against whom the Lord counts no iniquity, and in whose spirit there is no deceit. For when I kept silent, my bones wasted away through my groaning all day long. For day and night your hand was heavy upon me; my strength was dried up as by the heat of summer. *I acknowledged my sin to you*, and I did not cover my iniquity; I said, 'I will confess my transgressions to the Lord,' and you forgave the iniquity of my sin" (Psalm 32:1-5).

Here David first stated his conclusion, as he spoke of the blessedness of being forgiven. Then he explained that blessedness by acknowledging his own guilt and his miserable condition before he repented. But with genuine repentance came the deep assurance that he was forgiven. In sequence of time, the blessedness actually came after his repentance and assurance of forgiveness. But just as we often do, David gave the "bottom line" before explaining how he got there.

We must do as David did if we want to experience God's grace in our failures at mortifying sin. It's not that repentance earns God's forgiveness. Only the blood of Christ does that. God, however, does deal with us as a loving but firm father deals with his children. He accepts us unconditionally because we are His sons and daughters in Christ, but He disciplines us for our good. And in the administering of His discipline He withholds the assurance of His forgiveness until we, through repentance, are ready to receive it.

The Discipline of Grace

SERVING BY GRACE

> *As each has received a gift, use it to serve one another,*
> *as good stewards of God's varied grace.*
>
> (1 PETER 4:10)

We're so accustomed to thinking of spiritual gifts as ministry abilities that we lose sight of the ordinary meaning of the word. A *gift* is something given to us; something we don't earn. But even that fails to adequately convey the biblical sense. We tend to give gifts to people who in some sense deserve them because of their relationship to us or because they've done us a favor of some kind. But God gives spiritual gifts to people who don't deserve them. None of us deserves to be in God's service, whether teaching a children's Sunday school class or serving on some faraway mission field.

It's an awesome thing to attempt to speak on behalf of God. Yet that's exactly what we do when we teach or preach or write. It matters not whether our audience is one person or fifty thousand, whether they are kindergarten pupils or graduate theological students. Any time we say or write something that we hold out to be biblical truth, we're putting ourselves in the position of being God's spokesman.

Peter said, "If anyone speaks, he should do it as one speaking the very words of God" (1 Peter 4:11, NIV). When we teach the Scriptures, do we appreciate the awesomeness of our responsibility, to be speaking on God's behalf? Do we consider the accountability that comes with being entrusted with the divine message?

Paul himself was keenly conscious of his immense responsibility: "For we are not, like so many, peddlers of God's word, but as men of sincerity, as commissioned by God, in the sight of God we speak in Christ" (2 Corinthians 2:17). He knew God not only sent him, but observed him.

Transforming Grace

FAR BETTER

In your presence there is fullness of joy;
at your right hand are pleasures forevermore.

(PSALM 16:11)

The period between our death and the still-future resurrection of our bodies is usually called the *intermediate state*. The Bible actually tells us little about this period, but what it does say is very encouraging. In 2 Corinthians 5:8 Paul said that he "would prefer to be away from the body and at home with the Lord" (NIV), and in Philippians 1:23 he said, "My desire is to depart and be with Christ, for that is far better."

Taking Paul's statements along with Hebrews 12:22-24, we can say that in the intermediate state we'll be with Christ; we'll be in the presence of thousands upon thousands of angels in joyful assembly (perhaps still hearing those seraphs of Isaiah 6:1-3 who call out antiphonally, "Holy, holy, holy is the LORD Almighty"); we'll be with all believers of all ages; we'll be perfectly conformed to Christ in our spirits; and we'll be in a state that is far better than anything we can imagine.

It's difficult for us to visualize an existence in heaven without the benefit of our physical senses; or, for that matter, a physical brain. Yet we need to remember that God has existed eternally without a physical body. And even the angels apparently exist only in spirit (though some have assumed a physical body at times for specific purposes). Though we cannot understand how these things will be, we need to submit our minds to the teaching of Scripture and look forward to the time when we also will be with Christ, when our spirits will be made perfect, and when we'll be in a state that's far better than our best conditions on earth.

The Gospel for Real Life

THE INADEQUATE APOSTLE

By the grace of God I am what I am.

(1 CORINTHIANS 15:10)

Paul was conscious throughout his entire ministry of his utter unworthiness to be a servant of Christ. We see him expressing it again to the Corinthians: "For I am the least of the apostles, unworthy to be called an apostle, because I persecuted the church of God. But by the grace of God I am what I am, and his grace toward me was not in vain. On the contrary, I worked harder than any of them, though it was not I, but the grace of God that is with me" (1 Corinthians 15:9-10).

Paul freely admitted he didn't deserve his ministry; he was an apostle only by the grace of God — by God's unmerited favor. However, in the expression "by the grace of God I am what I am," the word *grace* can be taken in the context to mean either God's unmerited favor or God's enabling power. Considering his prior acknowledgment of unworthiness, his statement would appear to mean, "I am unworthy to be an apostle, but by God's unmerited favor I am one." But looking forward in this passage, to where Paul speaks about the effects of God's grace on his ministry, it would appear to mean, "By God's enabling power I am an effective apostle."

I believe both these meanings of grace are incorporated in Paul's statement. He wasn't giving us a technical treatise on grace and distinguishing its finer shades of meaning. Rather, Paul was speaking from his heart, saying that God's grace was sufficient for both his unworthiness and his inadequacy. He was saying, "I'm an apostle as a result of God's unmerited favor shown to me and as a result of God's enabling power at work in me."

Transforming Grace

A Rich Welcome

I will welcome you, and I will be a father to you, . . .
says the Lord Almighty.

(2 Corinthians 6:17-18)

What will it be like when we enter the presence of the Lord? The apostle Peter gave us an inspired perspective on this in 2 Peter 1:11, where he said, "There will be richly provided for you an entrance into the eternal kingdom of our Lord and Savior Jesus Christ." This is a picture of a grand and glorious homecoming.

At the end of World War II thousands of servicemen returned home from Europe and the Far East. As the various ships on which they returned arrived in ports here in the United States, they were greeted by cheering crowds and lively bands. And if relatives were able to be present, there was the added excitement of tearful hugs and joyful kisses. These servicemen received a rich welcome back home. This is the way it will be with us, only on a much grander scale.

Peter prefaced his words about this rich welcome with this instruction: "Therefore, brothers, be all the more diligent to make your calling and election sure, for if you practice these qualities you will never fall" (2 Peter 1:10). It might appear, upon a casual reading of this Scripture, that our rich welcome is actually dependent on our practicing these "qualities" mentioned in verses 5 through 7. However, the practice of these qualities — that is, pursuing the particular Christian virtues presented in verses 5 through 7 — is not the basis of the rich welcome. Rather, it's one of the means whereby we make our calling and election sure. It's a way we assure ourselves that we've been made new creations in Christ (2 Corinthians 5:17) and that we do indeed have the hope of eternal life.

The Gospel for Real Life

GRACE THAT WORKS HARDER

Our sufficiency is from God.

(2 CORINTHIANS 3:5)

If you feel incompetent in God's service you are in good company. Paul felt that way also: "Not that we are sufficient in ourselves to claim anything as coming from us, but our sufficiency is from God" (2 Corinthians 3:5).

If there's anyone in the history of the church who could have relied on his own God-given endowments, surely it would have been Paul. He was a brilliant theologian, a gifted evangelist, a tireless church planter, and a sound missionary strategist. He was also adept at cross-cultural minis-try — "To the Jews I became as a Jew, in order to win Jews. . . . To those outside the law I became as one outside the law" (1 Corinthians 9:20-21). Yet Paul, with all his abilities, acknowledged that we aren't competent in ourselves.

We are not competent, but God makes us competent. That's what Paul was saying in 1 Corinthians 15:10: "His grace toward me was not in vain. On the contrary, I worked harder than any of them." God's grace in its concrete expression of divine power was effective in Paul — so effective that Paul could say he worked harder than all the other apostles. At first glance, that statement seems to put Paul in a position of unconscionable boasting, and I used to be troubled by it. It seemed quite out of charac-ter with Paul's obviously genuine humility. But I've come to realize Paul wasn't boasting. He was exalting the grace of God. He was saying that God's grace at work in him was so effective it caused him to work harder than all of them. The grace of God motivated him, enabled him, and then blessed the fruits of his labors.

Transforming Grace

A PRECIOUS SIGHT

Gather to me my faithful ones.

(PSALM 50:5)

Sometimes when I focus too much on my own shortcomings — how often I've sinned, how little I've availed myself of all the blessings of God and opportunities that have come my way — I think I would like to somehow just slip in heaven's side door unnoticed. But that's because I focus too much on myself and try to anticipate my welcome on the basis of my performance.

There will be no slipping in the side door of heaven with our head hanging down and our tail between our legs. No, no, a thousand times no! Everyone who has been the object of God's calling and election will receive a rich welcome into Christ's eternal kingdom (2 Peter 1:10-11) — not because we deserve it, but because we've been clothed with the spotless robe of Christ's righteousness. Because we are united to Him who is the object of the Father's everlasting love and delight, we also will be received as objects of His love and delight.

We see something of God's perspective on our entrance into His eternal kingdom in Psalm 116:15: "Precious in the sight of the LORD is the death of his saints." Why is this true? We think of death as a parting. We think of "losing a loved one" through death. But from God's perspective, the death of a believer is just the opposite. It's a homecoming. It is precious in His sight.

Think of a World War II ship steaming into the harbor at war's end with servicemen lining the rails. That sight was precious in the eyes of the relatives eagerly watching. And this is just a pale picture of how God anticipates the arrival "home" of His sons and daughters from our own spiritual war of this life.

The Gospel for Real Life

Enlarging Our Horizons

He does according to his will . . . among the inhabitants of the earth.

(Daniel 4:35)

Most Christians tend to think of the sovereignty of God only in terms of its immediate effect upon us, or our families or friends. We're not too interested in the sovereignty of God over the nations and over history unless we're consciously and personally affected by that history.

But we must remember that God promised to Abraham and to his seed that all nations will be blessed through Christ (see Genesis 12:3; 22:18; Galatians 3:8). Someday that promise will be fulfilled for, as recorded in Revelation 7:9, John saw "a great multitude that no one could count, from every nation, tribe, people and language, standing before the throne and in front of the Lamb" (NIV). God has a plan to redeem people from all nations and to bless all nations through Christ.

As we look around the world today, we see over half of the world's population living in countries whose governments are hostile to the gospel, where missionaries are not allowed, and where national Christians are hindered from proclaiming Christ. How do we trust God for the fulfillment of His promises when the current events and conditions of the day seem so directly contrary to their fulfillment?

We must also look at the sovereignty of God and at His promises. He has promised to redeem people from every nation, and He has commanded us to make disciples of all nations. We must trust God by praying. We must learn to trust God for the spread of the gospel, even in those areas where it is severely restricted.

God is sovereign over the nations. He is sovereign even where every attempt is made to stamp out true Christianity. In all of these areas, we can and must trust God.

Trusting God

A HEART WARMED FOR WORK

I will run in the way of your commandments when you enlarge my heart!
(PSALM 119:32)

We must keep going back to His grace. Only the grace of God revealed in the gospel of Jesus Christ will give us the courage to get up again and keep on going even after we have failed for the umpteenth time. Only grace will allow us to be as honest about our sin as David was about his.

The desire to engage in the discipline of mortification comes only from the gratitude and joy of knowing that, however miserably I've failed, God's grace is greater than my sin.

The godly Scottish pastor Horatius Bonar expressed it this way: "It is forgiveness that sets a man working for God. He does not work in order to be forgiven, but because he has been forgiven, and the consciousness of his sin being pardoned makes him long more for its entire removal than ever he did before. An unforgiven man cannot work. He has not the will, nor the power, nor the liberty. He is in chains. . . . A forgiven man is the true worker, the true Law-keeper. He can, he will, he must work for God. He has come into contact with that part of God's character which warms his cold heart. Forgiving love constrains him. He cannot but work for Him who has removed his sins from him as far as the east is from the west. Forgiveness has made him a free man, and given him a new and most loving Master. Forgiveness, received freely from the God and Father of our Lord Jesus Christ, acts as a spring, an impulse, a stimulus of divine potency. It is more irresistible than law, or terror, or threat."[82]

The Discipline of Grace

WILLING TO BE A WORM

Fear not, you worm Jacob. . . . Behold, I make of you a threshing sledge.

(ISAIAH 41:14-15)

Years ago when God opened up for me a wider Bible teaching and writing ministry, I felt drawn to Isaiah 41:14-15. Though the promise was given to Israel, I sensed God allowing me to make a personal application — that He would indeed make me into a threshing sledge, a harvesting instrument in His hand. I also sensed that God required, as a condition of the promise, that I accept the description of "worm Jacob," not in a denigrating sense, but as a realization of my own personal weakness and helplessness.

I go back to that condition and promise almost every time I teach the Word of God or sit down to write, to acknowledge my own inability to accomplish anything for God and to lay hold of His promise to give me the power to minister for Him. God seems to keep saying, "As long as you're willing to acknowledge you're as weak and helpless as a worm, I'll make you strong and powerful like a threshing sledge with new, sharp teeth."

The gracious paradox of divine strength working through human weakness as taught in Scripture has been recognized through the centuries by the great teachers of the church. John Owen said, "Yet the duties God requires of us are not in proportion to the strength we possess in ourselves. Rather, they are proportional to the resources available to us in Christ. We do not have the ability in ourselves to accomplish the least of God's tasks. This is a law of grace. When we recognize it is impossible for us to perform a duty in our own strength, we will discover the secret of its accomplishment. But alas, this is a secret we often fail to discover."[83]

Transforming Grace

LIKE HIM IN BODY

This mortal body must put on immortality.

(1 CORINTHIANS 15:53)

As glorious as will be our "homecoming" at death, there will be an even more glorious time at the resurrection when our perfected spirits are united with our resurrection bodies. John refered to this in 1 John 3:2: "When he appears, we shall be like him, for we shall see him as he is" (NIV). At the resurrection we'll be like Jesus not only in spirit, but also in body.

Paul told us, "The Lord Jesus Christ . . . will transform our lowly body to be like his glorious body" (Philippians 3:20-21). Note the contrast Paul drew between our present lowly bodies and our future bodies that will be like His glorious body.

In this present life our bodies are subject to suffering, sickness, disabilities, decay, ugliness, aging, and finally death. It's not a pretty picture. The fact is, in this life, because of the curse of sin, our bodies are lowly bodies.

That's why Paul also wrote, "But we ourselves, who have the firstfruits of the Spirit, groan inwardly as we wait eagerly for adoption as sons, the redemption of our bodies" (Romans 8:23). We groan. Between the internal conflict with our sinful nature and the external struggles with our lowly bodies, as well as the frustrations of adverse circumstances that so frequently beset us, we groan. But this groaning is not without purpose. Instead it causes us, or should cause us, to wait eagerly for the redemption of our bodies.

Paul said it's in this hope that we're saved (Romans 8:24). God intends that the struggles of this life wean us from our attachments to this present world. Generally speaking, believers who have the least benefits of this life have the most vigorous hopes of heaven.

The Gospel for Real Life

KNOW YOUR ENEMY

Watch and pray that you may not enter into temptation.

(MATTHEW 26:41)

If we're going to watch against temptation, we need to be aware of its sources and behavior. To again use an analogy from warfare — and we are indeed engaged in spiritual warfare — we need some intelligence information about the enemy. The Bible speaks of three different sources of temptation waging war against the children of God: the world, the flesh, and the devil. We need to know how they operate and how they tempt us.

The world, or the sinful society in which we live, is characterized by the subtle and relentless pressure it brings to bear upon us to conform to its values and practices. It creeps up on us little by little. What was once unthinkable becomes thinkable, then doable, and finally acceptable to society at large. The Devil, or Satan, is the god of this world and the ultimate mastermind and strategist behind all the temptations that come to us from society. Beyond that, however, he often tempts us directly. He "prowls around like a roaring lion looking for someone to devour" (1 Peter 5:8, NIV).

As dangerous as the world and the devil are, neither is our greatest problem. Our greatest source of temptation dwells within us. It's what the apostle Paul called the flesh. It's the principle of sin that still remains within us, though it no longer exercises dominion. Paul called indwelling sin a law, or as we would say, a principle, that's at work within us constantly seeking to draw us into sin (Romans 7:21-25). Indwelling sin now wages guerrilla warfare against us, and as any military person will attest, that's the most difficult warfare to defend against.

The Discipline of Grace

SACRIFICIAL GRACE

> *They gave . . . beyond their means.*
>
> (2 CORINTHIANS 8:3)

When Paul wanted to challenge the Corinthian Christians to give generously toward the need of poorer believers in Jerusalem, he held up as
an example the Macedonian churches: "We want you to know, brothers, about the grace of God that has been given among the churches of
Macedonia, for in a severe test of affliction, their abundance of joy and
their extreme poverty have overflowed in a wealth of generosity on their
part. For they gave according to their means, as I can testify, and beyond
their means, of their own free will, begging us earnestly for the favor of
taking part in the relief of the saints" (2 Corinthians 8:1-4).

The generosity of the Macedonians was indeed remarkable. They gave
out of poverty; they gave beyond their ability, in disregard of their own
needs. What was the secret of such an outpouring of generosity? Paul said
the secret was *the grace of God* (verse 1). Here Paul used *grace* to mean a
working of the Holy Spirit in the lives of believers — as a concrete expression of God's unmerited favor.

Charles Hodge commented on this work of grace: "The liberality of
the Corinthians was due to the operation of the grace of God. The sacred
writers constantly recognize the fact that the freest and most spontaneous
acts of men, their inward states and the outward manifestations of those
states, when good, are due to the secret influence of the Spirit of God,
which eludes our consciousness."[84]

So it was the grace of God, not the superiority of their own character, that caused such an abundant outpouring of generosity from the
Macedonians. God intervened in their hearts by the power of His Spirit to
create this amazing generosity.

Transforming Grace

WHAT WILL OUR NEW BODY BE LIKE?

But God gives it a body as he has chosen.

(1 CORINTHIANS 15:38)

It is difficult for us to know what New Testament writers mean by saying we'll become like Christ in His glorious body. On this subject, we do well to stick to the wording of Scripture.

Paul wrote, "So is it with the resurrection of the dead. What is sown is perishable; what is raised is imperishable. It is sown in dishonor; it is raised in glory. It is sown in weakness; it is raised in power. It is sown a natural body; it is raised a spiritual body. If there is a natural body, there is also a spiritual body" (1 Corinthians 15:42-44).

And later in the same chapter: "Behold! I tell you a mystery. We shall not all sleep, but we shall all be changed, in a moment, in the twinkling of an eye, at the last trumpet. For the trumpet will sound, and the dead will be raised imperishable, and we shall be changed. For this perishable body must put on the imperishable, and this mortal body must put on immortality. When the perishable puts on the imperishable, and the mortal puts on immortality, then shall come to pass the saying that is written: 'Death is swallowed up in victory'" (1 Corinthians 15:51-54).

Paul emphasized the strong difference between the natural, mortal body and the spiritual, immortal body. But both are bodies. Our perfected spirits will be at home in our immortal bodies. What exactly this spiritual body looks like or how it functions, we do not know. We only know it will be like the Lord's glorious body, and in that we put our hope and expectations.

The Gospel for Real Life

KNOW YOURSELF

Sin is crouching at the door. Its desire is for you, but you must rule over it.
(GENESIS 4:7)

The evil desire within us constantly searches for occasions to express itself. It's like a radar system whose antenna is constantly scanning the environment for temptations to which it can respond. Some years ago, when I was continually indulging my desire for ice cream (which I don't do anymore), my eyes would automatically be drawn to an ice-cream store. It was uncanny. I could pass the signs of a score of stores without consciously seeing them, but I never failed to see the sign of an ice-cream store.

Recently I became interested in a certain model car. It was the same make as the one I drive, but a nicer, more expensive model. As soon as I became interested in that particular car, I noticed every one I passed on the street. I began to think of reasons why I needed that nicer model. It was roomier, more comfortable on a long trip, and had a better transmission. I finally concluded, rather reluctantly, that I really didn't need that car. But the point is, during that time my antenna was "tuned" for that model car.

Perhaps the indulgence with ice cream and the fixation on a nicer model car seem rather benign compared to temptations you've faced. You may be thinking, *Come on, let's talk about some real sins — covetousness, lust, envy, resentment, lying to customers, or cheating on exams.* Well, first of all, the indulgence in ice cream and the preoccupation with a nicer car may not be so benign, but either way, those issues demonstrate the principle: Our flesh is always searching out opportunities to gratify itself according to the particular sinful desires each of us has.

The Discipline of Grace

WITH HIM FOREVER

Where I am, there will my servant be also.

(JOHN 12:26)

While Paul in 1 Corinthians 15 emphasized the reality of an immortal, spiritual body, John in Revelation called our attention to the reality of our eternal presence with God: "And I heard a loud voice from the throne saying, 'Behold, the dwelling place of God is with man. He will dwell with them, and they will be his people, and God himself will be with them as their God. He will wipe away every tear from their eyes, and death shall be no more, neither shall there be mourning, nor crying nor pain anymore, for the former things have passed away'" (Revelation 21:3-4).

In the next chapter we read, "No longer will there be anything accursed, but the throne of God and of the Lamb will be in it, and his servants will worship him. They will see his face, and his name will be on their foreheads. And night will be no more. They will need no light of lamp or sun, for the Lord God will be their light, and they will reign forever and ever" (Revelation 22:3-5).

The day will come when our perfected spirits and immortal bodies are forever united. And in that glorious condition "we will be with the Lord forever" (1 Thessalonians 4:17, NIV). Hallelujah! At that time we will experience the full reality of the unsearchable riches of Christ.

Before we experience that glorious reality, we still live in this life. We're not just to wait for our hope of heaven, but to be actively and vigorously engaged in becoming more like Christ (the process called *sanctification*) and of extending the rule of His kingdom (the first three petitions of the Lord's Prayer in Matthew 6:9-13).

The Gospel for Real Life

THE REWARD OF GRACE

Who has given a gift to him that he might be repaid?

(ROMANS 11:35)

Every aspect of our ministry is by the grace of God. We're unworthy to minister, but God considers us worthy through Christ. We're inadequate to minister, but God makes us adequate through the powerful working of His Holy Spirit. We're not naturally given to self-sacrifice, but God gives us that spirit by His grace. All is of grace. No human worthiness or adequacy is required or accepted.

Such a strong, biblical emphasis on God's grace apart from human worth or adequacy leads to the question of the relationship of grace and rewards. Doesn't God promise rewards to His faithful servants? Didn't Paul himself teach that we must appear before the judgment seat of Christ to receive what is due us?

God does promise rewards, and we must all appear before the judgment seat of Christ (see Matthew 25:21; 2 Corinthians 5:10). But these rewards are rewards of grace, not of merit. We never by our hard work or sacrificial service obligate God to reward us.

If all our service to God is made possible by His undeserved favor and made effective by the Spirit's power, we've really brought nothing to Him that we didn't first receive from Him. The Puritan Samuel Bolton said, "If there was anything of man's bringing, which was not of God's bestowing, though it were never so small, it would overturn the nature of grace, and make that of works which is of grace."[85] But every thought, word, or deed emanating from us that is in any way pleasing to God and glorifying to Him has its ultimate origin in God, because apart from Him, there's nothing good in us (Romans 7:18).

Transforming Grace

ASSUMING GOD'S ROLE

Judge not, that you be not judged.
(MATTHEW 7:1)

It's easy to become judgmental toward anyone whose opinions are different from ours, then to hide our judgmentalism under the cloak of Christian convictions. Paul wrote, "Stop judging one another regardless of which position you take." Then he added, "Who are you to pass judgment on the servant of another? It is before his own master that he stands or falls. And he will be upheld, for the Lord is able to make Him stand" (Romans 14:4). Basically, Paul was saying, "Stop trying to play God toward your fellow believers in Christ. God is the Judge, not you."

That's what we're doing when we judge others whose preferences and practices are different from ours. We're arrogating to ourselves a role God has reserved for Himself. Perhaps this is what Jesus had in mind in the well-known words of Matthew 7:3 when He said, "Why do you see the speck that is in your brother's eye, but do not notice the log that is in your own eye?" Could that log in our eye be the log of judgmentalism, arrogating to ourselves the role of God?

Here we see Jesus using hyperbole to make His point. Physically, it's impossible to have a log in one's eye. But the log in one's own eye may well represent God's verdict on our sin of judgmentalism. If I'm correct, then the seriousness of the sin of judgmentalism is not so much that I judge my brother as that in so doing I assume the role of God.

We sin if we condemn the obviously flagrant sins of others without at the same time acknowledging that we ourselves are still sinners before God. One of the major objectives of this book is to help us stop doing that.

Respectable Sins

DEAD TO SIN'S GUILT AND DOMINION

For one who has died has been set free from sin.

(ROMANS 6:7)

"What shall we say then?" the apostle Paul asked in Romans 6:1. "Are we to continue in sin that grace may abound?" If we're justified freely by God's grace through the work of Christ, doesn't more sin increasingly magnify God's grace?

"By no means!" responded Paul. "How can we who died to sin still live in it?" (Romans 6:2).

Paul's response is not an impatient "How could you think such a thing?" Rather, as he demonstrated in the verses that follow, such a practice cannot occur because a fundamental change has occurred in our relationship to sin. The expression Paul uses for this decisive change is, "We died to sin."

What does Paul mean by that? It's fairly obvious he doesn't mean we died to the daily committal of sin. If that were true, no honest person could claim to be justified, because we all sin daily. Nor does it mean we died in the sense of being no longer responsive to sin's temptations, or else Peter's admonition to abstain from sinful desires (1 Peter 2:11) would be pointless. So what does Paul mean?

Conservative evangelical commentators have generally taken one of two positions in answering this question. Several have held that Paul refers exclusively to the guilt of sin. That is, through our union with Christ in His death, we died to sin's guilt. Other commentators say that Paul means we died to sin's reign and dominion in our lives. Because sin no longer exercises absolute dominion over us, we no longer can continue in sin as a predominant way of life. We struggle with sin, and we do sin, but sin no longer is our master.

I believe both views should be brought together.

The Gospel for Real Life

The Best Defense

Be watchful.

(1 Corinthians 16:13)

With all the enemies from the world and from Satan arrayed against us, and a guerrilla army of flesh within our own hearts, how can we effectively watch against the temptations that constantly beset us? The old adage "The best defense is a good offense" is good advice for watching against temptation. The best offense is meditation on the Word of God and prayer. It's surely no coincidence that they're the only two spiritual exercises that we are encouraged to do *continually*. We're to meditate on God's Word "day and night" (Psalm 1:2), and Paul exhorted us to "pray continually" (1 Thessalonians 5:17, NIV).

There is power in the Word of God to keep us from sin: "I have stored up your word in my heart, that I might not sin against you" (Psalm 119:11). For every temptation that you face, there are specific passages of Scripture that address that issue. If you're not aware of some, ask your pastor or another mature Christian to help you find them. Then memorize those verses, meditate on them, and pray over them every day, asking the Holy Spirit to bring them to your mind in times of need. Ask, also, that He will strengthen your will to enable you to obey the word that He brings to your mind. All of us are being influenced by sinful society, so we want to do all we can to continually bring the Word of God to bear upon our thinking.

Also remember that Jesus told us to watch and *pray* against temptation (Matthew 26:41). We aren't capable of watching by ourselves. "Unless the LORD watches over the city, the watchman stays awake in vain" (Psalm 127:1). Even with our best diligence, we need the extra dimension of the Lord watching for us.

The Discipline of Grace

DELIVERANCE FROM SIN

Consider yourselves dead to sin.

(ROMANS 6:11)

The guilt of our sin in Adam resulted in our being given over to sin's
dominion as a penal consequence. When a judge sentences a convicted
criminal to five years in prison, that sentence is the penal consequence
of his crime — analogous to what God did to Adam and all his posterity. Part of the penal consequence of Adam's sin was being delivered into
sin's bondage.

When the prisoner has served his five years, his penal consequences
are over. The broken law no longer has a claim against him. In that sense
he has ended his relationship to the law and its penal consequences. He
must continue to obey the law in the future, but the particular offense that
sent him to prison has been dealt with forever. To use Paul's expression,
he has died to the law and its penal consequences.

How does this apply to us? Let me paraphrase from the comments of
John Brown, a nineteenth-century Scottish pastor, theologian, and author
of several commentaries: "The wages of sin is death. Until the condemning sentence is executed, a person is subject to sin, both in its power to
condemn and its power to deprave [or exert dominion]. But let the penal
consequences be fully endured, let the law's penalty be fully paid, and the
person is at once delivered from sin's condemning power and its deprav-
ing influence or dominion. It's in this way that all that are in Christ Jesus,
all that have been justified by His grace, have died, not in their own
persons, but in the person of their Surety. They are therefore delivered
from the reign of sin — from its power to condemn, and therefore, also
from its power to rule in the heart and life."[86]

The Gospel for Real Life

ACCEPTED THROUGH CHRIST

It is through him that we utter our Amen to God for his glory.

(2 CORINTHIANS 1:20)

Even the good works we bring to God are in themselves defective, both in motive and performance. It is virtually impossible to purge our motives completely of pride and self-gratification. And we can never perfectly perform those good works. The best we can do falls short of what God requires, but the truth is, we never actually do the best we can, let alone what would meet God's perfect standard.

That is why Peter wrote, "You yourselves like living stones are being built up as a spiritual house, to be a holy priesthood, to offer spiritual sacrifices acceptable to God *through Jesus Christ*" (1 Peter 2:5). Our best works are acceptable to God only because they are made acceptable by the merit of Jesus Christ. But God does accept them through Christ; He accepts them on the basis of His grace.

Ernest Kevan quoted one of the Puritans on the imperfection of our works as follows: "We do not do all that is commanded but come short of our duty, and that which we do is imperfect and defective in respect of manner and measure; and therefore in justice deserves punishment, rather than reward: and consequently the reward, when it is given, is to be ascribed to God's undeserved mercy and not to our merit."[87]

So the entire Christian life is a life lived under grace from first to last, from beginning to end, all "to the praise of his glorious grace, which he has freely given us in the One he loves" (Ephesians 1:6).

Transforming Grace

DEFINITIVE SANCTIFICATION

You were sanctified.
(1 CORINTHIANS 6:11)

Our slavery to the dominion of sin was the result of our guilt incurred by Adam's sin, further aggravated by our own personal sin. Through our union with Christ in His death, however, our guilt, both from Adam's and from our own sins, was forever dealt with. Having then died with Christ to the guilt of sin, we died to, or were delivered from, the dominion of sin.

Whether we say we died to the dominion of sin, or we were delivered from the dominion of sin through our death to the guilt of sin, the result is the same. We no longer continue in sin as a dominant lifestyle. Sin no longer has dominion over us.

This death to, or deliverance from, sin's dominion is often called *definitive sanctification*. You're probably more or less familiar with the word *sanctification*, which historically has been used as a shorthand expression for Christian growth. Its basic meaning, however, is "separation," and in using the term *definitive sanctification* we're speaking of a decisive break—a decisive separation from sin as a ruling power in the believer's life. It's a point-in-time event occurring simultaneously with justification. It's a change wrought in us by the monergistic action of the Holy Spirit as He removes us from the kingdom of darkness and brings us into the kingdom of Christ (Colossians 1:13).

That's why Paul could write to the Corinthian believers as those who had already been sanctified, even though they were still quite immature in their Christian walk (see 1 Corinthians 1:2,30; 6:11). This definitive break with the dominion of sin, which is solely the work of the Holy Spirit, occurs in the life of everyone who trusts in Christ as Savior. There's no such thing as justification without definitive sanctification.

The Gospel for Real Life

PRAYING AGAINST TEMPTATION

God is faithful, and he will not let you be tempted beyond your ability.

(1 CORINTHIANS 10:13)

Jesus taught us to pray, "And lead us not into temptation, but deliver us from evil" (Matthew 6:13).

Here we see two requests: that we not be led into temptation, and that we be delivered from the Evil One. Because we know from James 1:13 that God does not tempt anyone, the first part must be understood as a request that God will not providentially bring us into the way of temptation. It is the prayer of the believer who sees his or her weaknesses and prays to not even encounter those temptations.

Of course, if we're praying not to be led into temptation, we should take steps ourselves to see that we do not *walk* into the way of temptation. Paul said in 1 Thessalonians 5:22, "*Abstain* from every form of evil." He exhorted the Corinthian church, "*Flee* from sexual immorality" and he told Timothy, "*Flee* youthful passions" (1 Corinthians 6:18; 2 Timothy 2:22). *Flee*, of course, denotes a stronger response than *abstain*, but both are necessary. We can abstain from certain temptations by not turning on the television or picking up certain magazines. But sometimes a temptation presents itself, and then we must flee. This is all part of watching.

The second request Jesus taught us in Matthew 6:13 is "deliver us from evil," or, in some translations, "from the evil one" — meaning, of course, Satan. We need to pray defensively against the attacks of Satan. Christ did defeat him on the cross (Colossians 2:15), and we must by faith lay hold of that victory as we pray that we will be delivered from his attacks.[88]

The Discipline of Grace

SOMETHING TO BELIEVE

Blessed is the man against whom the Lord will not count his sin.
(ROMANS 4:8)

We're free from both the guilt and the reigning power or dominion of sin in our lives. But of what use is this information to us? How can it help when we're struggling with persistent sin patterns and see ourselves giving in to sinful desires? Here's where Paul's instructions in Romans 6:11 can help us: "In the same way, count yourselves dead to sin but alive to God in Christ Jesus" (NIV).

Paul isn't telling us to *do* something but to *believe* something. We're to count on, or believe, that we're dead to sin.

We're dead to its guilt. God no longer counts it against us. We're no longer under condemnation (Romans 4:8; 8:1). This is not make-believe. You are indeed guilty in yourself, but God no longer regards you as guilty, because the guilt has already been borne by Christ as your substitute. The sentence has been served. The penalty has been paid. To use Paul's expression, you have died to sin's guilt.

When we're painfully conscious of sin in our lives, it's difficult to count on the fact that we're dead to its guilt. All the more reason to hold steadfast to the promise of God. Just as it seemed incredible to Abraham that he could have a son when he was nearly a hundred years old and Sarah's womb was dead, so it often seems incredible to us to believe that we've died to sin's guilt when it appears so ugly in our own sight. But just as Abraham did not weaken in faith, but believed the promise of God, so we must believe what God says to us. There is no condemnation for those who are in Christ Jesus. We have died to sin's guilt.

The Gospel for Real Life

Hundredfold Reward, by Grace

And everyone who has left houses or brothers or sisters . . .
for my name's sake, will receive a hundredfold.

(Matthew 19:29)

In the verses immediately preceding the parable of the workers in the vineyard in Matthew 20, Jesus promised a "hundredfold" reward, or ten thousand percent, to "everyone" who has sacrificed for Jesus' sake. God's rewards to us will not only be of grace, but will indeed be gracious — that is, generous beyond all measure.

So the grace of God in our service to Him does not negate rewards but rather makes them possible. As R. C. Sproul said, "But the blessing Christ promised, the blessing of great reward, is a reward of grace. The blessing is promised even though it is not earned. Augustine said it this way: Our rewards in heaven are a result of God's crowning His own gifts."[89]

This is the amazing story of God's grace. God saves us by His grace and transforms us more and more into the likeness of His Son by His grace. In all our trials and afflictions, He sustains and strengthens us by His grace. He calls us by grace to perform our own unique function within the body of Christ. Then, again by grace, He gives to each of us the spiritual gifts necessary to fulfill our calling. As we serve Him, He makes that service acceptable to Himself by grace, and then rewards us a hundredfold by grace.

In Romans 1:17, Paul spoke of the gospel as revealing "a righteousness that is by faith from first to last" — that is, from beginning to end. This is also an appropriate term for grace, for faith is no more than the response to and appropriation of the grace of God.

Transforming Grace

DO NOT LET SIN REIGN

If by the Spirit you put to death the deeds of the body, you will live.

(ROMANS 8:13)

We have died not only to sin's guilt but also to its reigning power in our lives. Although sin as an active principle is still with us, it can no longer reign supreme in our lives. We're united to Christ, and His Spirit has come to reside in us. We've been delivered from Satan's power and given a new heart (Ezekiel 36:26; Acts 26:18). However, as believers we experience a tension that's like a tug-of-war. Paul described it in Galatians 5:17: "For the sinful nature desires what is contrary to the Spirit, and the Spirit what is contrary to the sinful nature. They are in conflict with each other, so that you do not do what you want."

We must acknowledge this tension if we're to make progress in the Christian life. Indwelling sin is like a disease that we can't begin to deal with until we acknowledge its presence. But in the case of sin, we must also count on the fact that, though it still resides in us, it no longer has dominion over us. As Paul said, "For sin shall not be your master, because you are not under law, but under grace" (Romans 6:14).

Because we have the assurance that sin shall not be our master, we are not to let it reign in our mortal bodies so that we obey its evil desires (Romans 6:12). Rather we are, by the enabling power of the Spirit, to put to death the misdeeds of the body (Romans 8:13) and to abstain from sinful desires, which war against our souls (1 Peter 2:11). We're called to an active, vigorous warfare against the principle of sin that remains in us.

The Gospel for Real Life

Unquestionable Love

The Lord is . . . kind in all his works.

(Psalm 145:17)

The apostle John said, "God is love" (1 John 4:8). This succinct statement, along with its parallel one, "God is light" (1 John 1:5; that is, God is holy), sums up the essential character of God, as revealed to us in the Scriptures. Just as it is impossible in the very nature of God for Him to be anything but perfectly holy, so it is impossible for Him to be anything but perfectly good.

Because God is love, an essential part of His nature is to do good and show mercy to His creatures. Psalm 145 speaks of His "abundant goodness," of His "abounding in steadfast love" and being "good to all," of how "his mercy is over all that he has made" (verses 7-9). Even in His role of Judge of rebellious men, He declares, "I take no pleasure in the death of the wicked" (Ezekiel 33:11, niv).

When calamity after calamity seems to surge in upon us, we'll be tempted to doubt God's love. Not only do we struggle with our own doubts, but Satan seizes these occasions to whisper accusations against God: "If He loved you, He wouldn't have allowed this to happen." My own experience suggests that Satan attacks us far more in the area of God's love than either His sovereignty or His wisdom.

If we're to honor God by trusting Him, we must not allow such thoughts to lodge in our minds. As Philip Hughes said, "To question the goodness of God is, in essence, to imply that man is more concerned about goodness than is God. . . . To suggest that man is kinder than God is to subvert the very nature of God. . . . It is to deny God; and this is precisely the thrust of the temptation to question the goodness of God."[90]

Trusting God

MAKING LIGHT OF GOD'S DISCIPLINE

Do not regard lightly the discipline of the Lord.

(HEBREWS 12:5)

We're warned in Hebrews 12:5 not to regard lightly the Lord's discipline. It may be difficult for us to conceive of doing this, but one way is when we count His discipline of little value — as something only to be endured rather than as something for our profit.

We also despise God's discipline of adversity when we fail to see God's hand in the hardships we encounter. Instead of acknowledging them as from God, we tend to view adversities as chance occurrences; we don't seek God's purpose in the discipline, but instead focus entirely on finding relief.

The Scriptures tell us, however, that adversities are not chance occurrences; like our so-called blessings, they all come from the hand of God. This truth is scattered throughout the Bible. "In the day of prosperity be joyful, and in the day of adversity consider: God has made the one as well as the other" (Ecclesiastes 7:14). "I form light and create darkness, I make well-being and create calamity, I am the LORD, who does all these things" (Isaiah 45:7). "Is it not from the mouth of the Most High that good and bad come?" (Lamentations 3:38). "Does disaster come to a city, unless the LORD has done it?" (Amos 3:6).

Some Christians have difficulty with this truth and even deny it, because they cannot believe that a "God of love" is responsible for either the individual or public disasters that come to us. But the clear testimony of Scripture stands against all our protestations. So we need to recognize the hand of God in all the adversities we encounter and not make light of His discipline.

The Discipline of Grace

THE ONLY OBJECTIVE AUTHORITY

The Lord . . . bore witness to the word of his grace.

(ACTS 14:3)

We don't understand just how the Holy Spirit interacts with our human spirit, but we do know He most often uses His Word. He brings to our mind some Scripture particularly appropriate to the situation. He may do this through a sermon, a Christian book, the encouraging words of a friend, or our own reading or study of Scripture. In my case, since I've memorized so many Scriptures over the years, He often brings to my mind a memorized verse.

In Acts 20:32, Paul said to the Ephesian elders, "Now I commend you to God and to the word of his grace, which is able to build you up and to give you the inheritance among all those who are sanctified" (Acts 20:32). Earlier in verse 24, Paul had referred to "the gospel of the grace of God," the good news of salvation through faith in Christ Jesus. In verse 32, however, as he speaks of "the word of his grace, which is able to build you up," the reference is to the ongoing use of Scripture in our daily lives to build us up in the Christian faith. Paul specifically called this "the word of his grace," the Word through which we come to understand and appropriate God's grace in our daily lives.

The Bible is not merely a book about God; it is a book *from* God. "All Scripture is breathed out by God" (2 Timothy 3:16, NIV). The Bible is God's self-revelation to us all. He wants us to know about Himself and His provision for our salvation and our spiritual growth. It is God's only objective, authoritative communication to us.

Transforming Grace

LIKE ARMIES IN BATTLE

The spirit indeed is willing, but the flesh is weak.

(MATTHEW 26:41)

William Romaine (born 1714) was one of the leaders of the eighteenth-century revival in England, along with George Whitefield and the Wesley brothers. In his classic work on faith he wrote, "No sin can be crucified either in heart or life, unless it be first pardoned in conscience, because there will be want of faith to receive the strength of Jesus, by whom alone it can be crucified. If it be not mortified in its guilt, it cannot be subdued in its power."[91]

What Romaine was saying is that if you do not believe you are dead to sin's guilt, you cannot trust Christ for the strength to subdue its power in your life. So the place to begin in dealing with sin in your life is to count on the fact that you died to its guilt through your union with Christ in His death. This is an important truth you need to ponder and pray over until the Holy Spirit convinces you of it in both your head and heart.

Meanwhile, to make progress in the Christian life, we must acknowledge the continuing tension between our sinful nature and the Spirit of God within us.

Observing this "internal conflict," George Smeaton noted, "And the strange thing is, that in this conflict the power and faculties of the Christian seem to be occupied at one time by the one, and at another time by the other. The same intellect, will, and affections come under different influences, like two conflicting armies occupying the ground, and in turn driven from the field."[92]

With any two opposing forces, the direction of movement often goes back and forth until one eventually prevails. This is the way it will be with us until the Holy Spirit finally prevails.

The Gospel for Real Life

DISCOURAGED BY HIS DISCIPLINE

Do not regard lightly the discipline of the Lord,
nor be weary when reproved by him.

(HEBREWS 12:5)

Another improper response to God's discipline is to "be weary" when He reproves us. We tend to lose heart when we think God is disciplining us out of anger instead of out of love. Hebrews 12:6, however, explicitly states that "the Lord disciplines the one he loves." I acknowledge it's often difficult to sense God's love when we are undergoing His discipline, but we must by faith accept the testimony of Scripture.

The Puritan Samuel Bolton (1606–1654) wrote, "God has thoughts of love in all He does to His people. The ground of His dealings with us is love (though the occasion may be sin), the manner of His dealings is love, and the purpose of His dealings is love. He has regard, in all, to our good here, to make us partakers of His holiness, and to our glory hereafter, to make us partakers of His glory."[93]

When the writer of Hebrews told us not to lightly regard the Lord's discipline or be wearied by His reproof, his purpose was to encourage us. A good part of that encouragement must come from the realization that the hardships we encounter come from a God who is not only in sovereign control of every circumstance of our lives, but who also loves us, and who deals with us only on the basis of love. He's not only the sovereign ruler of His universe, but also our heavenly Father through the Lord Jesus Christ.

So in times of adversity, don't lose heart under it by failing to see His love in it.

The Discipline of Grace

CHRIST'S POWER, NOT OURS

*His divine power has granted to us all things
that pertain to life and godliness.*

(2 PETER 1:3)

We are not to wage this warfare against sin in the strength of our own willpower. Instead, just as we by faith look to Christ for our righteous standing before God, so by faith we're to look to Him for the enabling power to live the Christian life. This power comes as a result of our vital or living union with Him. Jesus referred to this union in John 15:1-5 when He called Himself the vine and us the branches. Just as the branches derive their life and nourishment from the vine, so we are to receive our spiritual life and power from Him.

All believers are spiritually united to Christ in such a way that our spiritual life comes from Him. We're not completely passive, however, in this relationship. Rather, we're to abide or remain in Him by faith. We're to actively rely on Christ for the enabling power we need to wage war against the sin that remains in us, to put on the positive virtues of Christlike character (called "the fruit of the Spirit" in Galatians 5:22-23), and to serve Christ effectively in all that He calls us to do.

The apostle Paul had in mind our union with Christ and the power that comes from Him in such Scriptures as Philippians 4:13, "I can do everything through him who gives me strength" (NIV), and Colossians 1:29, "To this end I labor, struggling with all his energy, which so powerfully works in me" (NIV). Paul waged war against indwelling sin, and he worked hard in ministry, but he did both in dependence on Christ and the power that comes through a living union with Him.

The Gospel for Real Life

WORD OF HIS GRACE

I commend you . . . to the word of his grace.

(ACTS 20:32)

We need to get beyond the "how-tos" of Scripture — how to raise children, manage finances, witness to unbelievers — and all other such utilitarian approaches to Scripture. Such practical instruction is indeed valuable, but we need to go beyond that. Our practical age has come to disparage a firm doctrinal understanding of Scripture as being of no practical value. But there's nothing more practical for our daily lives than knowing God. Only in Scripture has God revealed to us the truths about His person and His character.

But the Bible is more than merely objective truth; it's actually life-giving and life-sustaining. "It is no empty word for you, but your very life" (Deuteronomy 32:47). Growth in the grace of God requires growth in our assimilation of the Word of God. In the biological realm, assimilation is the process by which nourishment is changed into living tissue. In the spiritual realm, it's the process by which the written Word of God is absorbed into our hearts and becomes, figuratively speaking, living spiritual tissue.

How do we know God's grace is sufficient for our particular "thorns"? How do we rightly understand what it means to live "by the grace of God"? How do we learn about the "throne of grace" where we receive mercy and find grace to help us in our time of need? Where do we discover that God is the gracious landowner who gives us far, far more than we deserve? The answer to all these questions is the Scriptures. That's why Scripture is called the Word of His grace. God uses Scripture to mediate His grace to us. R. C. H. Lenski said, "God and the Word of his grace always go together; God lets his grace flow out through that Word."[94]

Transforming Grace

PROGRESSIVE SANCTIFICATION

*As you received from us how you ought to live,
and to please God, . . . do so more and more.*

(1 THESSALONIANS 4:1)

Warring against the sin that remains in us and putting on Christlike character is usually called *sanctification*. But because the term *definitive sanctification* is used to describe the point-in-time decisive deliverance from sin's dominion, it's helpful to speak of Christian growth as *progressive sanctification*. The word *progressive* indicates positive change. To use the tug-of-war analogy, it assumes that though the rope may move back and forth, over time it moves in the right direction until finally at the end of our lives we win the tug-of-war against sin.

There's no doubt this rope must move in the right direction. The New Testament writers assume our growth and continually urge us to pursue it. We're to pursue holiness "more and more," and to love each other "more and more" (1 Thessalonians 4:1,9-10). We're to possess the qualities of Christian character "in increasing measure" (2 Peter 1:8, NIV). However, we can always expect resistance. To stay with the tug-of-war analogy, although the Spirit who dwells within us is stronger than the sinful nature, that nature continues to "dig in its heels" every step of the way. And sometimes it will pull the rope in the wrong direction.

What is it then that will keep us going in the face of this internal conflict? The answer is the gospel. What will motivate us and keep us going — even in the midst of the tension between the Spirit and the sinful nature — is the assurance in the gospel that we have indeed died to the guilt of sin, that there's no condemnation for us who are in Christ Jesus, that the Lord will never count our sins against us, and that we're truly delivered from the reigning power of sin.

The Gospel for Real Life

HIS LOVING DISCIPLINE

The Lord . . . chastises every son whom he receives.

(HEBREWS 12:6)

In addition to disciplining those He loves, the Lord also, as our Father, "chastises" or punishes us. Punishment may serve one of two purposes: the execution of justice or the correction of character. When a person convicted of a crime is sent to prison, that's punishment in the execution of justice. When a loving parent punishes a child, it's for the correction of the child's character.

Although today we usually equate discipline with punishment, the biblical use of the word *discipline* had a broader meaning. Punishment would have been one aspect of the overall program of child-training. But all of God's discipline, including punishment for disobedience that He sends to us in the form of adversity, is administered in love and for our welfare. We must never equate His punishment of us with the negative emotions we often see in a human parent.

God does punish in the execution of justice. The Scriptures say, "God is just" (2 Thessalonians 1:6, NIV) and "'It is mine to avenge; I will repay,' says the Lord" (Romans 12:19, NIV). But as far as believers are concerned, God has already executed the justice we should have received on His Son on the cross. Christ fully satisfied the justice of God and turned away His wrath from us. Therefore, God's punishment of us is always corrective and always administered in love and for our welfare.

In times of adversity Satan will seek to plant the thought in our mind that God is angry with us and is disciplining us out of wrath. Here is another instance when we need to preach the gospel to ourselves. The gospel will reassure us that the penalty for our sins has been paid, that God's justice has been fully satisfied.

The Discipline of Grace

HEALTHY EXPOSURE TO GOD'S WORD

. All Scripture is . . . profitable for teaching, for reproof,
for correction, and for training in righteousness.

(2 TIMOTHY 3:16)

The close connection between God and the Word of His grace is illustrated in Romans 15:4-5: "For whatever was written in former days was written for our instruction, that through endurance and through the encouragement of the Scriptures we might have hope. May the God of endurance and encouragement grant you to live in such harmony with one another, in accord with Christ Jesus" (Romans 15:4-5).

Paul tells us here that we receive endurance and encouragement from Scripture. Then he names God as the source of endurance and encouragement. Endurance and encouragement are provisions of God's grace "to help us in our time of need." As we go to the throne of grace asking for it, God does provide. But He usually provides through Scripture.

If we are to appropriate the grace of God, we must regularly expose ourselves directly to the Word of God. It is not enough to only hear it preached or taught in our churches on Sundays, as important as those avenues are. We need a regular plan of reading, study, and yes, even memorization. Bible study and Scripture memorization earn no merit with God. We never earn God's blessing by doing these things, any more than we earn His blessing by eating nutritious food. But as the eating of proper food is necessary to sustain a healthy physical life, so the regular intake of God's Word is necessary to sustain a healthy spiritual life and to regularly appropriate His grace.

If we're to appropriate the grace of God, we must become intimate friends with the Bible. We must seek to know and understand Scripture's great truths about God and His character, and about man and his desperate need of God's grace.

Transforming Grace

SINS OF THE TONGUE

> *The tongue is a fire, a world of unrighteousness.*
>
> (JAMES 3:6)

The Bible is replete with warnings against sins of the tongue. The book of Proverbs alone contains about sixty such warnings. Jesus warned that we'll give account for every careless word we speak (Matthew 12:36). And then there is that well-known passage in James 3 where he speaks of the tongue's sinful effects, likening them to the spark that sets a forest ablaze.

The Scripture passage that has helped me most to deal with the sins of the tongue is Ephesians 4:29: "Let no corrupting talk come out of your mouths, but only such as is good for building up, as fits the occasion, that it may give grace to those who hear." This is an application of Paul's "put off / put on" principle that he set forth in Ephesians 4:22-24. The principle is that we're to put off the sinful traits of the old self and, at the same time, give diligence to putting on the gracious traits of the new self created in Christ.

As we look at Ephesians 4:29, we see that we're not to let any corrupting talk come out of our mouths. Corrupting talk is not limited to profanity or obscene speech. It includes all the various types of negative speech — including lying, slander, critical speech (even when true), harsh words, insults, sarcasm, and ridicule. Note Paul's absolute prohibition: *No* corrupting talk. None whatsoever. This means *no* gossip, *no* sarcasm, *no* critical speech, *no* harsh words. All these sinful words that tend to tear down another person must be put out of our speech. Think about what the church of Jesus Christ would look like if we all sought to apply Paul's words.

Respectable Sins

THE SECRET

The love of Christ controls us.
(2 CORINTHIANS 5:14)

We must always keep focused on the gospel. Horatius Bonar, nineteenth-century Scottish pastor and author, wrote: "The secret of a believer's holy walk is his continual recurrence to the blood of the Surety, and his daily [communion] with a crucified and risen Lord. All divine life, and all precious fruits of it, pardon, peace, and holiness, spring from the cross. All fancied sanctification which does not arise wholly from the blood of the cross is nothing better than Pharisaism. If we would be holy, we must get to the cross, and dwell there; else, notwithstanding all our labour, diligence, fasting, praying and good works, we shall be yet void of real sanctification, destitute of those humble, gracious tempers which accompany a clear view of the cross.

"False ideas of holiness are common, not only among those who profess false religions, but among those who profess the true. The love of God to us, and our love to Him, work together for producing holiness. Terror accomplishes no real obedience. Suspense brings forth no fruit unto holiness. No gloomy uncertainty as to God's favour can subdue one lust, or correct our crookedness of will. But the free pardon of the cross uproots sin, and withers all its branches. Only the certainty of love, forgiving love, can do this. . . .

"Free and warm reception into the divine favour is the strongest of all motives in leading a man to seek conformity to Him who has thus freely forgiven him all trespasses."[95]

Paul said the same thing very succinctly: "For Christ's love compels us" (2 Corinthians 5:14, NIV). To be compelled is to be highly motivated. We're to be motivated by Christ's love for us. And where do we learn of His love? Where do we hear Him say, "I love you"? In the gospel.

The Gospel for Real Life

All Hardship Is Discipline

It is for discipline that you have to endure.

(Hebrews 12:7)

All hardship of whatever kind has a disciplinary purpose for us. There's no such thing as pain without a purpose in the life of a believer. Every expression of discipline has as its intended end conformity to the likeness of Christ.

Can we tell if a particular adversity is related to some specific sin in our lives? Not with certainty, but my belief is that the Holy Spirit will bring such a connection to our attention if we need to know in order to deal with a particular sin. If nothing comes to mind, we can ask God if there's something He wants us to consciously learn. Beyond that, it's vain to speculate as to why God has brought a particular hardship into our lives. Part of the sanctifying process of adversity is its mystery — our inability to make any sense out of it.

Although all pain has a purpose in the mind of God, that purpose is usually hidden from us. As Paul wrote, "How unsearchable are his judgments and how inscrutable his ways!" (Romans 11:33). The Williams New Testament expresses Paul's thought in an even more forceful way: "How unsearchable His decisions, and how mysterious His methods!"[96] God's ways, being infinitely higher than our ways, will usually remain a mystery to us.

When we're unable to make any sense of our circumstances, we need to come back to the assurance in Hebrews 12:7: "God is treating you as sons." He is the one in charge of sanctification in our lives. He knows exactly what and how much adversity will develop more Christlikeness in us and He will not bring, nor allow to come into our lives, any more than is needful for His purpose.

The Discipline of Grace

The Word Stored Up

The law of his God is in his heart; his steps do not slip.
(Psalm 37:31)

I strongly advocate Scripture memorization. In our warfare against Satan and his emissaries, we're told to take "the sword of the Spirit, which is the word of God" (Ephesians 6:17). Charles Hodge commented on this statement: "In opposition . . . to all the suggestions of the devil, the safe, simple, and sufficient answer is the word of God. This puts to flight all the powers of darkness. The Christian finds this to be true in his individual experience. It dissipates his doubts; it drives away his fears; it delivers him from the power of Satan."[97]

To take up this sword, we must have it at hand, in our hearts. We must be like the psalmist who said, "I have stored up your word in my heart, that I might not sin against you" (Psalm 119:11). This principle of storing up God's Word has a much wider application than only keeping us from sin. The Word, stored in the heart, provides a mental depository for the Holy Spirit to use to mediate His grace to us, whatever our need for grace might be.

I recently received a phone call with disturbing news, and I went to bed that night feeling as if I'd just received an emotional kick in the stomach. The next morning, however, I awakened with 1 Peter 5:7 going through my mind: "Cast all your anxiety on him because he cares for you" (NIV). I was given grace by God's Spirit to believe that He did care in this specific situation. That is only one in a series of incidents occurring frequently in my life — and I'm sure in the lives of all other believers who store up God's Word in their hearts.

Transforming Grace

A BLESSING TO ALL

> *I will make you as a light for the nations,*
> *that my salvation may reach to the end of the earth.*
> (ISAIAH 49:6)

To explore what the apostle Paul called "the unsearchable riches of Christ" (Ephesians 3:8) — the gospel — we rightly examine our need of the gospel, the work of Christ in meeting that need, and the application of His work to our individual lives in justification, adoption, glorification, and sanctification. But if we stopped at that point, it could seem as if the gospel promotes only an attitude of pure self-interest on our part: *What will the gospel do for me?* Or at most, the gospel would be about God and me.

But the gospel is not about God and me. The gospel is about God and the world: "In Christ God was reconciling the *world* to himself" (2 Corinthians 5:19).

We're not to be a terminus point for the gospel, but rather a way station in its progress to the ends of the earth. God intends that everyone who has embraced the gospel become a part of the great enterprise of spreading the gospel. What our particular part may be will vary from person to person, but all of us should be involved.

The same Scriptures that in centuries past motivated the pioneers in world missions should motivate us today. A good starting point is Genesis 12:3, where God promises Abraham that "all peoples on earth will be blessed through you" (NIV). God repeats this promise in Genesis 22:18, where He more specifically says, "through your offspring all nations on earth will be blessed" (NIV). In Galatians 3:16 the apostle Paul identified this "offspring" as Christ. God's promise to Abraham, then, is that *all nations* will be blessed through Christ — that is, through His atoning work for us.

The Gospel for Real Life

SUBMISSION TO OUR FATHER'S DISCIPLINE

Submit yourselves therefore to God.

(JAMES 4:7)

To gain the most profit from the discipline of hardship, we need to submit to it. The author of Hebrews said that if we respected our fathers' discipline, how much more should we submit to God's discipline: "We have had earthly fathers who disciplined us and we respected them. Shall we not much more be subject to the Father of spirits and live?" (12:9). Our fathers' discipline was at best imperfect, both in motive and in application. But God's discipline is perfect, exactly suited to our needs.

How do we submit to God's discipline? Negatively, it means that we don't become angry at God, or charge Him with injustice, when difficult circumstances come into our lives. I believe even short-term anger toward God is sin, for which we need to repent. Though the anger may be an emotional response, it's still a charge of injustice against God. Surely that is sin. It's even more serious when someone allows anger toward God to continue over months or even years. Such an attitude amounts to a grudge against God and is actually rebellion. It is certainly not submitting to our heavenly Father.

Positively, we submit to God's discipline when we accept all hardship as coming from His loving hand for our good. This means that our primary response would be one of humble submission and trust. As Peter wrote, "Humble yourselves, therefore, under God's mighty hand, that he may lift you up in due time" (1 Peter 5:6). We should submit to God's providential dealings with us, knowing there's still much in our characters that needs improving. We should trust Him, believing that He's infinite in His wisdom and knows exactly the kind and extent of adversity we need to accomplish His purpose.

The Discipline of Grace

THE SPIRIT'S SWORD

> *Take . . . the sword of the Spirit, which is the word of God.*
> (EPHESIANS 6:17)

If you desire to appropriate God's grace, you must have the sword of the Spirit — the Word of God — available in your mind for the Spirit to use. In fact the structure of Ephesians 6:17 provides a very instructive insight into the interaction between the Holy Spirit and the believer. Paul said we're to take the sword of the Spirit. That's something we must do. And yet it is the Spirit's sword, not ours. *He* must make it effective. The bare quoting of Scripture does not make it effective in our hearts; only the Spirit can do that. But He will not make His sword effective unless we take it up.

Often God's Word is not made effective immediately. In fact, there are many times when I struggle over an issue for a period of days, mulling over several pertinent passages of Scripture and crying out for grace, before the Holy Spirit finally makes them effective and gives His grace, helping in time of need. The Spirit of God is sovereign in His working, and we cannot squeeze Him into the mold of our spiritual formulas: "Pray for grace, quote some verses, and receive a guaranteed answer."

God also has His own timetable. Sometimes He grants grace to help almost immediately. At other times, He allows us to struggle for days, perhaps even weeks or months, before we receive the grace to help. Regardless of the delays He may impose, we must continue to come to the throne of grace believing His promise to grant grace to help, and we must continue to resort to appropriate Scripture until He makes it effective in our hearts. Our responsibility is to take up the sword of the Spirit; His prerogative is to make it effective.

Transforming Grace

THE REIGN OF CHRIST

All things have been handed over to me by my Father.

(MATTHEW 11:27)

The concept of Christ's reign is stated most explicitly in the words of Jesus commonly known as the Great Commission: "All authority in heaven and on earth has been given to me. Go therefore and make disciples of all nations, baptizing them in the name of the Father and of the Son and of the Holy Spirit, teaching them to observe all that I have commanded you. And behold, I am with you always, to the end of the age" (Matthew 28:18-20).

Here Jesus first asserts His universal authority, then commands His disciples to go and make disciples — to bring people of all nations under the sway of His authority. Whatever other meanings we may include in the word *disciple*, it must capture this idea of coming under the reign and rule of Jesus Christ.

The *reign* of Christ among all nations is a parallel goal to that of bringing the *blessing* of Christ to all nations. The goal of Christ's universal *blessing* focuses on people's needs. They desperately need to be rescued from God's coming wrath, and to be redeemed from their futile, destructive ways of life.

The goal of Christ's *reign* focuses on His authority in the hearts of those people. Jesus came "to redeem us from all wickedness and to purify for himself a people that are his very own, eager to do what is good" (Titus 2:14). This speaks of the rule and reign of Christ in the heart of every individual believer.

Both these goals — the blessing and the reign of Christ — are accomplished through the successful proclamation of the gospel among all nations, or to the ends of the earth.

The Gospel for Real Life

SUBMITTING TO HIS DISCIPLINE

Shall we not much more be subject to the Father of spirits and live?

(HEBREWS 12:9)

John Owen said that to submit to the Father of our spirits denotes "an acquiescence in His sovereign right to do what He will with us as His own; a renunciation of self-will; an acknowledgment of His righteousness and wisdom in all His dealings with us; a sense of His care and love, with a due apprehension of the end of His chastisements; a diligent application of ourselves unto His mind and will, or to what He calls us to in an especial manner at that season; a keeping of our souls by persevering faith from weariness and despondency; a full resignation of ourselves to His will, as to the matter, manner, times, and continuance of our afflictions."[98]

Owen's quote is a mouthful, but I've used it because it's such a complete description of the attitude and response toward adversity we need to develop. I encourage you to go back over it several times until you fully grasp what he said.

Submitting to God's discipline doesn't mean we shouldn't pray for relief from the difficulty or seek legitimate means to gain relief. Sometimes the end God has in mind is to exercise our faith, so He brings us into straitened circumstances so that we might look up to Him and see His deliverance. But strengthening our faith is an important aspect of discipline.

The main thing is our attitude. We can pray earnestly to God for relief and still be submissive to Him regarding the outcome. Jesus is our supreme example in this as He prayed the night before His crucifixion, "My Father, if it is possible, may this cup be taken from me. Yet not as I will, but as you will" (Matthew 26:39, NIV).

The Discipline of Grace

SEEING GOD'S HAND

Humble yourselves . . . under the mighty hand of God.

(1 PETER 5:6)

Job and Joseph are examples of those who saw God's hand in their circumstances. In one day, Job's oxen were stolen, his camels carried off, his servants murdered. Lightning burned up his sheep, and a mighty wind struck the house of his oldest son, killing all his children. Later Job himself was afflicted with painful sores from head to feet. He responded, "The LORD gave, and the LORD has taken away" (Job 1:21). With respect to his own affliction he said, "Shall we receive good from God, and shall we not receive evil?" (2:10).

Note that Job ascribed his sufferings to the hand of God. He saw beyond the actions of evil men and the disasters of nature to the sovereign God who controlled those events. At the close of Job's story, we read that his relatives and friends "showed him sympathy and comforted him for all the evil that *the LORD* had brought upon him" (Job 42:11). Though the writer had himself reported the malicious activity of Satan in Job's life at the beginning of the narrative, he still ultimately ascribed Job's troubles to the Lord.

Joseph, when he finally revealed his identity to his wicked brothers who had sold him into slavery, saw beyond their evil acts and said, "It was not you who sent me here, but God" (Genesis 45:8). He recognized that God in His sovereignty used even the heinous sins of his brothers to accomplish His purpose.

If you and I are to appropriate God's grace in our times of need, we must see His sovereignty ultimately ruling in all the circumstances of our lives. And when those circumstances are difficult, disappointing, or humiliating, we must humble ourselves under His mighty hand.

Transforming Grace

MADE PERSONALLY

Blessed be the LORD . . . who alone does wondrous things.

(PSALM 72:18)

David said, "I praise you because I am fearfully and wonderfully made" (Psalm 139:14, NIV). We might say, "That's well enough for David; he was handsome, athletic, skilled in war, and a gifted musician. But look at me. I'm very ordinary physically and mentally." In fact, some people feel they don't even measure up to ordinary.

I understand people who feel that way. In addition to having hearing and vision disabilities, I've never been excited about my physical appearance. But God didn't give His own Son handsome features in His human body: "He had no beauty or majesty to attract us to him, nothing in his appearance that we should desire him" (Isaiah 53:2, NIV). Jesus, at best, was apparently nondescript in His physical appearance. This never bothered Him nor interfered with His carrying out His Father's will.

David praised God not because he was handsome but because *God made him.* Dwell on that thought: The eternal God, infinite in His wisdom and perfect in His love, personally made you and me. He gave you your body, your mental abilities, and your basic personality because that's the way He wanted you to be — and He loves you and wants to glorify Himself through you.

This is our foundation for self-acceptance. God sovereignly and directly created us to be who we are, disabilities or physical flaws and all. We need to learn to think like George MacDonald, who said, "I would rather be what God chose to make me than the most glorious creature that I could think of; for to have been thought about, born in God's thought, and then made by God, is the dearest, grandest, and most precious thing in all thinking."[99]

Trusting God

Our Task

May he have dominion . . . to the ends of the earth!
(Psalm 72:8)

As people believe the gospel and are saved, the reign of Christ is established in principle in their hearts. They're delivered from the kingdom of darkness and brought into the kingdom of Christ (Colossians 1:13). God's will is that this process be carried out among every nation on earth.

This, then, is our task: proclaiming the gospel in each nation so that people there will trust in Christ and be brought under His authority in their lives. We cannot quantify what it means for a nation to be "blessed," nor what is meant by "all the families of the nations will bow down before him" (Psalm 22:27, niv), but surely these expressions signify more than just a token few from each nation. Surely they promise a significant penetration of the gospel among every nation, tribe, people, and language.

Vast numbers of people still live in spiritual darkness. There is yet much spiritual ground to be possessed. We find ourselves in a situation similar to the Israelites after conquering much of Canaan, when God said to Joshua, "There are still very large areas of land to be taken over" (Joshua 12:24–13:1, niv). While we rejoice in the gospel's progress in many parts of the world, we acknowledge that there's more work to do before we can say every nation has been blessed.

When Jesus commissioned us to make disciples of all nations, He clearly intended that we meet this objective. Furthermore, He has the power to ensure that we do. He's not like a helpless football coach standing on the sidelines watching his vastly inferior team take a sound beating. While we don't know the final score, we do know that Jesus' "team" will eventually win. God will not be defeated by the powers of darkness.

The Gospel for Real Life

ADVERSITY'S GOAL

> *The LORD your God . . . led you through the great and*
> *terrifying wilderness . . . to do you good in the end.*
> (DEUTERONOMY 8:14-16)

The writer of Hebrews contrasted the finite wisdom of human parents in disciplining children with the infinite, infallible wisdom of God. Even the best human parents can only discipline as they think best. Their judgment is fallible, their actions are sometimes inconsistent and are often guided by the impulse of the moment. As is often observed, they have to learn by doing. Anyone who has tried to rear children in a godly, responsible manner knows there are times when parents simply do not know what is the appropriate manner or degree of discipline for a child.

God, however, always disciplines us for our good. He knows what is best for each one of us. He doesn't have to debate with Himself over what is most suitable for us. He knows intuitively and perfectly the nature, intensity, and duration of adversity that will best serve His purpose to make us partakers of His holiness. He never brings more pain than is needed to accomplish His purpose. Lamentations 3:33 expresses that sentiment this way: "For he does not willingly bring affliction or grief to the children of men" (NIV).

Returning to Hebrews 12:10: "God disciplines us for our good, that we may share in his holiness" (NIV). Observe how the writer equated our good with becoming more holy. Paul wrote in a similar manner when he said, "And we know that in all things God works for the good of those who love him. . . . For those God foreknew he also predestined to be conformed to the likeness of his Son" (Romans 8:28-29, NIV). To be conformed to the likeness of Christ and to share in God's holiness are equivalent expressions. That is the highest good to which the believer can aspire.

The Discipline of Grace

SUBMITTING TO HIS DISCIPLINE

God . . . gives grace to the humble.

(JAMES 4:6)

It's not enough to see God's mighty hand behind our adversities, nor to view Him as a loving Father disciplining His children. I've seen the doctrine of God's sovereignty in the Scriptures for so many years that I instinctively see His hand behind every circumstance. I regularly acknowledge, almost reluctantly sometimes, that all hardship is God's discipline, either corrective or remedial. The rub comes in submitting to it. Sometimes we resist it. But if we're to appropriate God's grace in our trial, we must first submit to His hand, which brought the trial.

God gives grace only to the humble, to those who are not only humble toward other people, but are humble, or submissive, under His mighty hand. John Lillie expressed this idea well: "'Humble yourselves, therefore,' receiving in silent, meek submission whatever humiliation it [God's hand] may now lay upon you. For this is your time of trial, and, when paternal rod meets thus with the child-like spirit, will be surely followed by another time of healing and joy." Then Dr. Lillie added this word of exhortation: "See that you do not frustrate the gracious purpose of God and lose the blessing of sorrow. Rather make that purpose yours also."[100]

After the death of my first wife, a friend sent me a sympathy card on which she had copied the following verse, apparently from an ancient hymn, which I've now put in my notebook to meditate on frequently when I pray: "Lord, I am willing to receive what You give, to lack what You withhold, to relinquish what You take, to suffer what You inflict, to be what You require."

We must have that spirit if we are to humble ourselves under God's mighty hand and receive the grace He has promised to give.

Transforming Grace

OUR RESPONSE

May people be blessed in him, all nations call him blessed!
(PSALM 72:17)

If God has promised that all nations will be blessed and that "all the ends of the earth will remember and turn to the LORD" (Psalm 22:27), how should we respond? I maintain that our response should begin with prayer. We should boldly and persistently plead in prayer the promises of God.

Daniel, one of the Bible's great men, is our example. He lived during the Babylonian captivity of Judah. He understood, from reading Jeremiah 29:10, that the captivity would last seventy years. So he took God at His word and began to pray that He would fulfill His promise to restore the Jews to their home (Daniel 9:1-19). He pleaded the promise of God. This is what we should do in response to God's promises of the success of the gospel. We should earnestly pray over such Scriptures as Genesis 22:18 and Psalm 22:27-28, asking God to fulfill His promises.

I'm dismayed at how little we Christians pray for the success of the gospel among the nations. If we honestly examine our prayers, we find that we give the greatest priority to our own earthly needs. Perhaps we even pray about our own or our loved ones' spiritual needs. But how many are praying about the spread of the gospel to the ends of the earth? How many are pleading the promises of God?

As a personal application of this challenge, I keep a small world map with my morning devotional material. I try to pray "around the world" over the course of a week, putting my finger on specific countries, especially those more resistant to Christianity, and asking God to bless them with a significant penetration of the gospel, so His name will be glorified among them.

The Gospel for Real Life

Hardship's Harvest

For the moment all discipline seems painful rather than pleasant.
(Hebrews 12:11)

I once knew a person who would recount some of the adversities her family was facing and would then put on a forced smile and say, "But we are victorious." She apparently thought believers should not admit pain. But the writer of Hebrews was honest. He said the discipline of hardship is painful.

"But later it yields the peaceful fruit of righteousness to those who have been trained by it" (Hebrews 12:11). This "fruit of righteousness" is essentially equivalent to sharing in His holiness. Discipline, then, is one of the chief means God uses to make us holy.

The discipline of hardship also produces peace for those who have been trained by it. This, wrote Philip Hughes, "bespeaks the rest and relaxation enjoyed by the victorious contestant once the conflict is over."[101] Hughes was speaking of the rest that comes to the believer when we go to be with the Lord. But there's also a peace to be enjoyed in this life for those who have learned to endure adversity as the evidence of God's fatherly hand upon them to make them more holy.

F. F. Bruce captured this thought well when he wrote, "The person who accepts discipline at the hand of God as something designed by his heavenly Father for his good will cease to feel resentful and rebellious; he has 'calmed and quieted' his soul [Psalm 131:2], which thus provides fertile soil for the cultivation of a righteous life, responsive to the will of God."[102]

The road to holiness is paved with adversity. If we want to be holy, we must expect the discipline of God through the heartaches and disappointments He brings or allows to come into our lives.

The Discipline of Grace

A BROADER HORIZON

Your kingdom come, your will be done, on earth as it is in heaven.

(MATTHEW 6:9-10)

Consider the prayer Jesus taught us in Matthew 6:9-13. It seems evidently intended as an example to be followed. Notice the sequence of the requests. The first three are that His name be hallowed, His kingdom come, and His will be done. There's a certain degree of overlap here: God's name will be hallowed as His kingdom comes in the hearts of people; God's will shall be done as people acknowledge the kingship of Christ in their lives and in their societies. All these requests will be answered through the successful advance of the gospel to the ends of the earth.

In seeking to stimulate us to lift up our eyes to God's great objective for all nations, I don't intend to minimize the importance of evangelism and disciple-making at home. What I'm seeking to do is to broaden our spiritual horizon, to get on our hearts what, according to Scripture, is on God's heart: The gospel is not just about God and me, or even about God and the people among whom I live and work. The gospel is about God and the world.

Obviously, there's more to carrying out the Great Commission than prayer. People must go to the ends of the earth. As I write this chapter, our son, daughter-in-law, and one-year-old grandson are preparing to go to one of the more difficult areas of the world. Is it hard to see them go to a people who are so resistant to the gospel? Absolutely! But if we're praying for the penetration of the gospel among those people, we must be prepared for God to use us or our loved ones to help answer those prayers.

The Gospel for Real Life

DESTINED FOR GLORY

*This light momentary affliction is preparing for us an
eternal weight of glory beyond all comparison.*

(2 CORINTHIANS 4:17)

Paul wrote that our sufferings produce perseverance, which in turn
produces character (Romans 5:3-4), and James said that the testing of our
faith develops perseverance, which leads to maturity (James 1:2-5). Our
ultimate hope, though, is not in maturity of character in this life, as valuable as that is, but in the perfection of character in eternity. John wrote,
"When he appears, we shall be like him, for we shall see him as he is"
(1 John 3:2, NIV). The often painful process of being transformed into His
likeness will be over. We shall be completely conformed to the likeness of
the Lord Jesus Christ.

Paul wrote, "I consider that our present sufferings are not worth
comparing with the glory that will be revealed in us" (Romans 8:18, NIV).
I visualize in my mind a pair of old-fashioned balance scales. Paul first
puts all our sufferings, heartaches, disappointments — all our adversities
of whatever kind from whatever source — onto one side of the balance
scales. Then he puts on the other side the glory that will be revealed in us.
As we watch, the scales do not balance, but completely bottom out on the
side of the glory that will be revealed in us.

This is not to say that our present hardships are not painful. We see
from Hebrews 12:11 that they are indeed painful, and we all know this
to some degree from experience. But we need to learn to look by faith
beyond the present pain to the eternal glory that will be revealed in us.

The God who disciplines us will also glorify us.

The Discipline of Grace

GRACE TO EACH OTHER

God has so composed the body . . .
that the members may have the same care for one another.

(1 CORINTHIANS 12:24-25)

Ministering grace is a two-way street. We're to pray for one another, encourage one another, teach and admonish one another, spur one another on, carry each other's burdens, share with one another, and so on. Truly the body of Christ should be constantly alive with this reciprocal ministry to one another.

Ministering grace to one another means being an agent available for the Holy Spirit to use to convey His grace to someone else. Allowing others to be ministers of grace to us takes some grace in itself, and we may need to pray, "Lord, help me to be transparent and open to my friend, even though doing so seems humiliating to me right now. And make my friend a minister of Your grace to me."

All of us, if we're exploiting this avenue of God's grace, should find ourselves at various times on both the receiving and the giving end. To borrow a principle of reciprocity from Paul's teaching on giving, "Your abundance at the present time should supply their need, so that their abundance may supply your need" (2 Corinthians 8:14).

How can we be ministers of grace to others? In the same three basic ways that they can be ministers to us: prayer, the Word of God, and help in submitting to God's providence. But there's a crucial difference between receiving and giving. In receiving we must give permission to the other person to share Scripture with us and to help us submit to God's providence. In giving, we must receive permission. Usually this means we must first earn the right to minister to the person through a relationship of mutual sharing, openness, and trust that we have already established.

Transforming Grace

MORE THAN ABLE

With God all things are possible.

(MATTHEW 19:26)

To take Christ's blessing and reign to the ends of the earth, not only must people go, but we must provide financial support for them or for modern communication means to reach places where people cannot go. Some of us must literally go, and all of us should participate in financial support. But the going is impotent and the financial support is futile if God doesn't go before us to open the eyes of the blind and turn them from darkness to light and from the power of Satan to God. And God does this as we plead His promises in prayer.

The scope of the Great Commission is vast, and the obstacles to its fulfillment are formidable. But as we pray let us remember the words of Paul: "Now to him who is able to do immeasurably more than all we ask or imagine, according to his power that is at work within us, to him be glory in the church and in Christ Jesus throughout all generations, for ever and ever! Amen" (Ephesians 3:20-21). God is more than able. The Great Commission *will* be fulfilled. Will you be a part of it? Will you help others discover the unsearchable riches of Christ that you now enjoy?

Meanwhile, I pray that you continue becoming more aware of those unsearchable riches you possess through your union with Christ. I pray you'll realize the abundant riches of your inheritance in Christ and will not rest content with the spiritual equivalent of "fifty cents to buy a sack of cornmeal." And I pray just as fervently that you will be challenged to get on board with God's great plan to bless all nations, so that the ends of the earth will turn to the Lord.

The Gospel for Real Life

GIVING FIRST TO GOD

See that you excel in this act of grace also.

(2 CORINTHIANS 8:7)

Some Christians think they cannot afford giving 10 percent of their income to God's work. I understand. When I left industry to become a staff trainee with The Navigators years ago, I took a 75 percent salary cut. I was financially shell-shocked. So I thought, "I can't afford to tithe. Surely, God accepts my sacrificial service as my giving." But God didn't let me get away with that. So I decided I would tithe my meager income and trust God to provide.

Later I was drawn to the story of Elijah and the widow of Zarephath (1 Kings 17:8-16). She was down to her last bit of flour and oil. She planned to prepare her last meal for her son and herself, and then die. Yet Elijah said to her in effect, "Feed me first, for God will provide for you." She did as Elijah instructed, and God did provide: "The jar of flour was not spent, neither did the jug of oil become empty, according to the word of the LORD that he spoke by Elijah" (verse 16). I began to pray over that verse, and I can tell you that throughout more than fifty years of ministry, God has always provided.

Giving back to God at least 10 percent of what He has given us is a tangible expression of our recognition that everything we have and our ability to earn comes from God (Deuteronomy 8:17-18).

Remember the infinite generosity of our Lord in giving Himself for our salvation: "Though he was rich, yet for your sake he became poor, so that you by his poverty might become rich" (2 Corinthians 8:9). Our giving should reflect the value we place on His gift to us.

Respectable Sins

Live by Grace

My grace is sufficient for you.
(2 Corinthians 12:9)

Learning to live by grace instead of by performance helps us accept the discipline of adversity. We realize that God is not disciplining us because of our bad performance but because of His love for us. We also learn to accept that whatever our situation, it's far better than we deserve. So we learn not to ask, "Why did this happen to me?" (meaning, What did I do to deserve such bad treatment from God?). We also learn, as Paul did with his thorn in the flesh, that God's grace is sufficient for us, however difficult and frustrating our circumstances might be. God's enabling grace will give us the inner spiritual strength we need to bear the pain and endure the hardship until the time when we see the harvest of righteousness and peace produced by it.

Far from being opposed to each other, grace and discipline — both God's discipline of us and our discipline of ourselves — are inextricably united together in God's program of sanctification. There's no question that God bases His discipline on grace. We are the ones who have problems with the relationship of grace and discipline, and who need to work at cultivating a proper relationship.

That work includes learning to preach the gospel to ourselves every day. We base the "duty" of discipleship on the gospel, resulting in the practice of a Christ-based acceptance with God and a Spirit-energized approach to the pursuit of holiness. In the joy and strength of knowing our sins are forgiven and sin's dominion is broken, we press on to become holy as He is holy. The so-called duty of discipleship then becomes a joy and a delight even though it requires vigorous effort.

The Discipline of Grace

DEEPER LONGING

That I may know him and the power of his resurrection.

(PHILIPPIANS 3:10)

As we concentrate on growing in our reverence and awe for God and in our understanding of His love for us, we will find that our desire for Him will grow. As we gaze upon His beauty, we'll desire to seek Him even more. And as we become progressively more aware of His redeeming love, we'll want to know Him in a progressively deeper way. But we can also pray that God will deepen our desire for Him. I recall reading Philippians 3:10 a number of years ago and realizing a little bit of the depth of Paul's desire to know Christ more intimately. As I read I prayed, "O God, I cannot identify with Paul's longing, but I would like to." Over the years God has begun to answer that prayer. By His grace I know experientially to some degree Isaiah's words, "My soul yearns for you in the night; in the morning my spirit longs for you" (Isaiah 26:9, NIV). I'm grateful for what God has done, but I pray I will continue to grow in this desire for Him.

In his book *Desiring God*, John Piper wrote, "[God] loves us and seeks the fullness of our joy that can be found only in knowing and praising Him, the most magnificent of all Beings."[103] One of the wonderful things about God is that He's infinite in all His glorious attributes, so never in our desire for Him will we exhaust the revelation of His person to us. The more we come to know Him, the more we'll desire Him. And the more we desire Him, the more we'll want to fellowship with Him and experience His presence. And the more we desire Him and His fellowship, the more we'll desire to be like Him.

Sources

Bridges, Jerry. *The Discipline of Grace*. Colorado Springs, CO: NavPress, 1994, 2006. Used by permission.

Bridges, Jerry. *The Fruitful Life*. Colorado Springs, CO: NavPress, 2006. Used by permission.

Bridges, Jerry. *The Gospel for Real Life*. Colorado Springs, CO: NavPress, 2002. Used by permission.

Bridges, Jerry. *Growing Your Faith*. Colorado Springs, CO: NavPress, 2004. Used by permission.

Bridges, Jerry. *Is God Really in Control?* Colorado Springs, CO: NavPress, 2006. Used by permission.

Bridges, Jerry. *The Practice of Godliness*. Colorado Springs, CO: NavPress, 1983, 1996, 2008. Used by permission.

Bridges, Jerry. *The Pursuit of Holiness*. Colorado Springs, CO: NavPress, 1978, 1996, 2006. Used by permission.

Bridges, Jerry. *Respectable Sins*. Colorado Springs, CO: NavPress, 2007. Used by permission.

Bridges, Jerry. *Transforming Grace*. Colorado Springs, CO: NavPress, 1991, 2008. Used by permission.

Bridges, Jerry. *Trusting God*. Colorado Springs, CO: NavPress, 1988, 2008. Used by permission.

NOTES

1. William S. Plumer, *Psalms* (1867; repr., Edinburgh, Scotland: Banner of Truth Trust, 1975), 557.
2. This statement is based on information from George Smeaton in his book *The Apostles' Doctrine of the Atonement* (Edinburgh, Scotland: Banner of Truth Trust, 1991 ed.), 15.
3. I am indebted to nineteenth-century pastor and author Henry A. Boardman for the idea of spelling out in detail what it means to obey the two great commandments. See his own version in: Henry A. Boardman, *The "Higher Life" Doctrine of Sanctification Tried by the Word of God* (1897; repr., Harrisonburg, VA: Sprinkle Publications, 1996), 190–191.
4. Quoted by permission from Mutua Mahiaini, from a letter written to The Navigators constituency in Kenya.
5. J. C. Ryle, *Holiness* (1952 ed., London: James Clarke & Co.), viii.
6. John Owen, *Communion with God,* ed. R. J. K. Law (Edinburgh, Scotland: Banner of Truth Trust, 1991), 117.
7. C. Samuel Storms, *The Grandeur of God* (Grand Rapids, MI: Baker, 1984), 124.
8. C. Samuel Storms, *The Grandeur of God* (Grand Rapids, MI: Baker, 1984), 125.
9. Matthew Henry, *A Commentary on the Whole Bible*, vol. 6 (Old Tappan, NJ: Revell, n.d.), 867.
10. Abraham Booth, *The Reign of Grace* (repr., Swengle, PA: Reiner Publications, 1976), 40, 48.
11. The statement that Jesus reaped what we have sown does not negate the application of this principle to us. It does, however, change the basis of its application. Jesus reaped the penal consequences of our disobedience. We reap the disciplinary consequences.
12. John Calvin, *Calvin's New Testament Commentaries*, vol. 10, *The Second Epistle of Paul to the Corinthians, and the Epistles to Timothy, Titus and Philemon*, ed. David W. Torrence and Thomas F. Torrance, trans. T. A. Smail (Grand Rapids, MI: Eerdmans, 1964), 371.
13. Andrew Bonar, *A Commentary on Leviticus* (1846; repr., Edinburgh, Scotland: Banner of Truth Trust, 1972), 218.
14. William Hendricksen, *Commentary on I and II Timothy and Titus* (London: Banner of Truth Trust, 1959), 370.
15. Attributed to John Berridge (1716–1793).
16. R. C. H. Lenski, *The Interpretation of St. Matthew's Gospel* (Minneapolis, MN: Augsburg, 1943), 758.
17. James Fraser, *A Treatise on Sanctification* (1774; rev. 1897, Audubon, NJ: Old Paths Publications, 1992), 418.
18. William Hendriksen, *A Commentary on the Gospel of John* (Edinburgh, Scotland: Banner of Truth Trust, 1961), 88–89.
19. Leon Morris, *The Atonement: Its Meaning and Significance* (Downers Grove, IL: InterVarsity, 1983), 153.
20. Charles Hodge, *Commentary on the Epistle to the Romans* (1886; repr., Grand Rapids, MI: Eerdmans, 1955), 290.

21. John Newton, "Come My Soul, Thy Suit Prepare," *Trinity Hymnal* (Philadelphia, PA: The Orthodox Presbyterian Church, 1961), hymn 531.

22. Some may question whether these are the words of Jesus or the words of John. In either case, however, they are words inspired by the Holy Spirit, so we can say they are the words of God.

23. George Smeaton, *The Apostles' Doctrine of the Atonement* (Edinburgh, Scotland: Banner of Truth Trust, 1991 ed.), 311.

24. Holiness "is characteristically Godlikeness" (G. B. Stevens, in *Hastings Bible Dictionary*, as quoted by W. E. Vine in *An Expository Dictionary of New Testament Words* [1940; single volume edition, London: Oliphants, Ltd., 1957], 227). Charles Hodge, writing on the phrase in Romans 6:19, "righteousness unto holiness," said, "The proximate result of obedience to God is inward conformity to the Divine image" (*Commentary on the Epistle to the Romans* [1886; repr., Grand Rapids, MI: Eerdmans, 1955], 209). A. W. Pink said, "Holiness . . . consists of that internal change or renovation of our souls whereby our minds, affections and wills are brought into harmony with God" (*The Doctrine of Sanctification* [Swengel, PA: Bible Truth Depot, 1955], 25).

25. Attributes as applied to God refer to His essential qualities and are inferred from Scriptures describing God. His attribute of holiness is taken from such passages as Exodus 15:11; Leviticus 19:2; Psalm 89:35; Isaiah 57:15; and 1 Peter 1:15-16.

26. Stephen Charnock, *The Existence and Attributes of God* (repr., Evansville, IN: Sovereign Grace Book Club, 1958), 449.

27. John Owen, *Communion with God*, ed. R. J. K. Law (Edinburgh, Scotland: Banner of Truth Trust, 1991), 13. Owen's three treatises on sin are *Of the Mortification of Sin in Believers*; *Of Temptation*; and *The Nature, Power, Deceit, and Prevalency of Indwelling Sin*. Those three volumes have been very influential in my own personal pursuit of holiness.

28. John's record does not say Jesus cried out. However, Mark says, "With a loud cry, Jesus breathed his last," and John indicates that "It is finished" were His last words. Putting together the two accounts, we are justified in saying, "Jesus cried out, 'It is finished.'"

29. Though believers never experience the wrath of God, we do, as occasion demands, experience the discipline of God. But the motivation behind the discipline is not God's wrath but His fatherly love (see Hebrews 12:5-6).

30. Jonathan Edwards, *The Works of Jonathan Edwards*, ed. Edward Hickman, vol. 1 (1834; Edinburgh, Scotland: Banner of Truth Trust, 1974), xx.

31. J. C. Ryle, *Holiness* (1952 ed., London: James Clarke & Co.), xv.

32. R. C. H. Lenski, *The Interpretation of St. Matthew's Gospel* (Minneapolis, MN: Augsburg, 1943), 758.

33. George W. Bethune, *The Fruit of the Spirit* (Swengel, PA: Reiner Publications, 1839), 117.

34. Philip E. Hughes, *The New International Commentary on the New Testament: Paul's Second Epistle to the Corinthians* (Grand Rapids, MI: Eerdmans, 1962), 36.

35. John Calvin, *Calvin's New Testament Commentaries*, vol. 10, *The Second Epistle of Paul to the Corinthians, and the Epistles to Timothy, Titus and Philemon,* ed. David W. Torrance and Thomas F. Torrance, trans. T. A. Smail (Grand Rapids, MI: Eerdmans, 1964), 21–22.

36. Thomas Lye, from a sermon titled "How Are We to Live by Faith on Divine Providence?" in *Puritan Sermons 1659–1689*, vol. 1, a collection of sermons by

seventy-five Puritan preachers, originally published in London at irregular intervals between 1660 and 1691 (Wheaton, IL: Richard Owen Roberts, Publisher, 1981), 374.

37. John Flavel, *The Works of John Flavel*, vol. IV (Edinburgh, Scotland: Banner of Truth Trust, 1982), 336–497.

38. John Murray, *The Epistle to the Romans, New International Commentary on the New Testament* series, vol. 1 (Grand Rapids, MI: Eerdmans, 1968), 294.

39. Stephen Brown (pastor of Key Biscayne Presbyterian Church), "The Song of Grace (Part 1), 1 Peter 5:6-14," cassette (Key Biscayne, FL: Key Life Tapes, 1990). He noted that our problem isn't that we made the gospel too good, but that we didn't make it good enough.

40. Richard Gilbert, "Sola Gratia and Sanctification," *Modern Reformation* (September/October 1990): 7.

41. Charles Hodge, *Commentary on the Epistle to the Romans* (1886; repr., Grand Rapids, MI: Eerdmans, 1955), 384.

42. John Murray, *The New International Commentary on the New Testament: The Epistle to the Romans*, vol. 2 (Grand Rapids, MI: Eerdmans, 1965), 111.

43. Paraphrased from Frederick William Faber, *Growth in Holiness* (1854; Westminster, MD: The Newman Press, 1960), 93.

44. Martin Luther, quoted in R. C. H. Lenski, *The Interpretation of St. Paul's Epistle to the Romans* (Minneapolis, MN: Augsburg, 1936), 746.

45. George Smeaton, *The Apostles' Doctrine of the Atonement* (Edinburgh, Scotland: Banner of Truth Trust, 1991 ed.), 248.

46. Stephen Charnock, as quoted by C. H. Spurgeon in *The Treasury of David*, vol. 2, Psalms 119–127 (1882–1887; repr., Grand Rapids, MI: Baker, 1984), 249.

47. Ernest F. Kevan, *The Grace of Law* (Grand Rapids, MI: Baker, 1976), 63.

48. Abraham Booth, *The Reign of Grace* (repr., Swengel, PA: Reiner Publications, 1976), 201.

49. William Law, *A Serious Call to a Devout and Holy Life*, rev. ed. (Grand Rapids, MI: Sovereign Grace Publishers, 1971), 6.

50. Charles Hodge, *An Exposition of the Second Epistle to the Corinthians* (London: Banner of Truth Trust, 1959), 133.

51. John Brown, *Expository Discourses on 1 Peter*, vol. 1 (1848; reprint edition, Edinburgh, Scotland: Banner of Truth Trust), 106.

52. Philip E. Hughes, *The New International Commentary on the New Testament: Paul's Second Epistle to the Corinthians* (Grand Rapids, MI: Eerdmans, 1962), 258.

53. Leon Morris, *The Apostolic Preaching of the Cross* (Grand Rapids, MI: Eerdmans, 1965), 59.

54. John Calvin, *Calvin's New Testament Commentaries*, vol. 8, *The Epistle of Paul to the Romans and to the Thessalonians*, ed. David W. Torrence and Thomas F. Torrence, trans. Ross Mackenzie (Grand Rapids, MI: Eerdmans, 1964), 263.

55. D. G. Kehl, *Control Yourself!* (Grand Rapids, MI: Zondervan, 1982), 25. This is an excellent book for those who want to pursue the subject of self-control further.

56. George W. Bethune, *The Fruit of the Spirit* (Swengel, PA: Reiner, 1839), 179.

57. Harold S. Kushner, *When Bad Things Happen to Good People* (New York: Avon Books, 1981), 6.

58. Samuel Bolton, *The True Bounds of Christian Freedom* (1645; repr., Edinburgh, Scotland: Banner of Truth Trust, 1978), 219.

P.163

59. Robert H. Bainton, *Here I Stand: A Life of Martin Luther* (Nashville: Abingdon, 1950), 44.

60. Robert H. Bainton, *Here I Stand: A Life of Martin Luther* (Nashville: Abingdon, 1950), 49.

61. The phrase "no merit of my own I claim" is a late twentieth-century revision of unknown origin of Mote's original line, "I dare not trust the sweetest frame."

62. Arthur W. Pink, *The Doctrine of Sanctification* (Swengel, PA: Bible Truth Depot, 1955), 200.

63. George Smeaton, *The Apostles' Doctrine of the Atonement* (Edinburgh, Scotland: Banner of Truth Trust, 1991 ed.), 239.

64. Arthur W. Pink, *The Doctrine of Sanctification* (Swengel, PA: Bible Truth Depot, 1955), 200.

65. The phrase "I tell you the truth" in verses 3 and 5 is literally "truly, truly." Among the Jews the repetition of a word was intended as an emphatic statement.

66. Charles Wesley, "And Can It Be That I Should Gain?" *Worship and Service Hymnal* (Chicago: Hope Publishing Company, 1957), 259. This historic, classic hymn appears in most standard hymnbooks; unfortunately, some leave out this particular stanza.

67. William Hendriksen, *New Testament Commentary: Exposition of Philippians* (Grand Rapids, MI: Baker, 1962), 120.

68. John Owen, *Temptation and Sin*, ed. James M. Houston (Portland, OR: Multnomah, 1983), 153.

69. Sinclair B. Ferguson, *John Owen on the Christian Life* (Edinburgh, Scotland: Banner of Truth Trust, 1987), 154.

70. 1 John 2:29; 3:9 (twice); 4:7; 5:1; 5:4; 5:18.

71. John Owen, *Temptation and Sin*, ed. James M. Houston (Portland, OR: Multnomah, 1983), 152.

72. Samuel Bolton, *The True Bounds of Christian Freedom* (1645; repr., Edinburgh, Scotland: Banner of Truth Trust, 1978), 220–221.

73. John Owen, *Temptation and Sin*, ed. James M. Houston (Portland, OR: Multnomah, 1983), 28.

74. G. Ch. Aalders, *Bible Students Commentary: Genesis*, vol. 1, trans. William Heynen (Grand Rapids, MI: Zondervan, 1981), 102.

75. J. A. Thompson, *The Tyndale Old Testament Commentaries: Deuteronomy: An Interpretation and Commentary* (Downers Grove, IL: InterVarsity, 1974), 134–135.

76. Philip E. Hughes, *The New International Commentary on the New Testament: Paul's Second Epistle to the Corinthians* (Grand Rapids, MI: Eerdmans, 1962), 451.

77. John Blanchard, *Truth for Life: A Devotional Commentary on the Epistle of James* (Welwyn, England: Evangelical Press, 1986), 268.

78. Philip E. Hughes, *The New International Commentary on the New Testament: Paul's Second Epistle to the Corinthians* (Grand Rapids, MI: Eerdmans, 1962), 443.

79. Harry Blamires, *Recovering the Christian Mind* (Downers Grove, IL: InterVarsity, 1988), 32–33.

80. John Owen, *Temptation and Sin,* ed. James M. Houston (Portland, OR: Multnomah, 1983), 41–42.

81. Gordon D. Fee, *The New International Commentary on the New Testament: The First Epistle to the Corinthians* (Grand Rapids, MI: Eerdmans, 1987), 37.

82. Horatius Bonar, *God's Way of Holiness* (1864; Durham, England: Evangelical Press, 1979), 51–52.

83. John Owen, *Temptation and Sin,* abridged by ed. James M. Houston (Portland, OR: Multnomah, 1983), 99.

84. Charles Hodge, *An Exposition of the Second Epistle to the Corinthians* (London: Banner of Truth Trust, 1959), 192.

85. Samuel Bolton, *The True Bounds of Christian Freedom* (1645; repr., Edinburgh, Scotland: Banner of Truth Trust, 1978), 94.

86. For the original quote, see John Brown, *Analytical Exposition of Paul the Apostle to the Romans* (1857; repr., Grand Rapids, MI: Baker, 1981), 93.

87. Ernest Kevan, *The Grace of Law* (Grand Rapids, MI: Baker, 1976), 190. Kevan quotes verbatim from the Puritans, including their seventeenth-century spelling and pronunciation. I have modernized both for the convenience of the reader.

88. Scripture indicates that God at times does allow Satan to tempt us, as he did Peter (Luke 22:31-32), but at least in that instance God was apparently using Satan to get at Peter's pride (see verse 33).

89. R. C. Sproul, "Suffering and Merit?" *Tabletalk* 13, no. 1 (February 1989), 5.

90. Philip E. Hughes, *Hope for a Despairing World* (Grand Rapids, MI: Baker, 1977), 18.

91. William Romaine, *The Life, Walk and Triumph of Faith* (1793; Cambridge, England: James Clarke & Co. Ltd., 1970 ed.), 280.

92. George Smeaton, *The Doctrine of the Holy Spirit* (1882; Edinburgh, Scotland: Banner of Truth Trust, 1958 ed.), 228.

93. Samuel Bolton, *The True Bounds of Christian Freedom*, rev. ed. (1645; Edinburgh, Scotland: Banner of Truth Trust, 1964), 25.

94. R. C. H. Lenski, *The Interpretation of the Acts of the Apostles* (Minneapolis, MN: Augsburg, 1934), 853.

95. Horatius Bonar, "God's Way of Holiness," as quoted in *Free Grace Broadcaster*, Issue 146 (October 1993): 32, Mt. Zion Bible Church, Pensacola, FL.

96. Charles B. Williams, *The New Testament in the Language of the People* (Nashville: Holman Bible Publishers, 1986), 351.

97. Charles Hodge, *A Commentary on the Epistle to the Ephesians* (1856; repr., Grand Rapids, MI: Baker, 1980), 389.

98. John Owen, as quoted by John Brown in *An Exposition of Hebrews* (1862; repr., Edinburgh, Scotland: Banner of Truth Trust, 1961), 626.

99. George MacDonald, quoted in J. R. Miller, "Finding One's Mission" (Swengel, PA: Reiner Publications, n.d.), 2.

100. John Lillie, *Lectures on the First and Second Epistle of Peter* (1869; repr., Minneapolis, MN: Klock & Klock Christian Publishers, 1978), 320.

101. Philip Hughes, *A Commentary on the Epistle to the Hebrews* (Grand Rapids, MI: Eerdmans, 1977), 532–533.

102. F. F. Bruce, *The Epistle to the Hebrews*, rev. ed., *New International Commentary on the New Testament* series (Grand Rapids, MI: Eerdmans, 1990), 346.

103. John Piper, *Desiring God* (Sisters, OR: Multnomah, 2003), 49.

About the Author

DR. JERRY BRIDGES is the best-selling author of such books as *The Pursuit of Holiness*, *Trusting God*, *The Practice of Godliness*, and *Respectable Sins*. Jerry is on staff with The Navigators' collegiate ministry. A popular speaker known around the world, Jerry lives with his wife, Jane, in Colorado Springs.